VOLUME FIFTY NINE

INTERNATIONAL REVIEW OF RESEARCH IN DEVELOPMENTAL DISABILITIES

Family-Focused Interventions

SERIAL EDITORS

ROBERT M. HODAPP
Vanderbilt Kennedy Center for Research on Human Development, Department of Special Education, Peabody College, Vanderbilt University, Nashville, TN, USA

DEBORAH J. FIDLER
Professor of Human Development and Family Studies, Colorado State University, Fort Collins, CO, USA

BOARD OF ASSOCIATE EDITORS

PHILIP DAVIDSON
University of Rochester School of Medicine and Dentistry

ELISABETH DYKENS
Vanderbilt University

MICHAEL GURALNICK
University of Washington

RICHARD HASTINGS
University of Warwick

LINDA HICKSON
Columbia University

CONNIE KASARI
University of California, Los Angeles

WILLIAM McILVANE
E. K. Shriver Center

GLYNIS MURPHY
University of Kent

TED NETTELBECK
Adelaide University

MARSHA MAILICK
University of Wisconsin-Madison

JAN WALLANDER
Sociometrics Corporation

VOLUME FIFTY NINE

INTERNATIONAL REVIEW OF RESEARCH IN DEVELOPMENTAL DISABILITIES

Family-Focused Interventions

Edited by

SUSAN HEPBURN
*Colorado State University,
Fort Collins, CO, United States*

Academic Press is an imprint of Elsevier
50 Hampshire Street, 5th Floor, Cambridge, MA 02139, United States
525 B Street, Suite 1650, San Diego, CA 92101, United States
The Boulevard, Langford Lane, Kidlington, Oxford OX5 1GB, United Kingdom
125 London Wall, London EC2Y 5AS, United Kingdom

First edition 2020

Copyright © 2020 Elsevier Inc. All rights reserved.

No part of this publication may be reproduced or transmitted in any form or by any means, electronic or mechanical, including photocopying, recording, or any information storage and retrieval system, without permission in writing from the publisher. Details on how to seek permission, further information about the Publisher's permissions policies and our arrangements with organizations such as the Copyright Clearance Center and the Copyright Licensing Agency, can be found at our website: www.elsevier.com/permissions.

This book and the individual contributions contained in it are protected under copyright by the Publisher (other than as may be noted herein).

Notices
Knowledge and best practice in this field are constantly changing. As new research and experience broaden our understanding, changes in research methods, professional practices, or medical treatment may become necessary.

Practitioners and researchers must always rely on their own experience and knowledge in evaluating and using any information, methods, compounds, or experiments described herein. In using such information or methods they should be mindful of their own safety and the safety of others, including parties for whom they have a professional responsibility.

To the fullest extent of the law, neither the Publisher nor the authors, contributors, or editors, assume any liability for any injury and/or damage to persons or property as a matter of products liability, negligence or otherwise, or from any use or operation of any methods, products, instructions, or ideas contained in the material herein.

ISBN: 978-0-12-822874-6
ISSN: 2211-6095

For information on all Academic Press publications
visit our website at https://www.elsevier.com/books-and-journals

Publisher: Zoe Kruze
Acquisitions Editor: Sam Mahfoudh
Editorial Project Manager: Shellie Bryant
Production Project Manager: Abdulla Sait
Cover Designer: Alan Studholme

Typeset by SPi Global, India

Contents

Contributors	*ix*
Preface	*xiii*

1. Reframing risk: Working with caregivers of children with disabilities to promote risk-taking in play   1

Patricia Grady-Dominguez, Kristina Ihrig, Shelly J. Lane, Jennifer Aberle, Kassia Beetham, Jo Ragen, Grace Spencer, Julia Sterman, Paul Tranter, Shirley Wyver, and Anita Bundy

1. Risky play: The accent should be on *play*	4
2. Benefits of risky play for children with disabilities	5
3. Parents and risk: Gatekeeping risky play for children with and without disabilities	7
4. Teachers and risk: Balancing duty of care and dignity of risk in play	10
5. TRiPS-R and TRiPS-T: Instruments to measure adults' tolerance of risky play	12
6. Using the TRiPS instruments in research and in practice	34
7. Summary and conclusion	40
Acknowledgment	41
References	41

2. Augmented naturalistic developmental behavioral intervention for toddlers with autism spectrum disorder: A community pilot study   47

Deanna M. Swain, Jamie Winter, Claire B. Klein, Amy Lemelman, Jennifer Giordano, Nicole N. Jablon, Kaori Nakamura, and So Hyun Kim

1. Introduction and change	48
2. Methods	51
3. Results	61
4. Discussion	64
5. Implications	68
Acknowledgments	68
References	68

3. Fathers, children, play and playfulness   71

Shelly J. Lane and Jennifer St. George

1. Introduction	72
2. Defining play and playfulness	73

v

3. Focusing on fathers	82
4. The father/child research project	90
5. Summary	97
6. Conclusion	98
Acknowledgments	98
References	98

4. Feasibility and acceptability of an online response inhibition cognitive training program for youth with Williams syndrome 107

Natalie G. Brei, Ana-Maria Raicu, Han Joo Lee, and Bonita P. Klein-Tasman

1. Introduction	108
2. Method	112
3. Results	119
4. Discussion	126
5. Conclusion	129
Acknowledgments	129
Source of funding	130
Conflict of interest	130
References	130
Further reading	134

5. The effect of parent personality on the acquisition and use of mindfulness skills during an MBSR intervention 135

Catherine M. Sanner, Hadley A. McGregor, Amanda E. Preston, and Cameron L. Neece

1. Current study	139
2. Method	140
3. Results	147
4. Discussion	153
Conflict of interest	158
References	158

6. A public health approach to family supports: Empowering families of children with autism through the ECHO model 163

Eric J. Moody, Haley A. Sturges, Sarah Zlatkovic, Ethan Dahl, Sandra Root-Elledge, and Canyon Hardesty

1. The public health approach to supporting families of children with ASD	169
2. Raising a child with ASD and family well-being	171

3. Public health programs for families of children with ASD	175
4. The problem of scaling up family support programs and the unique approach of ECHO for families	178
5. Conclusion	185
Acknowledgments	186
References	187

Contributors

Jennifer Aberle
Department of Health and Human Sciences, Colorado State University, Fort Collins, CO, United States

Kassia Beetham
School of Behavioural and Health Sciences, Australian Catholic University, Banyo, QLD, Australia

Natalie G. Brei
Catholic Social Services of Southern Nebraska, Lincoln, NE, United States

Anita Bundy
Department of Occupational Therapy, Colorado State University, Fort Collins, CO, United States; Faculty of Medicine and Health, University of Sydney, Camperdown, NSW, Australia

Ethan Dahl
Wyoming Institute for Disabilities, University of Wyoming, Laramie, WY, United States

Jennifer Giordano
Center for Autism and the Developing Brain, New York-Presbyterian Hospital, White Plains, NY, United States

Patricia Grady-Dominguez
Department of Occupational Therapy, Colorado State University, Fort Collins, CO, United States

Canyon Hardesty
Wyoming Institute for Disabilities, University of Wyoming, Laramie, WY, United States

Kristina Ihrig
Department of Occupational Therapy, Colorado State University, Fort Collins, CO, United States

Nicole N. Jablon
Center for Autism and the Developing Brain, New York-Presbyterian Hospital, White Plains, NY, United States

So Hyun Kim
Department of Psychiatry, Weill Cornell Medical College; Center for Autism and the Developing Brain, New York-Presbyterian Hospital, White Plains, NY, United States

Claire B. Klein
Department of Psychiatry, Weill Cornell Medical College, White Plains, NY, United States

Bonita P. Klein-Tasman
University of Wisconsin-Milwaukee, Milwaukee, WI, United States

Shelly J. Lane
Department of Occupational Therapy, Colorado State University, Fort Collins, CO, United States; Department of Occupational Therapy, University of Newcastle, Newcastle, NSW, Australia

Han Joo Lee
University of Wisconsin-Milwaukee, Milwaukee, WI, United States

Amy Lemelman
Department of Psychiatry, Weill Cornell Medical College; Center for Autism and the Developing Brain, New York-Presbyterian Hospital, White Plains, NY, United States

Hadley A. McGregor
Department of Psychology, Loma Linda University, Loma Linda, CA, United States

Eric J. Moody
Wyoming Institute for Disabilities, University of Wyoming, Laramie, WY, United States

Kaori Nakamura
Center for Autism and the Developing Brain, New York-Presbyterian Hospital, White Plains, NY, United States

Cameron L. Neece
Department of Psychology, Loma Linda University, Loma Linda, CA, United States

Amanda E. Preston
Department of Psychology, Loma Linda University, Loma Linda, CA, United States

Jo Ragen
Faculty of Medicine and Health, University of Sydney, Camperdown, NSW, Australia

Ana-Maria Raicu
Michigan State University, East Lansing, MI, United States

Sandra Root-Elledge
Wyoming Institute for Disabilities, University of Wyoming, Laramie, WY, United States

Catherine M. Sanner
Department of Psychology, Loma Linda University, Loma Linda, CA, United States

Grace Spencer
Faculty of Health, Education, Medicine and Social Care, Anglia Ruskin University, Cambridge, United Kingdom

Julia Sterman
Department of Occupational Therapy, University of Minnesota, Minneapolis, MN, United States

Jennifer St. George
Family Action Centre, University of Newcastle, Newcastle, NSW, Australia

Haley A. Sturges
Department of Psychology, University of Wyoming, Laramie, WY, United States

Deanna M. Swain
Department of Psychiatry, Weill Cornell Medical College, White Plains, NY, United States

Paul Tranter
School of Science, University of New South Wales, Sydney, NSW, Australia

Jamie Winter
Department of Psychiatry, Weill Cornell Medical College; Center for Autism and the Developing Brain, New York-Presbyterian Hospital, White Plains, NY, United States

Shirley Wyver
Department of Educational Studies, Macquarie University, Sydney, NSW, Australia

Sarah Zlatkovic
Wyoming Institute for Disabilities, University of Wyoming, Laramie, WY, United States

Preface

This special volume of the *International Review of Research in Developmental Disabilities* highlights recent work in developing and evaluating interventions that actively involve family members. We are pleased to offer a variety of perspectives on this complex topic, particularly at this time of uncertainty.

It is the fall of 2020; 7 months into the COVID-19 pandemic and mired in a period of socio-cultural upheaval unlike what most of us have witnessed directly in our lives. It is during times like these that we realize what matters most to us—*who* matters most to us. I would argue that the collection of people who matter most to you are your family, regardless of biological connection. A person could be considered "family" if there is a lasting, dependable relationship; a shared commitment to look out for each other, as Robert Frost defined family in his poem *The Death of a Hired Man*: "Home is the place where, when you have to go there, They have to take you in." Others would argue for a less transactional conception of family, where obligations to one another are rooted in connection and companionship, per David Byrne: "Home is where I want to be... But I guess I'm already there."

As Bronfenbrenner and others have emphasized—the family is a critical social context for development across the lifespan. Interventions that target a persistent change agent—such as a parent—have a greater likelihood of promoting change in child behavior due to increased opportunities to interact and promote learning in natural situations which promotes generalizability. Intervening at a family level is particularly important when the condition requires more adaptation from the family.

For this volume, we sought chapters that offered distinct perspectives and approaches to family-focused interventions. The chapters in this volume share a common interest in promoting adaptive outcomes for persons with disabilities and their families. They also differ in many aspects, such as the role of family members in the intervention, the outcomes they are targeting, and the underlying theory of change that has informed the development of their intervention.

We open the volume with three chapters that employ a caregiver-mediated approach to promote positive outcomes for young children with developmental disabilities. In "caregiver-mediated" interventions, highly skilled clinicians teach caregivers to deliver an evidence-based curriculum

xiii

to a family member (often a son or a daughter). In these models, caregivers collaborate with clinicians with the goal of improving child skills, such as functional communication, imitation or play. The caregiver is the agent of change and the clinician acts more like a coach or a facilitator than a therapist. The skills/behaviors of the caregivers are viewed as mediating the outcomes demonstrated by the child; and usually the wellbeing of the caregiver isn't an identified outcome of the intervention.

Patricia Grady and Anita Bundy present a compelling argument for encouraging parents of young children to promote exploration and risk-taking in play that will promote increased engagement, acquisition of adaptive skills, and possibly improve perceptions of efficacy and competence. An important implication of this line of work is the potential for coaching parents on how to assume competence instead of impairment. Such interventions could contribute significantly to increased self-efficacy in youth with developmental disabilities.

Deanna Swain and colleagues present a pilot study of a naturalistic developmental intervention (NDBI) for young children with autism. NDBIs emphasize the importance of active engagement of the child's caregivers in early intervention and this study adds to the empirical support for caregiver-mediated intervention in natural settings. This study is particularly strong in providing important contextual details in the discussion of the intervention development and delivery processes.

Shelly J. Lane and colleagues examine the importance of including fathers in play-based, naturalistic interventions and intentionally building strong father–child relationships. Clearly there is a dearth of work in understanding how to engage fathers in child therapies, as most caregiver-mediated research has focused on mothers. This chapter provides an insightful review of the literature, providing implications for research and practice.

In other family-focused intervention work, the role of the parent is not to deliver the intervention directly, but rather to facilitate or support their family member to participate in the intervention. Feasibility issues can significantly impede intervention studies, and its important in home-based interventions to understand the caregiver's perspective on the acceptability, usefulness, and degree of involvement required by caregivers for a youth with IDD to participate in an intervention.

Natalie Brei and Bonnie Klein-Tasman present a study that focuses on the development of a computerized educational program designed to improve cognitive skills in youth with Williams syndrome. Parents do not actually mediate the intervention, but they support its implementation in essential ways. Their input on what works and what they like and dislike about online interventions offers many important insights for clinicians wrestling with innovative ways to promote development in our clients from a distance. This chapter also highlights the necessity of partnering with parents and caregivers in the intervention development phase.

Finally, we offer two chapters that present methods for promoting positive child and family outcomes by directly intervening with the caregivers themselves, either through information and support or through specific skills training.

Catherine M. Sanner and Cameron Neece present an intervention study focused on moderators of a mindfulness-based approach to promoting caregiver well-being. This study is unique in its clear description of the intervention and its focus on characteristics of respondents that are associated with differential treatment outcomes. Understanding who tends to benefit from interventions is an important and often unexamined aspect of family-focused intervention studies. The authors also present a cohesive discussion of the potential of mindfulness strategies to promote lasting change for caregivers who are working to adapt to a disability, not change it.

We close this volume with a chapter that describes a family-focused intervention delivered in a public health context. Eric Moody and colleagues share data on the ECHO program in Wyoming, which is a telehealth platform designed specifically to connect people who have a shared interest in adapting and or managing a complex health condition. This chapter describes how this public health approach can be leveraged to support families of people with autism spectrum disorder across a vast, rural state.

We are grateful to the authors for their thoughtful contributions to this volume on family-focused interventions. Each of these chapters adds to our understanding of the processes and outcomes associated with collaborating with families in an intervention context, both in research and in practice.

SUSAN HEPBURN

CHAPTER ONE

Reframing risk: Working with caregivers of children with disabilities to promote risk-taking in play

Patricia Grady-Dominguez[a,*], Kristina Ihrig[a], Shelly J. Lane[a], Jennifer Aberle[b], Kassia Beetham[c], Jo Ragen[d], Grace Spencer[e], Julia Sterman[f], Paul Tranter[g], Shirley Wyver[h], and Anita Bundy[a,d]

[a]Department of Occupational Therapy, Colorado State University, Fort Collins, CO, United States
[b]Department of Health and Human Sciences, Colorado State University, Fort Collins, CO, United States
[c]School of Behavioural and Health Sciences, Australian Catholic University, Banyo, QLD, Australia
[d]Faculty of Medicine and Health, University of Sydney, Camperdown, NSW, Australia
[e]Faculty of Health, Education, Medicine and Social Care, Anglia Ruskin University, Cambridge, United Kingdom
[f]Department of Occupational Therapy, University of Minnesota, Minneapolis, MN, United States
[g]School of Science, University of New South Wales, Sydney, NSW, Australia
[h]Department of Educational Studies, Macquarie University, Sydney, NSW, Australia
*Corresponding author: e-mail address: Patricia.Grady@colostate.edu

Contents

1. Risky play: The accent should be on *play* — 4
2. Benefits of risky play for children with disabilities — 5
   2.1 Decision-making and autonomy — 6
   2.2 Emotional health — 6
   2.3 Physical health — 6
   2.4 Social competence and empathy — 7
3. Parents and risk: Gatekeeping risky play for children with and without disabilities — 7
4. Teachers and risk: Balancing duty of care and dignity of risk in play — 10
5. TRiPS-R and TRiPS-T: Instruments to measure adults' tolerance of risky play — 12
   5.1 Development of TRiPS-R and T-TRiPS — 13
   5.2 Psychometric evaluation of TRiPS-R data: A brief summary — 17
   5.3 Psychometric evaluation of TRiPS-R data: In-depth analysis — 19
   5.4 Psychometric evaluation of T-TRiPS: A brief summary — 29
   5.5 Psychometric evaluation of T-TRiPS: In-depth analysis — 30
6. Using the TRiPS instruments in research and in practice — 34
   6.1 Researchers — 37
   6.2 Therapists working with children with disabilities — 39
   6.3 Educators — 39
   6.4 A note for all practitioners interested in risky play — 39

7. Summary and conclusion   40

Acknowledgment   41

References   41

Abstract

Risky play is invigorating, challenging play with uncertain outcomes that optimizes children's development, health, and everyday well-being and creates opportunities to develop decision-making skills in low-consequence contexts, experience positive feelings such as confidence and courage, and enjoy health-promoting physical activity. Children with disabilities have fewer opportunities to engage in risky play, often because of the intervention of well-intentioned adults. In this paper, we define and examine the benefits of risky play for children with and without disabilities. Then, we examine the role of caregivers in "gatekeeping" risky play opportunities. We present two novel instruments that allow practitioners to assess caregivers' tolerance of risky play: the Tolerance of Risk in Play Scale-Revised (TRiPS-R) and the Tolerance of Risk in Play Scale-Teacher (T-TRiPS). We describe the results of psychometric analyses of these instruments, demonstrating evidence for construct validity and internal reliability of data collected using these instruments. Finally, we encourage practitioners who work with children with disabilities to employ these tools to promote risky play for the children they serve.

How do children learn the limits of their abilities if they are offered only activities where there is no risk of failure? Furthermore, if they are never allowed to experience discomfort, how do children develop physical skills, learn to regulate their emotions, extend themselves in social relationships or persevere in the face of cognitive challenges? (Niehues et al., 2013, p. 224).

Play is a leading context for children's growth, development, and learning. For the purpose of this paper, we define play simply as those activities done primarily for the sake of doing them. Manageable risk–taking is a natural and beneficial part of children's play. Risky play is challenging and exciting play with the possibility of physical injury, that affords opportunities for children to test their limits, explore boundaries, and learn to manage risk (Sandseter, 2009; Sandseter, Little, & Wyver, 2012). Kleppe, Melhuish, and Sandseter (2017) emphasized the ambiguity inherent in risky play, describing it as "play that involves uncertainty and exploration – bodily, emotional, perceptional or environmental – that could lead to either positive or negative consequences" (p. 9).

An extensive body of research suggests that risky play affords children with opportunities to overcome obstacles, experience well-being, and achieve physical and cognitive development (Brussoni, Olsen, Pike, & Sleet, 2012; Little & Eager, 2010). A recent systematic review concluded that risky play positively contributes to children's physical health and health behaviors, particularly by motivating physical activity (Brussoni et al., 2015).

Tovey (2007) noted that risky play gives children the opportunity to "learn at the very edge of their capabilities"—to push boundaries, innovate, and develop confidence and competence in physical, cognitive, and social skills (p. 82). Through risky play, children learn to recognize and manage real everyday risks, overcome fears, and balance impulsivity with careful reflection and decision-making (Caprino, 2018; Lavrysen et al., 2017).

Children of all abilities benefit from opportunities to develop courage, resilience, self-awareness, and skills through risky play. Unfortunately, children with disabilities may have fewer opportunities than their typically developing peers to participate in risky play (Beetham et al., 2019). Children with disabilities may be viewed by adults as less capable and in need of more protection from everyday risks and uncertainties (Bundy et al., 2015). A recent meta-analysis of injury prevention research found that children with both physical and cognitive disabilities had a greater risk of unintentional injuries than typically developing peers (Shi et al., 2015). The authors' explanation that children with disabilities have less innate ability to manage risks is consistent with conventional understanding. We propose an alternative explanation: because children with disabilities have fewer opportunities to engage in risky play, they are less capable of safely managing risk when confronted with real danger. More than likely, both factors create a perpetual cycle: slightly less skill leads to fewer opportunities, extending the skill gap between children with disabilities and typically-developing peers. Furthermore, children with disabilities (particularly cognitive disabilities) may need more opportunities to practice managing risks. Therefore, providing frequent opportunities for manageable risk-taking may enable them to improve this skill.

Adults who care for children (e.g., parents and teachers) may be the bridges or the barriers to risky play opportunities for children with disabilities (Sterman et al., 2016). In this paper, we explore the potential for both parents and teachers to promote risky play. We first describe literature about "competently-appropriate" risk-taking in play, and the benefits of this sort of play. Then, we explore parents' and teachers' role in "gatekeeping" risky play for children with and without disabilities. Finally, we present the results of two psychometric studies of instruments designed to evaluate parents' and teachers' risk tolerances.

Throughout the paper, we use the term "parents" broadly to refer to adults who are primary caretakers for children in their homes, regardless of biological relation. Similarly, we use the term "teachers" to refer to any school personnel responsible for creating or enforcing policies surrounding children's play. The term "competently-appropriate" refers to (children) having sufficient capability to undertake an activity. While this term may leave some feeling slightly perplexed, given adults' tendency to under-estimate children's capacities for risky play, we nonetheless selected it in favor of developmentally- or age-appropriate because of the wide range of abilities present at any particular age or developmental level.

1. Risky play: The accent should be on *play*

Recall your favorite childhood play experiences. Did you climb trees? Run through the woods? Wrestle with friends? Search for tadpoles in a swampy hole? Scramble to the top of polyhedral play structures? Race down steep hills on your bicycle—with friends or by yourself? Try to do something on your own without the usual adult assistance? Often, children's favorite ways to play involve an element of risk or danger. To define risky play, we draw from Sandseter's (2009) description: "thrilling and exciting forms of play that involve a risk of physical injury" (p. 3) and Sandseter et al.'s (2012) more broad definition: "play that provides opportunities for challenge, testing limits, exploring boundaries, and learning about risk." Many activities qualify as risky, but in order to be risky *play*, they must be essentially *playful*. That is, they must be intrinsically motivated and internally controlled, and involve the opportunity for some degree of suspension of reality (Skard & Bundy, 2008).

After extensive observations of children's play in two Norwegian preschools, Sandseter (2009) created a taxonomy describing types of risky play, outlining six types: play with great heights, play with high speeds, play with harmful tools, play with dangerous elements, rough and tumble play, or play where children can disappear/get lost. In a later study involving younger children (ages 1–3), Kleppe et al. (2017) added an additional category: play with impact. Table 1 is adapted from this publication, and describes the seven categories. Kleppe and colleagues also observed "vicarious risk" – a pre-risk-taking phase in which children become engaged while watching other children take risks. In our informal observations of children with disabilities, the authors of this paper have often witnessed children hanging back and watching peers take risks. Although these children were not participating explicitly, they often shared the ebullience of their peers. While this is not itself risky play, children can learn about risk-taking by watching others and gradually move towards taking risks themselves.

Table 1 Risky play categories.

Category	Risk	Examples
Great heights	Danger or injury from falling	• Climbing trees • Jumping from tall ledges • Balancing on top of jungle gyms • Hanging from monkey bars
High speed	Uncontrolled speed and pace that can lead to collision with something (or someone)	• Running at high speeds • Riding a bicycle down a hill • Skiing
Harmful tools	Can lead to injuries and wounds	• Using sharp tools for construction play • Cutting with scissors • Playing with ropes
Dangerous elements	Can be exposed to or injured by elements	• Playing near fire • Swimming in deep or icy water • Playing in darkness
Rough-and-tumble	Children can harm each other	• Wrestling • Play fighting • Chasing • High contact sports and games
Disappear/get lost	Children can disappear from the supervision of adults or get lost alone	• Exploring alone • Playing in an unfamiliar place
Impact	Injuries from crashing into objects/others	• Running into others • Running into fences or walls • Intentionally falling or crashing on the ground

Adapted from Kleppe, R., Melhuish, E. C., & Sandseter, E. B. (2017). Identifying and characterizing risky play in the age one-to-three years. *European Early Childhood Education Research Journal, 25*(3), 370–385.

2. Benefits of risky play for children with disabilities

There are myriad benefits of competently-appropriate risky play to physical health, development, and everyday well-being for both typically developing children and children with disabilities. Children with disabilities may gain even more benefits than their typically-developing peers. In this section, we describe several unique benefits that risky play may provide to children with disabilities.

2.1 Decision-making and autonomy

There is growing consensus that children and adults with disabilities should be involved in decision-making regarding medical care, education, daily lives, and futures (e.g., Adams & Levy, 2017). Indeed, the first principle of the United Nation's Convention on the Rights of Persons with Disabilities (UNCRC) is: "Respect for inherent dignity, individual autonomy including the freedom to make one's own choices, and independence of persons" (UNCRC, 2013). Decision-making requires careful consideration of risks and benefits—a difficult skill that requires practice. Through risky play, children with disabilities have opportunities to weigh risks and benefits in situations with minimal consequences. For example, a child considering whether she has the skills to jump from a high place safely uses the same general decision-making processes she will use later to weigh the risks and benefits of choices associated with independent living or medical care. In other words, the process of decision making in the context of risky play contributes to becoming an autonomous, empowered adult.

2.2 Emotional health

Children with disabilities (both cognitive and physical) often experience mental health comorbidities such as anxiety (Parkes et al., 2008; van Steensel & Heeman, 2017). Anxiety can have profoundly negative impacts on children's development – avoidant behavior may prevent children from seeking out novel opportunities to learn and grow. Play theorists have connected childhood mental health conditions to play deprivation (e.g., Brown, 2014). While this discourse is outside the scope of this paper, we take the position that access to free and risky play may help mitigate childhood anxiety.

Sandseter and Kennair (2011) described the "anti-phobic" effects of risky play. They proposed that, through risky play, children suspend fears and learn to manage anxiety and discomfort. Further, risky play is naturally uncertain – children must cope with unpredictability. Studies conducted by our research group and others (e.g., Hess & Bundy, 2003; Saunders, Sayer, & Goodale, 1999) suggest that playfulness can enhance children's natural coping abilities. Thus, providing regular and repeated opportunities for risky play may lead a child to be less anxious and more confident, and to cope more readily with fear and uncertainty in everyday life.

2.3 Physical health

Autism spectrum disorder (ASD), attention deficit hyperactive disorder (ADHD), and intellectual disability (ID) are among the most prevalent sources of childhood disability in the United States (Zablotsky et al., 2019). Recent meta-analyses connect all three conditions with higher rates of pediatric obesity than in typically-developing children (Kahathuduwa et al., 2019 [ASD], Cortese et al., 2016 [ADHD], Maiano, Hue, Morin, & Moullec, 2016 [ID]). Root causes of obesity vary (e.g., medication side effects, eating habits, sedentary behavior), but sufficient physical activity may be a powerful mediator (Powell, 2019). Studies suggest that risky play is associated with higher rates of habitual and acute physical activity – possibly because children are more engaged and, therefore, more likely to spend ample time at play (Brussoni et al., 2015; Engelen et al., 2013) Opportunities for risky play may combat childhood obesity and reduce the incidence of downstream health consequences for children with disabilities.

2.4 Social competence and empathy

Difficulty with social interactions is a hallmark characteristic of ASD (American Psychiatric Association, 2013) and is also prevalent among children with ADHD and many types of ID (Bora & Pantelis, 2016; Glasson et al., 2020). Children with these developmental disabilities may face exclusion by peers, leading to depression or other mental health concerns. Rough-and-tumble play, a form of risky play, provides a context for children to develop and practice social skills – particularly giving and interpreting social cues (Pellegrini & Smith, 1998). In order to keep play going, children must stifle aggression and recognize other children's playful intentions. Paradoxically, however, adults may prevent children with disabilities from engaging in this type of play out of fear that the children will become aggressive. Skilled playmates often assist by reminding the child that "they are just playing." If adults step back and allow the play to happen, they may find that all children can enhance their levels of empathy and acquire new and more complex social negotiation skills.

3. Parents and risk: Gatekeeping risky play for children with and without disabilities

Parents serve as gatekeepers to their children's play– they transport children to, allow, and disallow various types of play (Boxberger & Reimers, 2019). Parents are also primarily responsible for keeping their children safe—they may stifle play if they fear that it puts their child at risk of physical or emotional harm (Sterman, Naughton, Bundy, Froude, & Villeneuve, 2020b). In many parts of the Western World, parents' concerns for their children's safety may exceed the true dangers that these children face; hence parents place increasing restrictions on free outdoor play, leading to fewer opportunities to enjoy the benefits of risky play (Malone, 2007). In other words, unnecessary rules to prevent unlikely injury usurp play promotion (Wyver et al., 2010). This culture of "surplus safety" inhibits children's opportunities to experience the benefits of free play and competently-appropriate risk-taking (Buchanan, 1999) Wyver et al., 2010.

In the New Zealand State of Play Survey, Jelleyman, McPhee, Brussoni, Bundy, and Duncan (2019) investigated New Zealand parents' ($N=2003$) attitudes and practices towards risky play for their children (age 5–12). The authors administered a battery of mostly standardized and validated questionnaires that surveyed parents' beliefs about play, independent mobility, and children's health and safety. Parents generally believed that risky play and independent mobility supported children's growth and development, and that schools placed excessive limitations in the name of health and safety. However, when asked about their own children, most parents reported that their children seldom or never engaged in most forms of risky play. Additionally, more than half of parents felt that good supervision meant "knowing what their children were doing at all times" (p. 8). Many parents felt that, if children were unsupervised, they were likely to be injured in road crashes, ill-intentioned adults, or other frightening things. This study, the first of its kind, revealed the barriers parents place on children's free and risky play.

While the New Zealand State of Play Survey suggested the existence of limitations on children's play, few researchers have qualitatively explored parents' mindsets when enacting these limitations. Two studies by Niehues and colleagues began to explore this phenomenon for parents of children with and without disabilities. Niehues, Bundy, Broom, and Tranter (2015) examined parents' perceptions of, and responses to, risk and uncertainty in their children's lives. Thirty-seven parents participated. Ten had children with disabilities; 18 had faced perilous circumstances in their own lives, either due to their child's disability or their personal experiences (e.g., religious persecution). The remaining parents lived relatively risk-free lives. Interestingly, the parents who faced little risk expressed more fear of their children experiencing injury or failure. These parents acknowledged that they sometimes stifled children's opportunities to experience manageable uncertainties in favor of preventing minor injuries or being viewed as a "bad parent." On the other hand, parents who faced personal risk viewed challenging situations as opportunities for their children, with and without disabilities, to learn resilience, develop skills, and experience everyday wellbeing. While these parents acknowledged potential dangers and their own fears, they chose to provide their children with opportunities to manage risks.

In another paper, Niehues, Bundy, Broom, and Tranter (2016) explored six strategies adults used to make decisions about everyday risk-taking for their children. According to Niehues and colleagues, adults may: control (avoiding all risks), take time (reflect upon the child's abilities and the benefits of risk), develop trust (gain trust in the child's abilities), make positive appraisals (value the experiences of uncertainty), or let go (provide autonomy, support, and boundaries as needed to promote competently-appropriate risk-taking). Adults who faced risks in their own lives more easily selected and moved between these strategies for their children, while adults with less exposure to risk struggled to relinquish control.

Niehues et al.' (2015, 2016) work demonstrated the complexity of parents' decision-making around risk-taking and the impact these decisions have on children's everyday activities. Interestingly, parents of children with disabilities who participated in these studies were often more comfortable allowing their children to take risks than parents of typically-developing children. Some parents of children with disabilities acknowledged that everything presented more risk for their children than for other children, and that if they wanted their children to become independent adults, they had to begin early in allowing them to deal with risk. Nonetheless, parents' decision-making around risky play for children with disabilities is complicated. Sterman et al. (2016) conducted a qualitative synthesis of studies examining parents' decisions around active outdoor play for children with disabilities. Although they did not specifically examine risky play, outdoor play often affords risk-taking opportunities. Not surprisingly, they found that parents weighed myriad factors including finances, accessibility, and opinions of other adults alongside their child's needs and capabilities. Although Sterman et al. (2016) reviewed literature pertaining to children with disabilities, most parents likely consider these same factors.

When parents are intolerant of risk, their children have fewer chances to engage in risky play. When children do not engage in risky play, they do not learn to manage real, everyday risks. Vanskiver (unpublished master's thesis) investigated the relationship between parents' risk tolerance and children's ability to safely manage a pedestrian street crossing task. Parents completed a survey designed to measure their tolerance for risky play (Tolerance of Risk in Play Scale, which we describe in detail later in this paper). Children participated in a virtual reality task that simulated crossing the street. The children had to decide the right moment to cross the street so that they would not be hit by a virtual vehicle. Not surprisingly, parents' risky play tolerance significantly predicted children's performances on the street-crossing task, with lower tolerance scores predicting more hits and close calls ($R^2 = 0.29$, $F(1,16) = 6.52$, p less than 0.05). While this study did not examine this relationship for children with disabilities, we expect that the results would be similar – or potentially more significant. Because children with disabilities may need *more* opportunities to practice risk management than their peers, parents' risky play tolerance may be even more important to their safe decision-making.

4. Teachers and risk: Balancing duty of care and dignity of risk in play

Alongside parents, teachers are primarily responsible for supervising children's play. Thus, teachers are an important consideration if we desire to provide more opportunities for competently-appropriate risk-taking (Sterman, Naughton, Bundy, Froude, & Villeneuve, 2020a). While parents serve as gatekeepers of play at home and in the community, teachers have a similar role at school, particularly on the playground during recess. The often-opposing responsibilities of teachers to protect children from any potential of harm, while simultaneously providing rich opportunities for learning so children may develop into independent adults, can be summarized by the concepts "duty of care" and "dignity of risk." The juxtaposition of duty of care and dignity of risk is especially relevant when considering the responsibilities of teachers working with children with disabilities. Duty of care is defined by the law in relation to school liability; teachers are responsible for supervising children and preventing their exposure to situations that could result in injury (Newnham, 2000). Dignity of risk is the right of a person, especially those with a disability, to experience manageable exposure to risky situations in order to learn skills for risk management in anticipation of future autonomy (Woflensberger, Nirje, Olshansky, Perske, & Roos, 1972).

At school, the threat of liability following injury on the school playground is a significant concern for most teachers (Bundy et al., 2009). Injury may give rise to charges of negligence or failure to fulfill their duty of care. In reality, teachers are rarely negligent (Newnham, 2000). Instead, injuries may result from children seeking exciting play situations when opportunities for play are not challenging enough and therefore boring (Brussoni et al., 2015). Fear of liability has resulted in an imbalance between duty of care and dignity of risk with an emphasis on duty of care (Little, 2010). Further, teachers may perceive themselves as accountable to parents. Even if teachers know that they have not been negligent, they may fear calling a parent to report an injury (Sterman et al., 2019). Additionally, some teachers have personal reservations regarding risk and believe that all risky situations are dangerous, have high likelihood of resulting in injury, and should be avoided (van Rooijen & Newstead, 2016).

Even teachers who would allow their own children to engage in risky play may feel uncertain when supervising students engaging in risky play on the playground and interrupt the play in response (Bundy et al., 2009). The cultural shifts towards risk aversion and surplus safety (Gill, 2018; van Rooijen & Newstead, 2016; Wyver et al., 2010) make it difficult for teachers to feel they can allow risky play, without fear of consequence, even if they perceive associated benefits.

Little (2010) interviewed preschool teachers on their perspectives of risky play and safety during outdoor play. Even though many teachers acknowledged the value of risky play, they feared litigation, lack of support from school administration, and child health and safety regulations. Regulatory factors that limit play include playground structure guidelines (e.g., height, fall material, surface texture), teacher to child ratios on the playground, and school-specific play policy like restricting children to only going down a slide feet-first on their bottom (Ball, 2002); Little & Eager, 2010; van Rooijen & Newstead, 2016. Little (2010) acknowledged the contradictory perceptions held by teachers (i.e., on one hand children are competent and capable, but on the other hand, they are vulnerable and teachers must protect them) that cause conflict between teachers' pedagogical beliefs and their actions in the face of risk, furthering the imbalance between duty of care and dignity of risk.

In recent years, with increasing recognition of the benefits of risky play, many education programs have attempted to prioritize opportunities for such play at school during play outdoors and during physical education (Brussoni et al., 2015; Brussoni, Olsen, Pike, & Sleet, 2012; Wyver et al., 2010). These programs indicate that educators need to adopt a more nuanced view of risk, beyond good or bad, and understand that risky play holds opportunities for development including confidence, healthy lifestyle, resilience, social skills, and problem solving Brussoni et al., 2015; (Cooke, Wong, & Press, 2019). Nonetheless, several researchers (Cooke, Wong, & Press, 2019); Spencer et al., 2016 have found that, while societal understandings of risky play are shifting towards valuing these benefits, the initial reaction of teachers when supervising a child in a risky play situation is still to interrupt the play to protect themselves from negative consequences.

Despite the cultural shift towards permitting and even encouraging risky play in school, children with disabilities may still not have opportunities for this important play at school. Sterman et al. (2019) found that teachers perceived their students with disabilities as more vulnerable than typically-developing children; therefore, they felt they needed additional protection and supervision during play. In some schools, children with disabilities play on a separate playground, isolated from typically-developing peers. Without models for risky play, these children may not push their own boundaries. Furthermore, teachers may feel even more accountable to parents of children with disabilities or health concerns; as a result, they may be less lenient in permitting risky play. In order for a child of all abilities to enjoy the benefits of learning through the dignity of risk, teachers must seek a realistic balance between duty of care and dignity of risk.

5. TRiPS-R and TRiPS-T: Instruments to measure adults' tolerance of risky play

Understanding parents' and teachers' perceptions and practices surrounding risky play is the first step to providing opportunities for all children to engage in this health- and development-promoting play. The literature presented above suggests that both teachers and parents feel that free, risky play benefits children, but they struggle to balance this with their responsibility to protect children, be seen as good caregivers, and manage their own anxiety. For teachers, fears of litigation further influence their decisions around risky play. In an effort to better understand adults' practices related to risky play, our research group developed two instruments that assess adults' risk tolerance: the Tolerance of Risk in Play Scale-Revised (TRiPS-R) for parents, and the Tolerance of Risk in Play Scale-Teacher Version (T-TRiPS) for teachers. In this section, we describe development of TRiPS-R and T-TRiPS and the results of psychometric analyses of data gathered with these novel instruments.

5.1 Development of TRiPS-R and T-TRiPS

We derived TRiPS-R and T-TRiPS from the original Tolerance of Risk in Play Scale (Hill & Bundy, 2014). Members of our research group developed TRiPS to evaluate change in adults' risk tolerances as a result of an intervention entitled the Sydney Playground Project (SPP). SPP comprised a two-part intervention. The first component was child-directed: we placed recycled materials with no specific play purpose (i.e., tarps, tires, and barrels) on playgrounds during recess. The second component was adult-directed: we conducted group-based, constructive education sessions (Risk Reframing Workshops) with teachers and parents to encourage them to step back and allow the children to play without interference. We conducted the first round of this project in mainstream schools. A full description of the intervention can be found elsewhere (Bundy et al., 2011).

The original TRiPS contained 31 dichotomous items derived from Sandseter's (2009) six categories of risky play: (1) play with great heights, (2) play with high speed, (3) play with harmful tools, (4) play near dangerous elements, (5) rough-and-tumble play, and (6) play where children can 'disappear' or get lost. We designed TRiPS for use with parents, caregivers, and school staff. Each item asked the adult to decide whether they would allow a child to participate in an activity with some level of risk (e.g., "Do you let this child use 'adult tools' (e.g. hammer and nail, knife, scissors) unsupervised?" [*harmful tools*]).

Data gathered with TRiPS demonstrated strong construct validity and internal reliability based on Rasch analyses (Hill & Bundy, 2014). Despite promising psychometric properties, the authors described several limitations of the original instrument. They noted gaps along the hierarchy of items, suggesting that additional items were necessary to capture the most and least risk-tolerant adults. Further, they recommended separate instruments to evaluate school staff and parents/home caregivers, since these two groups supervised different types of play.

We created TRiPS-R to fulfill the need for a parent-specific version of the original TRiPS. TRiPS-R is a 30-item self-report survey that takes less than 15 min to complete; it is available both on paper and digitally. When we developed TRiPS-R, we were initiating the second round of SPP to take place in schools for children with disabilities. Therefore, we created TRiPS-R to be appropriate for parents of children with and without disabilities. First, we hypothesized that risk-tolerance would be lower for parents of children with disabilities; therefore, we added several easier items to the tool (e.g., "Do you allow this child play with other people's pets?") to improve sensitivity for lower levels of risk-tolerance. To improve the general usability of the instrument, we also revised items that were culturally specific to Australia (e.g., "Would you allow the child to play in the bush out of your sight?"), to improve the generalized usability of the instrument. Table 2 shows all items on TRiPS-R as well as abbreviated item names. Henceforth, we refer to items using the abbreviated names.

Table 2 TRiPS-R items and abbreviated item names.

TRiPS-R item	Abbreviated name
Do you trust this child to play by him/herself without constant supervision?	Play w/o supervision
Do you allow this child to play chase with other children?	Chase
Do you let this child go head first down a slippery dip/slide?	Slide
Do you allow this child to continue playing after s/he gets a scrape?	Scrape
Do you let this child continue to play very challenging activities even when you know s/he may not succeed?	Play challenging
Would you let this child climb a tree within your reach?	Tree within reach
Would you let this child roast marshmallows on an open fire?	Marshmallows
Do you allow this child to play-fight with sticks?[a]	Play-fight (sticks)[a]
Would you let this child walk on a slippery surface knowing there was a chance s/he may fall?	Slippery surface
Do you let this child use 'adult tools' (e.g. hammer and nail, knife, scissors) unsupervised?[b]	Adult tools
Do you allow this child to engage in rough and tumble play?	Rough and tumble
Would you let this child jump down from a height of 3–4 m/ 10–13 ft?	Jump 3–4
Do you allow this child play with other people's pets?	Other people's pets
Do you allow this child to go on school excursions?[c]	School excursions
Would you let this child swim in the ocean close to the shore while you were watching from the beach?	Ocean
Do you let this child resolve disagreements (without stepping in) if children are pushing or poking one another?	Physical disagreements

Table 2 TRiPS-R items and abbreviated item names.—cont'd

TRiPS-R item	Abbreviated name
Would you allow this child to play on equipment if you thought there was the potential s/he may break a bone?	Equipment (broken bone)
Do you let this child play in your yard unsupervised?	Yard unsupervised
Do you allow this child to play-fight, testing who is strongest?	Play-fight (strength)
Do you allow this child to play at other people's houses?	Others' houses
Do you wait to see how well this child manages challenges before getting involved?	Manages challenges
Would you let this child light a fire independently?	Light fire
Do you let this child resolve disagreements (without stepping in) if children are shouting, but not hitting?	Verbal disagreements
Would you let this child climb as high as s/he wanted in a tree?	Tree to desired height
Would you allow this child to ride a bicycle or scooter down a steep hill?	Steep hill
Do you allow this child to have sleep-overs at friends' houses?	Sleep-over
Would you let this child go off on their own in a new environment if you were able to watch them from afar?	New environment
Do you allow this child to choose what activities s/he will do on the weekend?	Weekend activities
Would you let this child balance on a fallen tree or other narrow surface about 2 m/6 ft above the ground?	Narrow surface
Do you encourage this child to take some risks if it means having fun during play?	Risks if fun
Would you allow this child to climb a tree beyond your reach?	Tree beyond reach

[a]Item removed from the TRiPS-R instrument after Rasch analysis.
[b]After initial analyses, item rephrased to "Do you allow this child to use 'adult tools' (e.g., hammer and nail, knife) unsupervised?"
[c]After initial analyses, item rephrased to "Would you allow this child to go on school or daycare excursions?"

Similarly, we designed T-TRiPS to fulfill the need for a teacher-specific instrument to evaluate risk tolerance. T-TRiPS was developed based on the original TRiPS, with items being modified or removed as they apply to the context of the teacher. T-TRiPS items reflect activities teachers commonly supervise their students doing during a school day. The T-TRiPS includes 25 items with dichotomous answers and 5 short answer questions probing teachers' personal experiences of risky play. Table 3 shows all items on T-TRiPS as well as abbreviated item names. Items reflect the six categories

Table 3 T-TRiPS items and abbreviated item names.

TRiPS-R item	Abbreviated name
Do you trust your students to play in the classroom without constant supervision?	Classroom w/o supervision
Do you let your students play chase with one another?	Chase
Would you let your students go head first down a slippery dip/slide?	Slide
Do you allow your students to continue playing after s/he gets a scrape?	Scrape
Do you let your students continue to play very challenging activities even when you know they may not succeed?	Play challenging
Would you let your students climb a tree or other surface within your reach?	Tree within reach
Would you let your students run in a place where there was an open fire or portable heater?	Open fire/heater?
Do you allow your students to playfight with sticks?	Play-fight (sticks)
Would you let your students walk on a slippery surface if there was a chance they may fall?	Slippery surface
Do you let your students use 'adult tools' (e.g. hammer and nail, knife, scissors) unsupervised?	Adult tools unsupervised
Do you allow your students to engage in rough and tumble play?	Rough and Tumble
Would you let the majority of your students jump down from a height of 34 m?	Jump 3–4
Would you allow your students to care for pets in the classroom?	Care for class pets
Would you let your students swim close to the pool edge while you were watching from the side?	Swim
Do you let your students resolve disagreements (without stepping in) if they are pushing or poking one another?	Physical disagreements
Would you allow your students to play on equipment if you thought there was the potential s/he may break a bone?	Equipment (broken bone)

Table 3 T-TRiPS items and abbreviated item names.—cont'd

TRiPS-R item	Abbreviated name
Do you allow your students to playfight, testing who is strongest?	Play-fight (strength)
Do you wait to see how well your students manage challenges before getting involved?	Manage challenges
Would you allow your student to ride a toy/bicycle down a steep hill?	Steep hill
Would you let your students climb as high as they wanted in a tree?	Tree to desired height
Do you let your students play in the playground unsupervised?	Playground w/o supervision
Do you let your students resolve disagreements (without stepping in) if the children are shouting but not hitting one another?	Verbal disagreements
Would you let your student(s) go off on their own in a new environment if you were able to watch them from afar?	New environment
Would you let your students balance on a fallen tree or other narrow surface 2 m above the ground?	Narrow surface
Do you encourage your students to take some risks if it means having fun during play?	Risks if fun

of risky play identified by Sandseter (2009) (great heights, high speed, harmful tools, dangerous elements, rough-and-tumble, disappear/get lost). The instrument can be completed in approximately 15 min.

In the sections that follow, we provide information about the psychometric properties of data gathered with TRiPS-R and T-TRiPS during the second round of SPP. For each instrument, we provide a brief summary followed by in-depth technical information regarding the statistical analyses. The former should be adequate for practitioners wanting to ensure that the assessments they use produce psychometrically-sound data. The second will be useful for researchers who require greater detail in publications and funding requests. We encourage readers to select the version that suits their needs.

5.2 Psychometric evaluation of TRiPS-R data: A brief summary

5.2.1 Participants and procedure

We collected data from 66 parents and caregivers of children ages 3–13 years. Most reporters were mothers born in Australia; they ranged in age from less than 20 years to greater than 56 years. The children they reported on ranged in age from 3 to 13 years; most (50/66) were male. Our participants comprised two groups: a group of parents whose children with disabilities participated in the second round of SPP ($n = 39$), and a group of parents who we recruited from pop-up adventure playgrounds (PUP) where children played with loose, recycled materials ($n = 27$). We presume the children from the PUP group were typically developing, although we did not collect that information. For the SPP group, we instructed parents to respond regarding their child who would participate in the intervention. For the PUP group, we instructed parents of multiple children to think of only one child when they responded to TRiPS-R; we gave no guidance for choosing. Reporters completed either a paper or an iPad version of the TRiPS-R. Reporters replied "yes" or "no" to each of 31 TRiPS-R items depending on if, under any circumstances, they would allow the child to do the activity.

5.2.2 Data analysis and results

We analyzed the data for evidence of construct validity and internal reliability using a statistical procedure called Rasch analysis. We tested the degree to which the data met two Rasch assumptions: (1) items that involved little risk would be easy for all respondents to allow their children to do (i.e., they would choose "yes"); and (2) parents who were more risk tolerant would be more likely to say "yes" to riskier activities than risk-intolerant parents.

Construct validity. The initial analyses revealed a need for minor revision to the TRiPS-R. After examining the results, we eliminated one item (*play-fighting with sticks*). Thus, the final version of TRiPS-R comprises 30 items. Data from 29 of the 30 items (96.7%) meet the specified assumptions. Thus, we concluded that there was good evidence for construct validity.

External validity. In addition to scoring TRiPS-R items, we asked parents to report the extent to which they encouraged their child to take risks: often, sometimes, seldom/never. Using analysis of variance and *t*-tests, we found that parents who said they more often encouraged risk-taking also achieved significantly higher TRiPS-R scores than parents who said they seldom or never encouraged risk taking.

Internal reliability. The Rasch-generated person reliability index of 0.88 revealed excellent evidence for internal reliability. That is, given a similar data set, there is high likelihood that the level of caregiver tolerance would be the same. The analysis also revealed approximately four levels of caregiver risk tolerance: very high, moderately high, relatively low, and very low.

5.3 Psychometric evaluation of TRiPS-R data: In-depth analysis

We used Rasch modeling to examine evidence for construct validity, external validity, and internal reliability of TRiPS-R data collected during the second round of the SPP, as well as additional data collected with a cohort of typically-developing children. Box 1. contains the eight research questions (RQs) we sought to answer.

5.3.1 Participants

We recruited a convenience sample of parents of children aged 3 to 13 years. We drew this sample from two sources. First, we recruited parents from the five primary school programs for children with disabilities in New South

---

BOX 1 Research questions (RQs) pertaining to construct validity, external validity, and internal reliability of the TRiPS-R/T-TRiPS.

Construct validity

- **RQ1**: Do individual items on the TRiPS-R/T-TRiPS correspond with the Rasch model of the latent variable (i.e., do responses on items correlate positively with increased total measure)?
- **RQ2**: Do data from 95% of items on the TRiPS-R/T-TRiPS conform to the expectations of the Rasch model, as measured by acceptable goodness-of-fit statistics?
- **RQ3**: Do data from 95% of persons who completed the TRiPS-R/T-TRiPS conform to the expectations of the Rasch model, as measured by acceptable goodness-of-fit statistics?
- **RQ4**: Is the spread of item difficulties on the TRiPS-R/T-TRiPS sufficient to capture levels of the latent variable among the sample measured?
- **RQ5**: Does the principal components analysis of linearized residuals suggest additional underlying constructs (i.e., multidimensionality) of the TRiPS-R/T-TRiPS?

External validity

- **RQ6**: Do parents/teachers who report frequently encouraging their children to take risks obtain higher scores on the TRiPS-R/T-TRiPS than parents/teachers who report less frequent risk encouragement?

Internal reliability

- **RQ7**: Does data collected with the TRiPS-R/T-TRiPS demonstrate sufficient internal reliability, as measured by person reliability index?
- **RQ8**: How many levels of risk tolerance can the TRiPS-R/T-TRiPS reliably discriminate, as measured by number of strata associated with the measure?

Wales, Australia that participated in the second round of the SPP. We also recruited parents from Pop-Up Playgrounds (PUP) hosted by Reverse Garbage in NSW (https://reversegarbage.org.au/). At PUPs, Reverse Garbage provides recycled loose materials (e.g., pipes, tires, fabric) for children to use in play. We recruited parents of children ages 3 and older to complete TRiPS-R while their children played on the PUP. While we presumed that most children attending the PUPs were typically developing, we did not specifically ask parents about their children's development. We received 39 surveys from the Sydney Playground Project cohort and 27 surveys from the PUPs. Because the Rasch model is robust to missing data, we included all 66 surveys, although 5 participants (7.6%) left questions blank (range 2 to 16 blank items). Table 4 contains demographic information about participants. Of note, the sample for this study comprised few fathers or parents of children aged 11–13. Additionally, more parents responded regarding their male children (55/66), likely due to the high proportion of SPP participants with ASD, which is more frequently diagnosed in males. Clearly, further research is indicated.

5.3.2 Procedure
We administered TRiPS-R via an online platform. All respondents had the option to complete the survey on iPads provided by the research team, or using a paper and pencil copy. We instructed all parents of multiple children to think of only one child when they responded to TRiPS-R. For those involved in the SPP, they were to think of the child participating in the intervention. We gave no instruction to parents of children participating in the PUP regarding selection of a child. Before completing TRiPS-R, participants responded to an additional question used to evaluate external validity: "How often do you encourage this child to take everyday risks? (Never, Seldom, Sometimes, Often)".

5.3.3 Analysis
We conducted Rasch analyses using Winsteps ([Version No. 4.5.2]; Linacre, 2020), a Rasch-specific statistical program. We transformed the 'yes' and 'no' responses to '1' and '0' respectively. For this analysis, we employed the dichotomous Rasch model (DRM). The DRM is based upon core assumptions detailed elsewhere (Wright & Stone, 1979). Here, we provide a brief description of these assumptions with respect to the present study.

The DRM assumes that items measure aspects of a unidimensional construct called the 'latent trait' – in this case, tolerance of risk in play.

Table 4 Demographic information for TRiPS-R psychometric study participants (N = 66).

Variable	PUP (*n* = 27)	SPP (*n* = 39)	Total
Respondent's relationship to child			
Mother	17	33	50
Father	7	2	9
Other	3	4	7
Respondent's age (years)			
≤20	0	1	1
21–25	1	0	1
26–30	2	1	3
31–35	7	3	10
36–40	6	8	14
41–45	6	14	20
46–50	0	4	4
50–55	1	1	2
≥ 56	0	2	2
No response	4	5	9
Respondent's national origin			
Australia	19	22	41
Other	3	7	10
No response	5	10	15
Child's age (years)			
3–4	12	4	16
5–7	12	21	33
8–10	2	13	15
11–13	1	1	2
Child's gender			
Female	9	7	16
Male	18	32	50

According to the model, all respondents are more likely to score higher (i.e., respond 'yes') to easier items. Additionally, the DRM assumes that people who are more risk tolerant are more likely to respond 'yes' to more difficult items. Through Rasch analysis, we transformed raw data into a log-odds unit ('logit') scale. The logit scale is a true-interval scale with a mean of 0.0 logits and standard deviation of 1.0 logits. Both items and respondents are assigned measures along a single hierarchy representing the construct. For the items, measures represent difficulty. For persons, measures represent risk tolerance.

Using the DRM, we examined several sources of evidence for construct validity and internal reliability. *Point-measure correlations, goodness-of-fit statistics, item spread*, and *principal components analysis* provided evidence for construct validity. *Congruence with self-reported risk tolerance* provided evidence for external validity. A *person reliability index* and *strata* calculated from that index provided evidence for internal reliability.

Point-measure correlations. To determine if each item corresponds with the latent variable (i.e., that "yes" on each item indicates more tolerance to risk), we examined Pearson point-measure correlation coefficients between observations and item measure. In the Rasch model, positive point-measure correlations suggest that items align with the construct (Bond & Fox, 2015). Of note, the magnitude of these correlations is less important than the directionality. We hypothesized that all point-measure correlations would be positive.

Goodness-of-fit Statistics. We examined two types of goodness-of-fit statistics for items: mean-square ($MnSq$) and standardized (Z_{std}) fit statistics. For each type of fit statistics, Winsteps provides two versions: infit and outfit. Infit statistics are "inlier-sensitive" or information-weighted to reduce the influence of off-target responses (i.e., people whose overall scores are far from the item measure). Outfit statistics are unweighted and typically reflect fit problems due to outliers. Mean-squares show the amount of distortion of the measurement system. Ideal mean-square value is 1.0. We expected values between 0.5 and 1.5 for both persons and items to indicate productive measurement. Standardized values test the hypothesis that the data fit the model perfectly; their desired value is 0.0. We considered values between -2.0 and $+2.0$ to be acceptable for measurement. We selected items for further examination if both infit or both outfit statistics failed to conform to the expectations of the model. We selected all criteria for goodness-of-fit statistics based on Linacre (2002).

Item spread. We assessed the spread of items in two ways. First, we compared the mean item measure and the mean person measure. In the Rasch model, the mean item measure is set at 0.0 logits. A mean person measure close to 0.0 indicates a match between the sample's risk-tolerance and the scale difficulty. Second, we visually inspected the Winsteps-generated Wright map. The Wright map provides a hierarchy of items and persons along a logit scale, ranging from lowest to higher measures. Large gaps indicate a need for more items, while items grouped together suggest redundancy.

Principal component analysis. While goodness-of-fit statistics and other evidence described above examine the extent to which the construct is unidimensional, principal component analysis of linearized residuals (PCA) provide evidence of the strength of additional dimensions in the data (i.e., multidimensionality). We considered a second dimension to be strong enough to refute unidimensionality of the construct if the following three conditions were met (Linacre, 2018). (1) There were contrasts with eigenvalues ≥ 3 (i.e., with the strength of more than 2 items). (2) Item subsets within contrasts demonstrated disattenuated correlations less than 0.57, indicating that item subsets likely measure different latent variables. (3) The strength of the contrast is markedly larger than a contrast that would be expected by chance alone (as determined by running PCA with Winsteps-generated simulated data files of the Rasch dimension only). According to Wright and Stone (1979), unidimensionality is essential to good construct measurement; evidence of multiple dimensions suggests that the items should be scored as multiple, separate instruments.

Congruence with self-report. To evaluate external validity of TRiPS-R, we conducted an analysis of variance (ANOVA) to identify significant differences in TRiPS-R scores among parents who reported different frequencies of risk encouragement. We grouped parents based on their responses to the question: "How often do you encourage this child to take everyday risks?", ("Seldom/Never," "Sometimes," and "Often"). We hypothesized that parents who reported more frequent risk-encouragement would achieve higher scores on TRiPS-R (i.e., have more tolerance of risk in play). We conducted post-hoc analyses using pairwise t-tests.

Person-reliability index. The person reliability index is the Rasch equivalent to Cronbach's alpha and represents the likelihood that measures could be reproduced with a similar data set (Wright & Masters, 1982). We required a person reliability index ≥ 0.80 to establish strong evidence for internal reliability.

Strata. The strata value is an alternative measure of reliability that represents the number of levels of risk-tolerance that the measure can distinguish

(Wright & Masters, 1982). Winsteps generates a separation index (G), which we converted to strata using the formula:

$$Strata = \frac{4G + 1}{3}$$

We required a strata value of ≥ 2.0 to establish evidence for sufficient internal reliability.

5.3.4 Results

Rasch analysis is an iterative process. We made several changes to the instrument based on the results of our analyses. Most of these changes were based on examination of goodness-of-fit statistics generated by Winsteps. Table 5 contains item difficulty measures, standard errors, and goodness-of-fit statistics from our initial analysis. During the initial analyses, all items demonstrated acceptable infit statistics ($MnSq$ 0.5–1.5 and Z_{std} −2.0–2.0). However, two items (*play-fight [sticks]*, and *weekend activities*) had both $MnSq$ and Z_{std} outfit statistics outside of the desirable range, suggesting that outlying responses contributed to statistical failure to fit. Additionally, one item (*school excursions*) had acceptable infit statistics and acceptable Z_{std} outfit statistics, but outfit $MnSq$ of 2.05. Linacre (2002) noted that $MnSq$ values greater than 2 indicate enough unpredictability to seriously degrade the measurement system. We closely examined these three items for sources of error. Through iterative analysis and cross-referencing with comments left on each survey question, we identified and removed seven individual responses deemed to be errors. Most of these errors were in response to *school excursions*; the children in question did not attend schools that offered excursions. After removing these responses, *play-fight [sticks]* continued to show outfit statistics outside our acceptable range (*play-fight [sticks]*). Additionally, *adult tools* showed unacceptable outfit statistics. We ultimately removed *play-fight [sticks]* as several comments suggested that responses reflected opposition to violence as instead of intolerance of risk. We chose to keep *adult tools* but to remove the references to scissors, as several parents commented that they were comfortable with scissors but not the other tools described. We revised *school excursions* to include day care and preschool outings. We also changed this question to, "Would you allow this child…" instead of "Do you allow this child…" in the event that some children (especially very young children) do not have the opportunity for school excursions. The final instrument comprises 30 items. All subsequent results represent the 30 retained items with original wording as shown in Table 2. Table 6 displays the measures, standard errors, and goodness-of-fit statistics for the final instrument.

Table 5 Item measures and goodness-of-fit statistics from initial TRiPS-R.

Item	Measure	MnSq (Infit)	Z_{std} (Infit)	MnSq (Outfit)	Z_{std} (Outfit)
Play w/o supervision	0.05	0.93	−0.42	0.95	−0.02
Chase	−2.81	0.95	0.05	0.33	−0.45
Slide	−0.37	1.13	0.79	0.98	0.12
Scrape	−4.02	0.93	0.24	0.19	−0.52
Play challenging	−1.97	0.85	−0.42	1.06	0.34
Tree within reach	−1.58	0.97	−0.03	0.69	−0.24
Marshmallows	0.05	1.13	0.84	1.30	0.86
Play-fight (sticks)[a]	2.37	1.39	2.48	2.32	2.81
Slippery surface	−0.05	1.06	0.43	0.97	0.07
Adult tools[a]	2.80	1.29	1.69	1.99	1.88
Rough and tumble	−1.58	1.02	0.14	0.96	0.19
Jump 3–4	3.28	0.98	−0.03	0.90	0.01
Other people's pets	−0.97	1.03	0.20	0.95	0.11
School excursions[a]	−1.58	1.28	1.12	2.02	1.33
Ocean	1.17	1.01	0.10	0.89	−0.34
Physical disagreements	0.99	0.99	−0.03	1.04	0.25
Equipment (broken bone)	0.33	0.73	−1.85	0.61	−1.26
Yard unsupervised	−0.07	0.88	−0.72	0.76	−0.52
Play-fight (strength)	0.33	0.92	−0.51	0.81	−0.49
Others' houses	−1.33	0.92	−0.27	0.95	0.14
Manages challenges	−2.71	0.85	−0.18	0.28	−0.55
Light fire	4.56	0.93	−0.07	1.07	0.40
Verbal disagreements	0.77	0.96	−0.21	0.91	−0.23
Tree to desired height	1.23	0.80	−1.41	0.71	−1.18
Steep hill	1.97	1.01	0.11	0.87	−0.38
Sleep-over	1.69	1.00	0.08	0.89	−0.33
New environment	−0.36	0.91	−0.50	0.81	−0.25
Weekend activities	−1.30	1.30	1.26	4.02	2.84
Narrow surface	1.42	0.87	−0.89	0.77	−0.89
Risks if fun	−3.17	1.12	0.39	1.22	0.60
Tree beyond reach	0.86	0.62	−2.86	0.51	−2.13

[a]Misfitting item.
MnSq, mean-square fit statistics; Z_{std}, standardized fit statistics.

Table 6 Item measures and goodness-of-fit statistics for final TRiPS-R.

Item	Measure	MnSq (Infit)	Z_{std} (Infit)	MnSq (Outfit)	Z_{std} (Outfit)
Play w/o supervision	0.16	0.98	−0.07	1.15	0.50
Chase	−2.78	0.98	0.11	0.34	−0.34
Slide	−0.27	1.16	0.93	1.01	0.18
Scrape	−4.00	0.93	0.23	0.18	−0.57
Play challenging	−1.92	0.83	−0.49	0.99	0.27
Tree within reach	−1.52	0.98	−0.01	0.66	−0.27
Marshmallows	0.16	1.19	1.18	1.52	1.27
Slippery surface	0.06	1.12	0.73	1.06	0.29
Adult tools[a]	3.04	1.37	2.03	2.38	2.12
Rough & tumble	−1.52	1.04	0.25	0.99	0.24
Jump 3–4	3.56	1.03	0.22	0.98	0.19
Other people's pets	−0.90	1.06	0.38	1.06	0.30
School excursions	−2.74	0.94	0.03	0.39	−0.24
Ocean	1.33	1.06	0.43	0.95	−0.10
Physical disagreements	1.14	1.01	0.13	1.12	0.50
Equipment (broken bone)	0.46	0.74	−1.78	0.62	−1.19
Yard unsupervised	0.04	0.90	−0.56	0.81	−0.34
Play–fight (strength)	0.46	0.94	−0.34	0.80	−0.51
Other's houses	−1.25	0.92	−0.28	1.10	0.37
Manages challenges	−2.67	0.87	−0.13	0.29	−0.45
Light fire	4.99	1.01	0.16	1.46	0.73
Verbal disagreements	0.91	0.98	−0.05	0.95	−0.07
Tree to desired height	1.40	0.81	−1.29	0.70	−1.13
Steep hill	2.17	1.08	0.56	0.92	−0.15
Sleep–over	1.88	1.05	0.39	0.95	−0.08
New environment	−0.26	0.95	−0.23	0.95	0.06
Weekend activities	−1.40	1.27	1.08	0.93	0.15
Narrow surface	1.59	0.9	−0.67	0.83	−0.58
Risks if fun	−3.14	1.15	0.44	1.39	0.71
Tree beyond reach	1.01	0.64	−2.52	0.52	−1.95

[a]Misfitting item.
MnSq, mean–square fit statistics; Z_{std}, standardized fit statistics.

Point-measure correlations. All items demonstrated positive point-measure correlations throughout each iterative analysis. Final point-measure correlations ranged from 0.11–0.73, suggesting that all items progressed in the same direction as the overall measure (RQ1).

Goodness-of-fit statistics. Twenty-nine of 30 items (96.7%) conformed to the expectations of the Rasch model for both infit and outfit statistics, suggesting strong construct validity (RQ2).

Item spread. The mean logit measure of participants in this study was 1.36, while the mean logit measure of items was fixed at 0.0. A higher mean person measure suggests that many of the items are easy for respondents to endorse. An imbalance of easy and difficult items can lead to imprecise measurement at the tails of the measure. However, visual inspection of the Wright map (Fig. 1) suggested that items (right side of figure) spread across various levels of the respondent risk tolerance (left side of figure). Although several items appear redundant (i.e., occupy similar spaces along the construct; [e.g., *narrow surface*; *tree to desired height*]), items sufficiently capture the range of risk tolerance among the intended population (RQ4). No participants obtained the maximum raw score, although three had estimated scores above the measurable range of item difficulties. None fell below this range. One important purpose of the TRiPS-R is to identify parents who are very risk intolerant. Thus, possible ceiling effects are not a major limitation of this measure.

Principal component analysis. PCA results did not suggest multidimensionality (RQ5). Although the PCA revealed a contrast with eigenvalue 2.77, explaining 4.6% of the variance in raw scores, the Rasch construct explained a much larger portion of the variance (48.8%). Although the contrast was larger than our threshold eigenvalue of 2.5, the disattenuated correlations for the three clusters of items in the contrast ranged from 1.0–0.82. This suggests that the components align along the Rasch construct, and can be considered "threads" of a unidimensional construct (Linacre, 2018).

Congruence with self-report. Fig. 2 displays the mean scores and quartile ranges for each group. Table 7 contains means and standard deviations for each group, reported in logits. As we expected, mean logit scores were higher for parents who reported that they more frequently encouraged risks. The ANOVA was significant ($F = 3.77$, $p = 0.03$). Pairwise t-tests (also displayed in Table 7) indicated that only the "Never/Seldom" group differed significantly from the "Often" group ($t = -2.27$, $p_{adj} = 0.03$). "Sometimes" and "Often" approached significant difference ($t = -1.88$, $p = 0.06$).

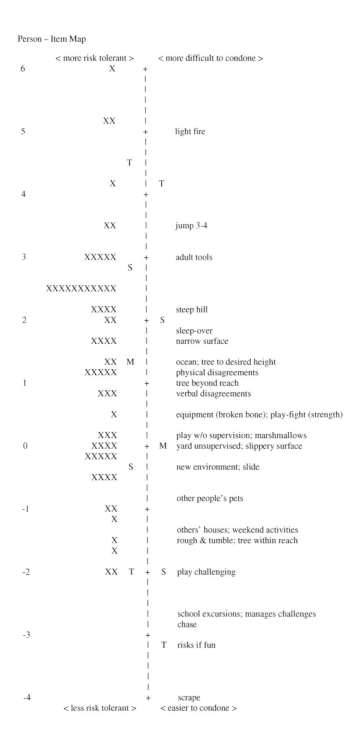

Fig. 1 Wright Map of the TRiPS-R Construct. *Notes.* Construct displayed along a common logit scale (far left). Left side of the map displays approximate participant measures (X); right side of the map displays approximate item measures. *M* = Mean. *S* = 1 standard deviation. *T* = 2 standard deviations.

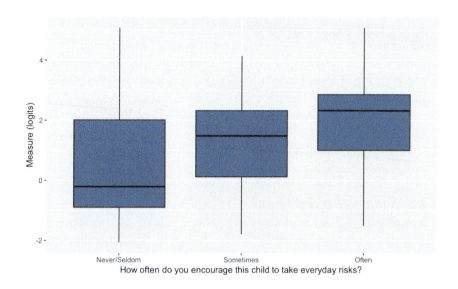

Fig. 2 Mean TRiPS-R Scores by self-reported frequency of encouraging everyday risks (N=66).

Table 7 Group means and pairwise comparisons of TRiPS-R scores and self-reported risk encouragement.

			Pairwise t-tests (t [p])	
Response	N	Mean (SD)	Sometimes	Often
Seldom	14	0.53 (1.99)	−1.52 (0.13)	−2.27 (0.03)
Sometimes	37	1.18 (1.38)		−1.88 (0.06)
Often	15	2.04 (1.76)		

Person reliability index. The person reliability index for the TRiPS-R was 0.88 (RQ7), suggesting strong evidence for internal reliability.

Strata. We found a separation value of 2.68, corresponding to a strata value of 3.91. This suggests that the TRiPS-R can reliably distinguish nearly 4 levels of performance. This exceeded our desired strata value of 2.0.

5.4 Psychometric evaluation of T-TRiPS: A brief summary
5.4.1 Participants and procedure
We collected data from 99 preschool and primary school teachers of children ages 4–12 years and diagnosed with ASD and/or ID. The teachers we

surveyed came from school participating in SPP. Teachers ranged in age from younger than 20 years to older than 56 years, and included lead and assistant teachers. Duration of teachers' experience teaching children with disabilities ranged from 4 months to 29 years. Approximately half of the participants reported growing up in Australia; the remainder were born in other nations but taught in Australia. Reporters completed either a paper or an iPad version of T-TRiPS. Reporters replied "yes" or "no" to each of 25 T-TRiPS items depending on if, under any circumstances, they would allow children in their classroom to participate in the activity.

5.4.2 Data analysis and results

We analyzed the data for evidence of construct validity and internal reliability using a statistical procedure called Rasch analysis. We tested the degree to which the data met two Rasch assumptions: (1) items that involved little risk would be easy for all respondents to allow their students to do (i.e., they would choose "yes"); and (2) teachers who were more risk tolerant would be more likely to say "yes" to riskier activities than risk-intolerant teachers.

Construct validity. Data from all 25 of T-TRiPS (100%) meet the specified assumptions. Thus, we concluded that there was good evidence for construct validity.

External validity. In addition to scoring T-TRiPS items, we also asked caregivers to report the extent to which they encouraged their child to take risks: often, sometimes, seldom/never. Using analysis of variance, we examined differences in scores between groups based on their response to this question. We did not find significant differences between groups based on their responses to this question. We hypothesize teachers may have difficulty differentiating between their personal beliefs on risky play and the professional expectations and rules of the schools they work for when reporting their tolerance of risky play. This warrants further investigation.

Internal reliability. The Rasch-generated person reliability index of 0.80 revealed excellent evidence for internal reliability. That is, given a similar data set, there is high likelihood that the level of teacher tolerance would be the same. The analysis also revealed approximately three levels of teacher risk tolerance: high, moderate, and low.

5.5 Psychometric evaluation of T-TRiPS: In-depth analysis

5.5.1 Participants

We recruited teachers from schools that participated in the second round of the SPP. A total of 99 preschool and primary school teachers of children, ages 4–12 years and diagnosed with ASD and/or ID, completed the instrument. Teachers ranged in age from younger than 20 years to older than 56 years and included lead and assistant teachers. Duration of teachers' experience teaching children with disabilities ranged from 4 months to 29 years ($M = 10.14$; $SD = 4.99$). Of the 99 participants, 48.4% reported growing up in Australia. Table 8 provides detailed demographic information about study participants.

5.5.2 Procedures
Participants completed T-TRiPS immediately prior to the pre-intervention risk reframing workshops. Teachers chose between an electronic (iPad) and pencil-and-paper versions of T-TRiPS. A research assistant entered data from paper assessments into the online platform.

5.5.3 Analysis
Analytical procedures for T-TRiPS were identical to those of TRiPS-R, with the exception of external validity (see below). Box 1 contains a brief summary of our research questions.

Congruence with self-report. To evaluate external validity of T-TRiPS, we conducted an analysis of variance (ANOVA) to identify significant differences in T-TRiPS scores among teachers who reported different frequencies of risk encouragement. We grouped teachers based on their responses to the question: "How often do you encourage your students to take everyday risks?", ("Seldom/Never," "Sometimes," and "Often"). We hypothesized that teachers who reported more frequent risk-encouragement would achieve higher scores on T-TRiPS (i.e., have more tolerance of risk in play).

5.5.4 Results
Our initial analyses did not suggest a need to remove or revise any T-TRiPS items. Therefore, subsequent results reflect the full, 25-item instrument. Table 9 contains difficulty measures and goodness-of-fit statistics for each item.

Point-measure correlations. All items demonstrated positive point-measure correlation. Point-measure correlations ranged from 0.15–0.56, suggesting that all items progressed in the same direction as the overall measure (RQ1).

Goodness-of-fit statistics. Twenty-five of 25 items (100%) conformed to the expectations of the Rasch model for both infit and outfit statistics, suggesting strong construct validity (RQ2).

Table 8 Demographic information for T-TRiPS psychometric study participants ($N=99$).

Variable	n
Teacher's age (years)	
≤ 20	3
21–25	7
26–30	20
31–35	20
36–40	11
41–45	8
46–50	8
50–55	7
≥ 56	9
No response	6
Experience teaching (years)	
<1–4	30
5–9	29
10–19	28
≥ 20	11
No response	1
Age of students (years)	
4–6	15
7–9	27
10–12	9
Multiple age groups	48
Teacher's national origin	
Australia	48
Other	23
No response	28

Table 9 Item measures and goodness-of-fit statistics for T-TRiPS.

Item	Measure	MnSq (Infit)	Z_{std} (Infit)	MnSq (Outfit)	Z_{std} (Outfit)
Classroom w/o supervision	1.09	1.26	2.24	1.47	1.76
Chase	−3.76	0.81	−0.32	1.49	0.78
Slide	−0.77	0.94	−0.52	0.85	−0.53
Scrape	−3.49	0.90	−0.14	0.79	−0.03
Play challenging	−3.26	1.15	0.52	1.60	0.96
Tree within reach	−0.26	1.00	0.03	1.04	0.27
Open fire/heater	3.11	1.04	0.23	0.83	−0.11
Play-fight (sticks)	2.84	1.16	0.71	1.37	0.80
Slippery surface	0.11	0.88	−1.37	0.85	−0.73
Adult tools unsupervised	2.60	0.94	−0.22	0.62	−0.79
Rough and tumble	−0.05	0.88	−1.31	0.79	−1.10
Jump 3–4	2.72	1.00	0.10	1.21	0.56
Care for class pets	−1.15	1.23	1.65	1.22	0.75
Swim	−0.96	1.02	0.21	0.85	−0.45
Physical disagreements	0.69	1.07	0.71	0.97	−0.07
Equipment (broken bone)	0.32	1.20	2.11	1.26	1.29
Play-fight (strength)	1.88	1.09	0.61	0.98	0.06
Manage challenges	−3.24	1.01	0.16	0.78	−0.10
Steep hill	0.79	1.01	0.17	0.91	−0.38
Tree to desired height	2.39	0.80	−1.00	0.55	−1.12
Playground w/o supervision	1.87	0.86	−0.98	0.70	−0.86
Verbal disagreements	−0.68	1.02	0.21	1.19	0.80
New environment	−0.34	0.86	−1.42	0.80	−0.94
Narrow surface	1.02	0.83	−1.64	0.76	−1.02
Risks if fun	−3.47	0.78	−0.50	0.27	−1.11

Item spread. The mean logit measure of participants in this study was 0.19, while the mean logit measure of items was fixed at 0.0. A higher mean person measure suggests an imbalance of easier items. However, the small difference between mean person and mean item measure suggests that the item spread sufficiently captures the levels of risk tolerance in this sample. However, visual inspection of the Wright map (Fig. 3) reveals several gaps along the hierarchy; further, 8 items achieved very similar levels of difficulty (i.e., located on the same line), suggesting some item redundancy.

Principal component analysis. PCA results did not suggest multidimensionality (RQ5). The largest contrast in the PCA had eigenvalue of 2.29, smaller than our desired threshold of less than 3. The PCA also revealed that the person and item measures explained 48.5% of the variance in raw scores.

Congruence with self-report. Fig. 4 displays the mean scores and quartile ranges for each group. Table 10 contains means and standard deviations for each group, reported in logits. We did not find that mean logit scores were higher for teachers who reported that they more frequently encouraged risks. The ANOVA was not significant ($F=0.48$, $p=0.617$). Teachers may have difficulty reporting their risk tolerance because of the challenge of differentiating between their personal and professional perspectives of risky play. We hypothesize many teachers of children with disabilities may report their willingness to encourage risky play more aligned with the expectations of their duty of care as teachers, erring on the side of caution so as not to be perceived as negligent. For some teachers, it is possible that even if they do understand the benefits of risky play and are personally more risk tolerant they may be caught between these two perspectives and report less tolerance of risk in play. Thus, the external validity of the T-TRiPS warrants further investigation.

Person reliability index. The person reliability index for T-TRiPS was 0.80 (RQ7), suggesting strong evidence for internal reliability.

Strata. We found a separation value of 2.01, corresponding to a strata value of 3.01. This suggests that T-TRiPS can reliably distinguish 3 levels of performance. This exceeded our desired strata value of 2.0.

6. Using the TRiPS instruments in research and in practice

The findings described here suggest that TRiPS-R and T-TRiPS are valid and reliable instruments useful for measuring adults' tolerance for children's risk-taking in play. However, the samples for both studies were

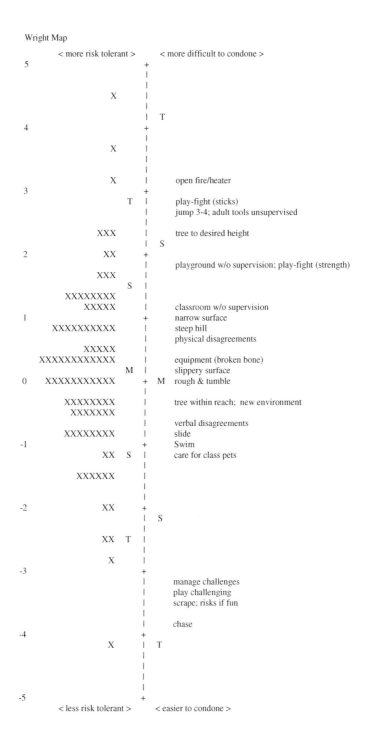

Fig. 3 Wright Map of the T-TRiPS Construct. *Notes.* Construct displayed along a common logit scale (far left). Left side of the map displays approximate participant measures (X); right side of the map displays approximate item measures. M = Mean. S = 1 standard deviation. T = 2 standard deviations.

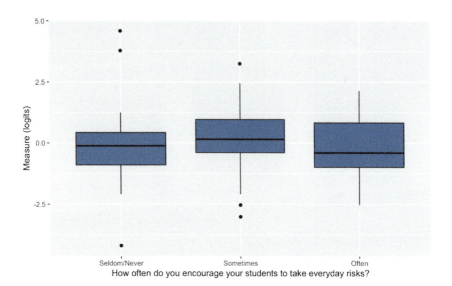

Fig. 4 Mean T-TRiPS scores by self-reported frequency of encouraging everyday risks ($N=99$).

Table 10 Group means and pairwise comparisons of T-TRiPS scores and self-reported risk encouragement.

Response	N	Mean (SD)
Never/seldom	14	0.03 (1.94)
Sometimes	37	0.18 (1.17)
Often	15	−0.16 (1.33)

relatively small, and participants did not reflect all potential respondents. Additionally, the relationship between teachers' self-reported risk tolerance and the risky play they will actually allow remains unclear. Ongoing and future studies will provide additional opportunities to evaluate the psychometric properties of data using these tools.

TRiPS-R and T-TRiPS are useful instruments for both researchers and practitioners who work with children with and without disabilities. In this section, we provide suggestions and examples of projects that may benefit from these instruments.

6.1 Researchers

TRiPS-R and T-TRiPS are effective tools for evaluating interventions designed to increase adults' tolerance for risky play. So far, we have used TRiPS-R and T-TRiPS to evaluate Risk Reframing Workshops (described above; Brussoni et al., 2018; Bundy et al., 2015). Studies using both tools are underway. We encourage researchers to design and evaluate other interventions to address adults' risk tolerance using the TRiPS instruments. Interventions may take a different approach (e.g., experiential, play-based interventions), or target other populations (e.g., parents of children with physical disabilities).

In addition to intervention evaluation, the TRiPS suite of instruments may prove useful for elucidating better understandings about adults' tolerance for risky play. For example, we used the TRiPS instruments to examine the progression of risk tolerance with age. Using the original TRiPS, Hill and Bundy (2014) found, as expected, that adults were more tolerant of risky play for older children compared to younger children. We examined this relationship using the data we collected with both TRiPS-R and T-TRiPS and did not reproduce these results. On TRiPS-R, parents of older children showed a non-significant tendency to score *lower* (i.e., have less risk tolerance; $F=1.29$, $p=0.28$; see Fig. 5). On T-TRiPS, teachers

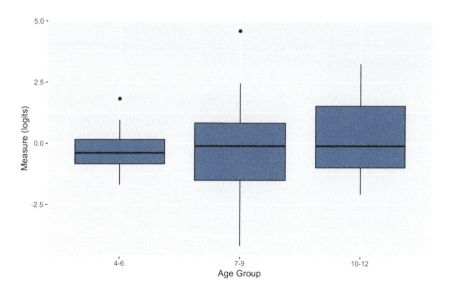

Fig. 5 Mean TRiPS-R scores by children's age ($N=66$).

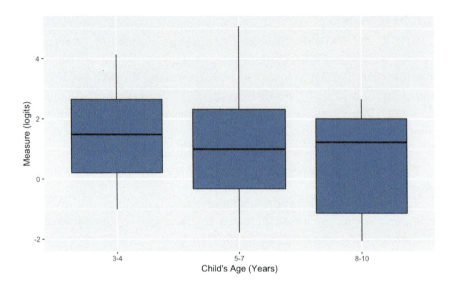

Fig. 6 Mean T-TRiPS scores by ages of children taught (N=48). *Note.* We excluded teachers who taught multiple age groups from this analysis.

remained stable across age ($F=0.16$, $p=0.86$; see Fig. 6). We hypothesize that this may be related to the population of adults who completed the instruments; many had (or taught) children with ASD and/or ID. It is possible that, as these children grow older, the consequences of risky play increase. For example, a child with ASD may have an outsized reaction to a minor injury compared to a typically-developing child. Another explanation may be that older children who participated in the SPP study (where most TRiPS-R and T-TRiPS data were collected) had more significant disabilities than the younger children in the study. Many children in Australia transfer into mainstream schools as they age; the children in this study all remained in specialized programs. Additionally, for the TRiPS-R, parents in the PUP group reported on younger children than in the SPP group. These children were more likely to be typically-developing, and therefore, parents may have been more risk tolerant (Beetham et al., 2019) – this could account for the higher scores in the youngest age group on the TRiPS-R. Given the relatively small samples in these two studies, more research is warranted to better understand the relationships among disability status, children's age, and adults' risk tolerance. However, findings of this nature demonstrate the usefulness of the TRiPS instruments for research purposes.

6.2 Therapists working with children with disabilities

TRiPS-R can serve as useful tools for goal setting in family contexts. Therapists (e.g., occupational therapists or psychologists) working with families who have a child with a disability should consider parents' risk tolerance as a part of their holistic assessment. Administering TRiPS-R may be an impactful way to open a conversation about risky play. The TRiPS-R contains a hierarchy of risky play items (as shown on the Wright maps, Fig. 1). Parents who are very intolerant of risk will likely only endorse items with a low measure (e.g., *tree within reach*). To gently increase parents' risk tolerance, practitioners might suggest they try permitting a slightly more challenging activity, such as playing at another child's house. As they witness children succeeding and benefiting from risky play, parents may begin to move up the hierarchy and develop trust in children's skills. Alternatively, children may participate in goal setting by choosing activities that they would like to try but that adults do not allow. This will promote not only risky play, but also autonomy and self-advocacy.

6.3 Educators

Teachers (and all educators) who aim to increase their own risk tolerance may use the T-TRiPS as a self-assessment. After evaluating their own risk tolerance, teachers may choose activities that fall slightly beyond their risk tolerance. Like parents, teachers may benefit from witnessing children's participation in these activities. This graded approach will allow teachers to work towards providing opportunities for risky play. Additionally, teachers may use the instrument to open discussions with school administration surrounding policies for risky play. Employing the T-TRiPS in a school can create an environment that is more amenable to children's development through risky play.

6.4 A note for all practitioners interested in risky play

It is tempting to consider adults' tolerance for risky play only as an individual construct – a personality trait that, with intervention, may be flexible to change. However, we note that risk tolerance is largely influenced by aspects of the environment. For example, a parent who lives in an apartment on a busy road may have access to fewer safe play spaces for their child as a parent who lives in a home with a backyard on a large suburban street (Karsten, 2005). Further, risky play and risk tolerance should not be decoupled from societal concerns including racism, poverty, and structural marginalization

(Giles, Bauer, & Darroch, 2019; Gerlach, Jenkins, & Hodgson, 2019). Children of low socioeconomic status often want to play outside independently from adults but feel stuck inside due to lack of safe places to play and parents' work schedules (Veitch, Salmon, & Ball, 2007a, 2007b) In the United States, non-white children are disproportionately represented within the child welfare system (Child Welfare Information Gateway, 2016). Parents who are Black, Indigenous, or otherwise non-white are more likely to be reported to child welfare, and their children are more likely to be taken into out-of-home care, than white parents. Faced with the very real risk of losing their children from an accusation of negligence for letting their children play independently too far from home, parents of color may be less likely to allow their children to play outside without close parental supervision. Having a child with a disability may compound this fear – they, too, are more likely to be involved in the child welfare system (Child Welfare Information Gateway, 2018). Solutions to this intersectional, insidious structural disparity are beyond the scope of this paper, and will require widespread anti-racist policy efforts. However, the authors of this paper encourage researchers and practitioners to take social and environmental factors into consideration when examining and seeking to change adults' risk tolerance.

7. Summary and conclusion

Drawing from Sandseter and colleagues' work (Sandseter, 2009; Sandseter et al., 2012), we defined risky play as thrilling and exciting play that provides opportunities for challenge, testing limits, exploring boundaries, and learning about risk. We argued that all children benefit from risky play: they gain opportunities to push boundaries, innovate, and develop confidence and competence in physical, cognitive, and social skills. They learn to recognize and manage real everyday risks, overcome fears, and balance impulsivity with careful reflection and decision-making (Caprino, 2018; Lavrysen et al., 2017). We further argued that children with disabilities may need more, not fewer, opportunities to practice managing risks. When an adult views a child as less capable than peers, that adult is likely to try to protect the child from all risk, including risky play. Even if some adults support risky play in theory, fear of liability may lead them to prevent children from taking part. Reduced consequences are a defining characteristic of play. A child who is "protected from" risky play will have less experience managing risk in safe places and, therefore is likely to be less capable of making good decisions when confronted with real danger.

The benefits of risky play are considerable but the challenges of promoting it are incontrovertible. Not only is there some possibility that a child may be injured, but adults also fear social consequences (e.g., being perceived as an irresponsible or "bad" parent or teacher) and, sometimes, litigation. Despite these challenges, adults (and most often, parents or teachers) are the gatekeepers to their children's play. Thus, there is a need for interventions to help parents and teachers reframe risky play (i.e., consider the benefits) and shift their behavior to allow children more control. To support the development of such interventions, as well as basic research exploring adults' risk tolerance, we developed TRiPS-R and T-TRiPS, assessments to examine parents' and teachers' tolerance for risky play and evaluate the impact of interventions.

Engaging in risky play helps children take responsibility for their actions, learn what they are capable of doing, and develop autonomy. Additionally, risky play confers benefits for children's emotional and physical health. And while reframing risk is crucial for parents, teachers and others who serve in caregiving roles, it is relevant to anyone with an interest in, or mandate for, children, especially administrators, health care workers and policy makers. If children are to reap the benefits of risky play, all those involved in maintaining children's well-being need to understand the benefits of such play, as well as their own levels of risk (in)tolerance.

Acknowledgment

The authors acknowledge the contributions of Dr. Michelle Villeneuve. Parts of this paper were completed in partial fulfillment of the degree of Master of Science at Colorado State University for Kristina Ihrig.

References

Adams, R. C., & Levy, S. E. (2017). Shared decision-making and children with disabilities: Pathways to consensus. *Pediatrics, 139*(6), 1–9.

American Psychiatric Association. (2013). *Diagnostic and statistical manual of mental disorders* (5th ed.). Washington, DC: APA.

Ball, D. J. (2002). *Playgrounds—Risks, benefits, and choices.* London, UK: Health and Safety Executive.

Beetham, K., Sterman, J., Bundy, A. C., Wyver, S., Ragen, J., Engelen, L., et al. (2019). Lower parent tolerance of risk in play for children with disability than typically developing children. *International Journal of Play, 8*(2), 174–185.

Bond, T. G., & Fox, C. M. (2015). *Applying the Rasch model: Fundamental measurement in the human sciences* (3rd ed.). Mahwah, NJ: L. Erlbaum.

Bora, E., & Pantelis, C. (2016). Meta-analysis of social cognition in attention-deficit/hyperactivity disorder (ADHD): Comparison with healthy controls and autistic spectrum disorder. *Psychological Medicine*, *46*(4), 699–716.

Boxberger, K., & Reimers, A. (2019). Parental correlates of outdoor play in boys and girls aged 0–12—A systematic review. *International Journal of Environmental Research and Public Health*, *16*(2), 190.

Brown, S. L. (2014). Consequences of play deprivation. *Scholarpedia*, *9*(5), 30449.

Brussoni, M., Brunelle, S., Pike, I., Sandseter, E. B. H., Herrington, S., Turner, H., et al. (2015). Can child injury prevention include healthy risk promotion? *Injury Prevention*, *21*(5), 344–347. Chicago.

Brussoni, M., Gibbons, R., Gray, C., Ishikawa, T., Sandseter, E. B., Bienenstock, A., et al. (2015). What is the relationship between risky outdoor play and health in children? A systematic review. *International Journal of Environmental Research and Public Health*, *12*, 6423–6454.

Brussoni, M., Ishikawa, T., Han, C., Pike, I., Bundy, A., Faulkner, G., et al. (2018). Go play outside! Effects of a risk-reframing tool on mothers' tolerance for, and parenting practices associated with, children's risky play: Study protocol for a randomized controlled trial. *Trials*, *19*(173), 1–9.

Brussoni, M., Olsen, L. L., Pike, I., & Sleet, D. A. (2012). Risky play and children's safety: Balancing priorities for optimal child development. *International Journal of Environmental Research and Public Health*, *9*, 3134–3148.

Buchanan, C. (1999). Building better playgrounds: A project for parents? *UAB Magazine*, *19*(3). Retrieved from http://main.uab.edu/show.asp?durki=25353.

Bundy, A. C., Luckett, T., Tranter, P. J., Naughton, G. A., Wyver, S. R., Ragen, J., et al. (2009). The risk is that there is "no risk": A simple, innovative intervention to increase children's activity levels. *International Journal of Early Years Education*, *17*(1), 33–45.

Bundy, A. C., Naughton, G., Tranter, P., Wyver, S., Baur, L., Schiller, W., et al. (2011). The Sydney playground project: Popping the bubblewrap—Unleashing the power of play: A cluster randomized controlled trial of a primary school playground-based intervention aiming to increase children's physical activity and social skills. *BMC Public Health*, *11*, 1–9.

Bundy, A. C., Wyver, S., Beetham, K. S., Ragen, J., Naughton, G., Tranter, P., et al. (2015). The Sydney playground project—Levelling the playing field: A cluster trial of a primary school-based intervention aiming to promote manageable risk-taking in children with disability. *BMC Public Health*, *15*, 1–6.

Caprino, F. (2018). When the risk is worth it: The inclusion of children with disabilities in free risky play. In *47-48. Today's children, tomorrow's parents* (pp. 40–47).

Child Welfare Information Gateway. (2016). *Racial disproportionality and disparity in child welfare*. Washington, DC: U.S. Department of Health and Human Services.

Child Welfare Information Gateway. (2018). *The risk and prevention of maltreatment of children with disabilities*. Washington, DC: U.S. Department of Health and Human Services.

Cooke, M., Wong, S., & Press, F. (2019). Towards a re-conceptualisation of risk in early childhood education. *Contemporary Issues in Early Childhood*. https://doi.org/10.1177/1463949119840740.

Cortese, S., Moreira-Mala, C. R., Fleur, D. S., Morcillo-Penalver, C., Rohde, L. A., & Faraone, S. V. (2016). Association between ADHD and obesity: A systematic review and meta-analysis. *American Journal of Psychiatry*, *173*(1), 34–41.

Engelen, L., Bundy, A. C., Naughton, G., Simpson, J. M., Bauman, A., Ragen, J., et al. (2013). Increasing physical activity in young primary school children—It's child's play: A cluster randomised controlled trial. *Preventive Medicine*, *56*(5), 319–325.

Gerlach, A., Jenkins, E., & Hodgson, K. (2019). Disrupting assumptions of risky play in the context of structural marginalization: A community engagement project in a Canadian inner-city neighborhood. *Health & Place*, *55*, 80–86.

Giles, A. R., Bauer, M. E., & Darroch, F. E. (2019). Risky statement?: A critique of the position statement on active outdoor play. *World Leisure Journal, 61*(1), 58–66.

Gill, T. (2018). *Playing it safe? A global white paper on risk, liability and children's play in public space.* Bernard van Leer Foundation.

Glasson, E. J., Buckley, N., Chen, W., Leonard, H., Epstein, A., Skoss, R., et al. (2020). Systematic review and meta-analysis: Mental health in children with neurogenetic disorders associated with intellectual disability. *Journal of the American Academy of Child & Adolescent Psychiatry, 59*(9), 1036–1048.

Hess, L. M., & Bundy, A. C. (2003). The association between playfulness and coping in adolescents. *Physical & Occupational Therapy in Pediatrics, 23*(2), 5–17.

Hill, A., & Bundy, A. C. (2014). Reliability and validity of a new instrument to measure tolerance of everyday risk for children. *Child: Care, Health and Development, 40*(1), 68–76.

Jelleyman, C., McPhee, J., Brussoni, M., Bundy, A., & Duncan, S. (2019). A cross-sectional description of parental perceptions and practices related to risky play and independent mobility in children: The New Zealand state of play survey. *International Journal of Environmental Research and Public Health, 16*(2), 262–281.

Kahathuduwa, C. N., West, B. D., Blume, J., Dharavath, N., Moustaid-Moussa, N., & Mastergeorge, A. (2019). The risk of overweight and obesity in children with autism spectrum disorders: A systematic review and meta-analysis. *Obesity Reviews, 20,* 1667–1679.

Karsten, L. (2005). It all used to be better? Different generations on continuity and change in urban chilren's daily use of space. *Children's Geographies, 3*(3), 275–290.

Kleppe, R., Melhuish, E. C., & Sandseter, E. B. (2017). Identifying and characterizing risky play in the age one-to-three years. *European Early Childhood Education Research Journal, 25*(3), 370–385.

Lavrysen, A., Bertrands, E., Leyssen, L., Smets, L., Vanderspikken, A., & De Graef, P. (2017). Risky-play at school: Facilitating risk perception and competence in young children. *European Early Childhood Education Research Journal, 25*(1), 89–105.

Linacre, J. M. (2002). What do infit, outfit, mean-square and standardized mean? *Rasch Measurement Transactions, 16*(2), 878. Retrieved from https://www.rasch.org/rmt/rmt162f.htm.

Linacre, J. M. (September 2, 2018). *Detecting multidimensionality in Rasch data using Winsteps table 23.* Retrieved from YouTube. https://www.youtube.com/watch?v=sna19Qem E50&t=638s.

Linacre, J. M. (2020). *Winsteps (version 4.5.2) [computer software].* Beaverton, OR: Winsteps.com.

Little, H. (2010). Finding the balance: Early childhood practitioners' views on risk, challenge and safety in outdoor play settings. In *Australian Association for Research in Education Conference* (pp. 1–12). Melbourne, Australia.

Little, H., & Eager, D. (2010). Risk, challenge and safety: Implications for pay quality and playground design. *European Early Childhood Education Research Journal, 18*(4), 497–513.

Maiano, C., Hue, O., Morin, A. J., & Moullec, G. (2016). Prevalence of overweight and obesity among children and adolescence with intellectual disabilities: A systematic review and meta-analysis. *Obesity Reviews, 17,* 599–611.

Malone, K. (2007). The bubble-wrap generation: Children growing up in walled gardens. *Environmental Education Research, 13*(4), 513–527.

Newnham, H. (2000). When is a teacher or school liable in negligence? *Australian Journal of Teacher Education, 25*(1), 46–51.

Niehues, A. N., Bundy, A., Broom, A., & Tranter, P. (2015). Parents' perception of risk and the influence on children's everday activities. *Journal of Child and Family Studies, 24,* 809–820.

Niehues, A. N., Bundy, A., Broom, A., & Tranter, P. (2016). Reframing healthy risk taking: Parents' dilemmas and strategies to promote children's well-being. *Journal of Occupational Science, 23*(4), 449–463.

Niehues, A. N., Bundy, A., Broom, A., Tranter, P., Ragen, J., & Engelen, L. (2013). Everyday uncertainties: Reframing perceptions of risk in outdoor free play. *Journal of Adventure Education & Outdoor Learning, 13*(3), 223–237.

Parkes, J., White-Koning, M., Dickinson, H. O., Thyen, U., Arnaud, C., Beckung, E., et al. (2008). Psychological problems in children with cerebral palsy: A cross-sectional European study. *The Journal of Child Psychology and Psychiatry, 49*(4), 405–413.

Pellegrini, A. D., & Smith, P. K. (1998). Physical activity play: The nature and function of a neglected aspect of play. *Child Development, 69*(3), 577–598.

Powell, F. (2019). Childhood obesity: Getting back to the basics. *DNP Qualifying Manuscripts, 14*, 1–14.

Sandseter, E. B. (2009). Characteristics of risky play. *Journal of Adventure Education and Outdoor Learning, 9*(1), 3–21.

Sandseter, E. B., & Kennair, L. E. (2011). Children's risky play from an evolutionary perspective: The anti-phobic effects of thrilling experiences. *Evolutionary Psychology, 9*(2), 257–284.

Sandseter, E. B., Little, H., & Wyver, S. (2012). Do theory and pedagogy have an impact on provisions for outdoor learning? A comparison of approaches in Australia and Norway. *Journal of Adventure Education and Outdoor Learning, 12*(3), 167–182.

Saunders, I., Sayer, M., & Goodale, A. (1999). The relationship between playfulness and coping in preschool children: A pilot study. *American Journal of Occupational Therapy, 53*(2), 221–226.

Shi, X., Shi, J., Wheeler, K. K., Stallones, L., Ameratunga, S., Shakespeare, T., et al. (2015). Unintentional injuries in children with disabilities: A systematic review and meta-analysis. *Injury Epidemiology, 21*(2), 1–13.

Skard, G., & Bundy, A. (2008). The test of playfulness. In *Play in occupational therapy for children* (2nd ed., pp. 71–94). St. Louis, MO: Mosby.

Spencer, G., Bundy, A., Wyver, S., Villeneuve, M., Tranter, P., Beetham, K., et al. (2016). Uncertainty in the school playground: Shifting rationalities and teachers' sense-making in the management of risks for children with disabilities. *Health, Risk & Society, 18*(5–6), 301–317.

Sterman, J. J., Naughton, G. A., Bundy, A. C., Froude, E., & Villeneuve, M. A. (2020a). Is play a choice? Application of the capabilities approach to children with disabilities on the school playground. *International Journal of Inclusive Education, 24*(6), 579–596.

Sterman, J. J., Naughton, G. A., Bundy, A. C., Froude, E., & Villeneuve, M. A. (2020b). Mothers supporting play as a choice for children with disabilities within a culturally and linguistically diverse community. *Scandinavian Journal of Occupational Therapy, 27*(5), 373–384.

Sterman, J., Naughton, G., Froude, E., Villeneuve, M., Beetham, K., Wyver, S., et al. (2016). Outdoor play decisions by caregivers of children with disabilities: A systematic review of qualitative studies. *Journal of Developmental and Physical Disabilities, 28*, 931–957.

Sterman, J., Villenueve, M., Spencer, G., Wyver, S., Beetham, K., Naughton, G., et al. (2019). Creating play opportunities on the school playground: Educator experiences of the Sydney Playground Project. *Australian Occupational Therapy Journal, 67*(1), 62–73.

Tovey, H. (2007). *Playing outdoors: Spaces and places, risk and challenge.* New York, NY: McGraw Hill.

United Nations Committee on the Rights of Persons with Disabilities. (2013). *Convention on the rights of persons with disabilities.* Retrieved from https://www.un.org/disabilities/documents/convention/convoptprot-e.pdf.

van Rooijen, M., & Newstead, S. (2016). Influencing factors on professional attitudes towards risk-taking in children's play: A narrative review. *Early Child Development and Care, 187*(5), 946–957.

van Steensel, F. J., & Heeman, E. J. (2017). Anxiety levels in childen with autism spectrum disorder: A meta-analysis. *Journal of Child and Family Studies, 26*, 1753–1767.

Veitch, J., Salmon, J., & Ball, K. (2007a). Children's active free play in local neighborhoods: A behavioral mapping study. *Health Education Research, 23*(5), 870–879.

Veitch, J., Salmon, J., & Ball, K. (2007b). Children's perception of the use of public spaces for active free-play. *Children's Geographies, 5*(4), 409–422.

Woflensberger, W. P., Nirje, B., Olshansky, S., Perske, R., & Roos, P. (1972). The dignity of risk. In *The principle of normalization in human services*. Toronto, Canada: National Institute of Mental Retardation.

Wright, B. D., & Masters, G. N. (1982). *Rating scale analysis: Rasch measurement*. Chicago, IL: Mesa.

Wright, B. D., & Stone, M. H. (1979). *Best test design: Rasch measurement*. Mesa.

Wyver, S., Tranter, P., Naughton, G., Little, H., Sandseter, E. B., & Bundy, A. (2010). Ten ways to restrict children's freedom to play: The problem of surplus safety. *Contemporary Issues in Early Childhood, 11*(3), 263–277.

Zablotsky, B., Black, L. I., Maenner, M. J., Schieve, L. A., Danielson, M. L., Bitsko, R. H., et al. (2019). Prevalence and trends of developmental disabilities among children in the United States: 2009-2017. *Pediatrics, 144*(4), 1–19.

CHAPTER TWO

Augmented naturalistic developmental behavioral intervention for toddlers with autism spectrum disorder: A community pilot study

Deanna M. Swain[a,*], Jamie Winter[a,b], Claire B. Klein[a], Amy Lemelman[a,b], Jennifer Giordano[b], Nicole N. Jablon[b], Kaori Nakamura[b], and So Hyun Kim[a,b]

[a]Department of Psychiatry, Weill Cornell Medical College, White Plains, NY, United States
[b]Center for Autism and the Developing Brain, New York-Presbyterian Hospital, White Plains, NY, United States
*Corresponding author: e-mail address: dms4001@med.cornell.edu

Contents

1. Introduction and change	48
1.1 Best practice recommendations	49
1.2 Evidence for NDBIs	50
1.3 Barriers to community implementation	50
1.4 Study aims	51
2. Methods	51
2.1 Participants	51
2.2 Development and rationale of current service model	51
2.3 Clinician training	53
2.4 NDBI programming	54
2.5 Procedure	57
2.6 Service level measures	58
2.7 Patient level behavioral change measures	58
2.8 Statistical analyses	60
3. Results	61
3.1 Implementation and service outcomes	61
3.2 Patient level behavioral change outcomes	62
4. Discussion	64
5. Implications	68
Acknowledgments	68
References	68

International Review of Research in Developmental Disabilities, Volume 59
ISSN 2211-6095
https://doi.org/10.1016/bs.irrdd.2020.09.003

© 2020 Elsevier Inc.
All rights reserved.

Abstract

In the United States, all families with children under the age of 3 years with disabilities or delays in development are eligible to receive public Early Intervention (EI) services. Many researchers are investigating Naturalistic Developmental Behavioral Interventions (NDBI), which have shown positive outcomes for young children with ASD. However, NDBIs have been mostly developed and implemented in university laboratories, and their effectiveness when delivered in community settings is not well understood. This pilot study introduces a comprehensive treatment model implemented in a community-based early intervention program that prioritizes caregiver empowerment, caregiver-clinician partnerships, and evidence-based practice (i.e., NDBI). Clinicians reported high satisfaction with the model, positive attitudes toward NDBI, and frequent use of NDBI strategies when providing care to families. Results also show that families across a range of socioeconomic backgrounds received services and children showed significant improvements in cognitive, social communication, and adaptive skills over the course of treatment. Caregivers demonstrated improvements in their ability to use NDBI strategies when interacting with their child. This study provides preliminary support that an evidence-based NDBI treatment program can be adapted to a community-based setting with high acceptability and positive behavioral change at the family level. Future research efforts should include caregiver input regarding model acceptability and examine effectiveness through direct comparison to a control group.

1. Introduction and change

Advancements in screening and increased awareness have led to early identification of children with Autism Spectrum Disorder (ASD). In turn, families can access intervention services sooner, which has been shown to result in improved longitudinal outcomes (Dawson, 2008; Reichow, 2012). The Individuals with Disabilities Education Act (IDEA, 2004) mandates that all states in the United States provide services for children under the age of three with disabilities or developmental delays and that these services be provided in a family capacity–building manner. However, the federal mandate allows for each state to decide on inclusion criteria and treatment delivery options, leading to significant variability. Furthermore, systematic reviews of community-based early intervention (EI) programs demonstrate smaller gains in child developmental outcomes compared to research trials of evidence-based practice (EBP), suggesting a significant gap between research and practice in community settings (Nahmias, Pellecchia, Stahmer, & Mandell, 2019). As a result, it is imperative to refine methods for effective incorporation of EBP into community settings for children with ASD.

Naturalistic Developmental Behavioral Interventions (NDBIs; Schreibman et al., 2015) provide a suitable match for integration into community-based EI services because they show strong evidence for treatment effectiveness and efficacy and include caregivers as an active treatment component. NDBIs share a core set of behavioral and developmental principles (e.g., following the child's lead, modeling and prompting for social communication, imitating play; Schreibman et al., 2015). Although NDBIs demonstrate strong empirical support for positive treatment outcomes in children with ASD (see details below), the evidence is often based on research studies implemented in university-based settings that provide 1:1 programming using highly constrained samples. Community-based EI services, however, are frequently provided in group settings and include families with diverse backgrounds, but the use of evidence-based practices has been inconsistent (Stahmer, Collings, & Palinkas, 2005). EI providers also often take an eclectic approach to deliver treatment in community settings, rather than strictly following manualized treatment programs. In the current study, we attempted to bridge this gap between research and community implementation by exploring the program feasibility of integrating NDBI strategies within a state-funded EI program. We provide preliminary findings to support evidence for future directions and adaptations of similar models.

1.1 Best practice recommendations

In addition to the IDEA guidelines, Zwaigenbaum et al. (2015) put forth the most recent set of best practice recommendations for EI programs serving children with ASD. Based on a review of the data, researchers call for the use of interventions that combine developmental and behavioral approaches, target core ASD symptoms, actively involve families, and incorporate family dynamics, beliefs, and support into treatment considerations. Caregiver involvement is critical to maximize the effectiveness of EI and the generalizability of treatment gains. A review of the roles played by caregivers in school-based interventions suggests that very few treatment packages focus on caregivers as recipients, agents, and collaborators (Rispoli, Mathes, & Malcolm, 2019), limiting caregivers' ability to advocate for their priorities and goals in treatment. Therefore, the EBPs implemented in the community-based EI program presented in the current study prioritize involvement of the caregivers as collaborators in addition to recipients and agents of treatment change.

1.2 Evidence for NDBIs

The principles guiding NDBIs, including teaching in natural environments and socially-rewarding contexts, are designed to enhance generalization of skills across people and settings (Bruinsma, Minjarez, Schreibman, & Stahmer, 2020; Schreibman et al., 2015). NDBIs apply behavioral strategies in a developmentally appropriate manner (i.e., targeting behaviors appropriate to developmental level and trajectory), target ASD symptoms, and teach parents to learn and implement the strategies in home and community settings. In a recent meta-analysis of NDBIs, significant treatment effects have been found for cognitive, language, and play skills (Tiede & Walton, 2019).

Preliminary efforts have been made to adopt NDBIs into community settings. For example, Early Start Denver Model (ESDM) was altered to be delivered in a group-based format in preschool classes (Vivanti, Duncan, Dawson, & Rogers, 2017). Preliminary findings for 27 preschoolers with ASD suggest this adaptation is both feasible and effective (Vivanti et al., 2014). High satisfaction ratings were reported by caregivers and staff. Children in the ESDM groups as well as children in a similar community-based educational program showed significant increases in cognitive and adaptive skills, with the ESDM group demonstrating significantly greater gains in receptive language. In another study, toddlers with ASD enrolled in EI classrooms were randomly assigned to receive treatment as usual or Joint Attention, Symbolic Play, Engagement, and Regulation (JASPER; Kasari, Gulsrud, Wong, Kwon, & Locke, 2010) for 10 weeks (Shire et al., 2017). Results demonstrated significantly increased rates of joint engagement, play skills, and social communication functioning for those in the JASPER condition. These initial studies show promise for community implementation of NDBIs and lend support to continued study of adapting EBP into community settings.

1.3 Barriers to community implementation

The average amount of time for university-based research to translate into publicly available EBPs ranges from 15 to 20 years (Proctor et al., 2009). Traditionally, this process involves a series of steps; only in the final step do researchers adapt the treatment to community settings. This gap in research and practice has led to the field of implementation science, which calls on more efficient methods to translate EBPs into community settings through stakeholder participation and evaluation (Odom, Cox, & Brock,

2013). Stakeholder participation can help identify barriers, fit, and maintenance of incorporating EBP into community settings.

1.4 Study aims

The current study examines program feasibility of adapting NDBI strategies to a community-based EI program through the following aims: (1) Examine implementation and service level outcomes to provide an account of treatment components and acceptability of service provision from a clinician standpoint; and (2) Evaluate patient-level outcomes by examining behavioral changes in children and caregivers.

2. Methods

2.1 Participants

For the evaluation of implementation and service level outcomes, stakeholder input was provided from clinicians in a New York State (NYS) funded EI Program at the Center for Autism and the Developing Brain (CADB) at Weill Cornell Medicine. Clinicians consisted of four individuals who served the role of parent coach and four who provided additional services (e.g., speech therapy [ST], occupational therapy [OT], Social Work). All individuals served in the program for at least 6 months prior to participating in the survey.

For the evaluation of patient-level outcomes, participants included 34 families of toddlers (79.4% male; $M_{age} = 25.62$ months) with a diagnosis of ASD enrolled in the EI program at CADB. Primary caregivers were characterized as the caregiver receiving the majority of parent coaching instruction; however, multiple family members and service providers participated in various capacities in treatment delivery. Additional baseline child and caregiver characteristics can be found in Table 1. The present study was approved by the Weill Cornell Institutional Review Board and informed consent was obtained from all participants' caregivers.

2.2 Development and rationale of current service model

The conceptualization of the CADB service model originated in collaborative discussions among clinicians, researchers, and NYS EI liaisons. The initial vision of the model included a comprehensive package of EBP that prioritized active caregiver involvement through caregiver-clinician partnerships. In an effort to provide high-quality care to an

Table 1 Patient level demographic information ($n = 34$).

Child	Mean (SD) or n (%)	Range	Primary caregiver	Mean (SD) or n (%)	Range
Age (months)	25.62 (4.72)	17–33	Age (years)	35.56 (4.71)	27–44
Sex (males)	27 (79.4)		Sex (females)	34 (100)	
Race			Race		
Caucasian	17 (50)		Caucasian	20 (58.8)	
African American	2 (5.9)		African American	3 (8.8)	
Asian	3 (8.8)		Asian	3 (8.8)	
Biracial	8 (23.5)		Biracial	1 (2.9)	
Hispanic	3 (8.8)		Hispanic	7 (20.6)	
Other	1 (2.9)		Other	–	
			Education		
Cognitive Measure			BA/BS or above	27 (79.4)	
Verbal ratio IQ	65.49 (35.85)	10–136	Below BA/BS	7 (20.6)	
Nonverbal ratio IQ	87.62 (22.43)	28–121	Income[a]		
ADOS-2			Less than $35,000	3 (8.8)	
CSS-SA	7.24 (2.06)	4–10	$66,000–$80,000	3 (8.8)	
CSS-RRB	7.76 (1.69)	5–10	$81,000–$100,000	1 (2.9)	
			$101,000–$130,000	6 (17.5)	
			$131,000–$160,000	4 (11.8)	
			Over $161,000	14 (41.2)	
			English primary language[b]	23 (67.6)	

[a]Income level was not reported for three families.
[b]Primary language information was not reported for five families.
Notes. CSS-SA, calibrated severity score social affect; CSS-RRB, calibrated severity score restricted and repetitive behaviors.

increased number of families, the model was designed to serve as a bridge to local resources (i.e., provide families with time-limited, high quality care with a goal of supporting families to transition to other community-based services after leaving the EI program). As a result, the model presented to families includes 6 months of services from a multidisciplinary team that serve the family unit. The emphasis on caregiver education and empowerment serves as the crux of the program. Clinicians enter the program with and receive high levels of training in ASD. Finally, the program serves as a training model through the inclusion of post-doctoral fellows and research assistants that participate as assistants in the classroom instruction.

Due to the comprehensive nature of the model, a single NDBI did not fully serve the range of programmatic needs. The model adopts a "technical eclectic approach" (p. 36; Bruinsma et al., 2020) which uses the core strategies of various NDBI treatment packages. Eclectic interventions (Reed, 2015) refer to the use of a combination of strategies or practices. While some findings have suggested that eclectic interventions may be inferior to EBP (Zachor, Ben-Itzchak, Rabinovich, & Lahat, 2007), when the strategies are conceptually grounded, selected from EBP, and implemented to a high standard, positive results have been demonstrated (Odom, Hume, Boyd, & Stabel, 2012). The majority of programming for parent coaching and classroom instruction followed the principles and procedures of ESDM; however, parent education and support groups, ST, and OT utilized EBP from their own disciplines as well as common components of NDBIs. As a result, the full model can best be described as augmented NDBI.

2.3 Clinician training

The group and individual-based interventions were implemented by a multi-disciplinary team consisting of a Board-Certified Behavior Analyst (BCBA), a Special Education Teacher, an Occupational Therapist, a Social Worker, Speech Language Pathologists, Psychologists, Post-Doctoral Fellows in Psychology, and research assistants. The team was led by an experienced interventionist with extensive training in multiple NDBIs (J.W., psychologist and BCBA).

All clinicians entered CADB with Master's level training or higher and previous knowledge and clinical experiences with young children with ASD and their families. Although our model was based on more general NDBI strategies, all clinicians received Introductory and Advanced Training Workshops in ESDM. Research assistants ranged in degree of previous experience with ASD and entered with bachelor's degrees in Psychology. Research assistants received a two-hour introductory course to NDBI and behavioral strategies, as well as ongoing supervision and weekly case updates. All clinicians achieved fidelity on the ESDM fidelity rating in the beginning of the study.

2.4 NDBI programming

Admission to participate in the program occurred on a rolling basis, with a maximum of six children per group at a time. Program participation included up to 6 months of approximately 13 h of service delivery per week, which consisted of group and individualized services for children and their families. The program consisted of both child- and caregiver-focused intervention in individual and group settings. Details of the treatment targets, EBP components, location, and hours of services offered for each treatment modality are provided in Table 2. Provision of services offered at our center does not encapsulate the full amount of services used by families; many families received services (e.g., Applied Behavior Analysis) outside of our center.

Child-focused services. Child services were designed to include 360 min (3 × 120 min) of NDBI group intervention per week in a classroom setting. The foundational classroom intervention was based on the principles and core strategies of NDBIs (Bruinsma et al., 2020; Schreibman et al., 2015) including three-part contingency, environmental arrangement, shared control, natural reinforcement, prompting, prompt fading, balanced turns, modeling, imitation of child language, play and behavior, broadening of attentional focus, and child choice or child-initiated teaching episodes. These strategies were then applied to the following activities: free play, circle time for welcome and songs, art, small group play, gym or outdoor gross motor activity, snack, and closing circle time. Within the classroom, ratios of adult support to child ranged from 1:1 to 1:3, based on the needs of the children and EI mandates for specific children requiring a 1:1 support. Classroom instruction included a "lead clinician," who set the daily activities and objectives, and an assistant teacher, as well as push-in ST and OT as needed, and assistance from post-doctoral fellows and research assistants.

Besides group-based intervention in a classroom setting, individual intervention was provided to each family including clinic- and/or home-based special instruction of NDBI components and parent coaching. All families received a total of 3h of individual, caregiver-mediated intervention;

Table 2 Description of comprehensive NDBI early intervention model.

Focus	Description	Treatment targets	EBP program/strategy examples	Location	Amount
Child	Group-based instruction	• Communication skills • Social skills • Play skills • Personal independence skills	• NDBI strategies • Peer-mediated instruction • Exercise • Parent-implemented intervention • Visual support[a] • Schedules[a] • Augmentative and Alternative Communication[a]	Clinic	3 × 120 min (360 min total)
	Parent-mediated special instruction			Clinic, home and community[b]	3 × 60 min (180 min total)
	Speech therapy	• Communication skills • Feeding • Play skills • Social skills	• (Prelinguistic) milieu teaching (naturalistic intervention, modeling, time delay) • Communication temptations • Indirect language stimulation/facilitated play • Augmentative and Alternative Communication[a]	Clinic	2 × 30 min (60 min total[c])
	Occupational therapy	• Motor skills • Personal independence skills • Feeding • Play skills • Sensory processing/modulation • Physical/mental stamina	• Activity analysis (functional behavior assessment) • Sensory integration • Specialized therapeutic equipment	Clinic	2 × 30 min (60 min total[c])
	Total amount				11 h

Continued

Table 2 Description of comprehensive NDBI early intervention model.—cont'd

Focus	Description	Treatment targets	EBP program/strategy examples	Location	Amount
Caregiver	Psychoeducation group	• ASD knowledge • Behavior management • Toilet training • Feeding problems • Sleep problems • Parent advocacy	• NDBI strategies • Differential reinforcement • Extinction • Visual supports • Social stories/narratives • Schedules	Clinic	1 × 60 min (60 min total)
	Support group	• Parenting stress • Self-awareness • Cognitive distortions	• Cognitive Behavioral Therapy • Mindfulness-based intervention	Clinic	1 × 60 min (60 min total)
	Individual support			Clinic	1 × 30 min
	Total amount				2.5 h

[a]Strategies included according to child's developmental needs.
[b]Home-based services offered to families who live within 30-min driving radius of center.
[c]Average amount of services utilized by families. However, families may not be eligible or may opt for fewer or more hours based on current external service utilization;
NDBI strategies = Naturalistic Behavioral Developmental Intervention strategies.

however, the location of service provision differed for families. For those families who lived within a 30-min driving radius of CADB, 2 of the 3 h of individual parent coaching sessions were provided in the home. Based on family preference and eligibility, children could also receive additional services, such as ST and OT.

Caregiver-focused services. To emphasize caregiver empowerment and education, caregiver specific services included 60 min of caregiver support group and 60 min of psychoeducation group for all caregivers as well as 30-min individual meetings with a Social Worker as needed. Material for the caregiver psychoeducation group was modular and covered topics such as ASD diagnostic overview, common difficulties experienced in ASD, behavioral strategies, and transitioning in the educational system. The caregiver support group was process based (i.e., instruction driven by input from parents and/or clinicians) and primarily focused on Cognitive-Behavioral Therapy and mindfulness principles. Each group session concluded with a brief mindfulness meditation practice.

2.5 Procedure

Following NYS EI evaluation, confirmed diagnosis of ASD, and families agreeing to receive EI services at CADB, a start date was assigned based on when the next family was expected to transition out of the program. New families participated in a graduated entry process starting with individualized services in the first week and transitioning into all available services in the following weeks. During the initial team meeting, caregivers were informed of research opportunities, recruited to participate in the current study, and provided with information regarding clinic policy and expectations; participation in services were not contingent on research involvement. Families were also encouraged to provide a description of child strengths and areas of concern to prioritize family goals and input. Each family was assigned a parent coach, who provided individualized services and helped coordinate care amongst the clinicians at CADB. During the first individualized sessions, parent coaches completed the ESDM Checklist (Rogers & Dawson, 2009), which combines caregiver report on child behavior in the home and community settings as well as clinician observations of child behavior in the home and clinic settings. Parent coaches worked collaboratively with families to create a comprehensive set of treatment objectives, which spanned across developmental domains (e.g., receptive and expressive communication, joint attention). Parents were encouraged to obtain a copy of "An Early Start for Your Child with

Autism: Using Everyday Activities to Help Kids Connect, Communicate, and Learn" (Rogers, Dawson, & Vismara, 2012). Weekly parent coaching sessions focused on implementation of NDBI strategies (e.g., gaining child attention, turn-taking, imitation) and parents were given handouts that summarized these strategies as needed. Parent coaches coordinated care internally (e.g., weekly clinician meetings) and externally (e.g., consultations with other child providers outside of CADB).

2.6 Service level measures

Feasibility and acceptability. Based on previous literature (Bowen et al., 2009; E. Proctor et al., 2011), a study-specific survey assessed clinician level of satisfaction and program feasibility. Clinicians reported levels of perceived appropriateness of services to children and families, including attitudes toward NDBI principles and adoption of principles into clinical care based on eight questions (e.g., "The core components of NDBI are beneficial for participants in the EI program," "I use the core components of NDBI in my treatment within the EI program," and "Caregivers benefit from participating in the EI program."). Answers were based on a Likert-scale, which ranged from 1 (*Strongly Disagree*) to 7 (*Strongly Agree*).

Equity. Equity was measured by exploring the range of socio-economic status, racial, and language backgrounds for families served by the current model.

Patient-centeredness and service utilization. Service utilization was quantified via review of billing records. One participant was excluded from the analyses due to incomplete billing files available. Percentages of families who received each type of service were calculated by dividing the number of families who received the service by total number of families in the current dataset. Due to variability in treatment duration, total duration estimates were provided for each service based on start and end billing dates. In an effort to standardize outcomes, weekly estimates of service use were calculated by dividing total hours billed (per service) by the total number of weeks the family participated in CADB EI services.

2.7 Patient level behavioral change measures

Data were taken from clinical practice as usual; thus, the number of cases varied across different measures. All measures were included in analyses if completed within 4 months before and 2 months after treatment start date (Time 1; means range from 1.5 months before [IQ] to 0.3 months after treatment start [MONSI-CC]) as well as 1 month before and 4 months after treatment exit (Time 2; means range from 0.0 months [BOSCC] to 0.3 months after treatment end [VABS]). Due to variability of collection dates, total time between measures was included as a covariate in all analyses. All measures were administered and rated by examiners who were blind to the treatment goals and utilization at treatment entry and exit.

Child developmental levels. Measures of cognitive skills and developmental abilities included the Mullen Scales of Early Learning (MSEL; Mullen, 1995), Bayley Scales of Infant Development (Bayley; Bayley, 2006) and Differential Ability Scales, Second Edition-Early Years (DAS-II; Elliott, 2007). The Bayley was used for one participant at program entry and the DAS-II was used for one participant at both timepoints and two participants at exit only; all other participants received the MSEL. Following the recommendation from the literature (Bishop, Guthrie, Coffing, & Lord, 2011), we used mental ages from these measures to capture meaningful changes from different measures across time points. Nonverbal mental age (NVMA) was calculated by averaging the age equivalents (in months) of the Cognitive and Fine Motor subtests on the Bayley, Visual Reception and Fine Motor subtests on the MSEL, and Picture Similarities and Pattern Construction subtests on the DAS-II. Verbal mental age (VMA) was calculated by averaging the age equivalents on Receptive and Expressive Language subscales of the MSEL, the Receptive and Expressive Communication subtests of the Bayley, and Verbal Comprehension and Naming Vocabulary subtests on the DAS-II. Full pre/post data were available for 30 children; 4 additional children had data available for one time point.

Child autism symptom severity. The Autism Diagnostic Observation Schedule, 2nd Edition (ADOS-2; Lord, Rutter, DiLavore, et al., 2012) is a semi-structured, standardized measure used to diagnose and assess ASD. The ADOS-2 yields calculated calibrated severity scores (CSS) in two domains, Social Affect (SA) and Restricted and Repetitive Behaviors (RRB; Gotham, Pickles, & Lord, 2009), which allow comparison of scores across different ADOS Modules. Twenty-nine participants (85.3%) were administered the Toddler Module, 2 (5.9%) Module 1, and 3 (8.8%) Module 2. Full pre/post data for ADOS-2 were available for 28 children; 6 additional children had data available for one time point.

The Brief Observation of Social Communication Change (BOSCC; Grzadzinski et al., 2016), a new treatment outcome measure, shows high reliability and validity for minimally verbal children with ASD using 12-min clinician-child interactions (Kim, Grzadzinski, Martinez, & Lord, 2019).

Like the ADOS-2, the BOSCC yields scores from two subdomains, social communication (SC) and RRB. Lower scores indicate better social communication skills and fewer RRBs. The BOSCC has shown to be more sensitive at capturing subtle changes in social communication behaviors compared to the ADOS-2 (Grzadzinski et al., 2016; Kim et al., 2019). Full pre/post data for the BOSCC were available for 17 children; 3 additional children had data available for one time point.

Child adaptive functioning. The Vineland Adaptive Behavior Scales, 2nd and 3rd Editions (VABS; Sparrow, Balla, & Cicchetti, 2005) is a standardized, semi-structured measure of adaptive behavior based on caregiver report. Changes in VABS scores were measured by AE across four domains: Communication, Daily Living Skills, Socialization, and Motor Skills. Full pre/post data for VABS were available for 20 families; 8 additional children had data available for one of the time points.

Caregiver implementation of NDBI strategies. The Measure of NDBI Strategy Implementation-Caregiver Change (MONSI-CC; Vibert et al., 2020) is an observational measure of caregivers' implementation of NDBI strategies. The MONSI-CC coding scheme was applied to 12-min, standardized play samples of the children playing with specific sets of toys and bubbles in a clinic with a caregiver. The MONSI-CC yields five subdomains (Environmental Set-Up, Child-Guided Interactions, Active Teaching and Learning, Opportunities for Social Communication, and Natural Reinforcement and Scaffolding), and an overall Total Score. Higher scores indicate higher frequency, effectiveness, and appropriateness of NDBI strategies. The MONSI-CC was available for 6 families due to the late introduction of the measure to the study.

2.8 Statistical analyses

For the evaluation of service-level outcomes, program feasibility was assessed by averaging individual scores on the clinician survey. Levene's test for equality of variances was used to determine differences in variance across groups (i.e., parent coaches and non-parent coaches) and independent sample t-tests were run to examine group mean differences. For the evaluation of patient level outcomes, Generalized Linear Mixed Models (GLMM) were used to determine whether significant improvements in developmental skills, autism symptom severity (ADOS-2; BOSCC), and adaptive functioning (VABS) were observed while controlling for baseline cognitive levels, symptom severity, language level, and age. GLMM control for missing data; we therefore included cases with missing timepoints (Krueger & Tian, 2004). Due to small sample size for MONSI-CC, one-tailed paired sample *t*-tests were run to determine caregiver level change. Effect sizes were calculated to indicate the magnitudes of changes over time using Cohen's d.

3. Results

3.1 Implementation and service outcomes

Feasibility and acceptability. Out of 16 clinicians currently or previously involved in the treatment program, 8 anonoymmously completed the survey (50%). Clinicians were highly satisfied with services provided to families ($M=6.50$, $SD=0.76$) and believed that services were beneficial for children ($M=SD$, 6.88, $=0.35$) and their caregivers ($M=6.88$, $SD=0.35$). In regard to perception of NDBI, clinicians reported that they understood the core components well ($M=6.50$, $SD=1.07$), believed the core components were beneficial for participants ($M=6.63$, $SD=0.74$), and used them in their clinical practice ($M=6.25$, SD 1.75). The lowest rating, although still a mean of 5.63 ($SD=1.3$), was regarding agreement with appropriateness of program length (min $=4$, max $=7$). There were no significant differences between clinicians who served as parent coaches ($n=4$) and those who did not ($n=4$; $ps>0.1$); however, those clinicians who did not serve as parent coaches reported significantly more variability in their response to the usage of core components of NDBI into their treatment and their impression on the benefit of NDBI for participants ($F=7.74$, $p=0.03$ and $F=13.5$, $p=0.01$, respectively).

For open ended questions, clinicians noted several strengths and barriers at the service and client levels. Strengths of the proposed model were recognized around the following themes: high level of clinician training, use of and focus on EBP, and increased caregiver involvement and focus. Challenges faced in the particular program included the following: administration confusion and time (e.g., scheduling, billing), length of program being too short for certain families, limited availability of slots for eligible children and minimal resources of some families (e.g., limits in finances and time). Fifty percent ($n=4$) identified the 6-month, rotating structure of the current model as both of benefit and challenge, especially for some families who need additional help.

Equity. Families served by the current EI program varied in income, race, and education. Total family income ranged from less than \$20,000 ($n=2$, 5.9%) to over \$161,000 ($n=14$, 41.2%). Half of the children identified as Caucasian ($n=17$). Approximately 80% ($n=27$) of primary caregivers attained a baccalaureate degree or higher. Twenty-one percent of caregivers reported speaking a primary language other than English ($n=2$, Spanish; $n=3$, Portuguese, $n=1$, Korean).

Patient-centeredness and service utilization. On average, families received a mean of 23 weeks of classroom services (range: 13–28 weeks, $SD=3.3$ weeks). Twenty-three families (67.7%) received parent-coaching in the clinic and home. The remaining families received all parent coaching only in the clinic. Most children received ST (94.1%, $n=32$) and OT (73.5%, $n=25$) services at CADB averaging 22 ($SD=5.2$) and 17 ($SD=7.5$) weeks respectively. Thirty-two families (94.1%) attended parent group sessions (psychoeducation and support combined) for an average of 19 ($SD=6.5$) weeks and 13 families (38.2%) utilized individual social support services for an average of 14 ($SD=6.8$) weeks.

The mean weekly averages for classroom hours was 5.1 (range: 3.4–6.0 h, $SD=0.70$ h) and 2.4 h of parent coaching combining in-home and clinic sessions (range: 0.9–3.7 h, $SD=0.66$ h). For those who utilized the services, mean weekly average use of ST and OT was 0.8 ($SD=0.23$) and 0.6 ($SD=0.33$) hours, respectively. The mean weekly average use of parent groups was 0.9 h ($SD=SD0.42$) and 0.4 ($SD=0.03$) hours of individual social work. Overall, families received on average 9.9 h (range: 6.7–12.8, $SD=1.66$) of treatment at CADB per week.

3.2 Patient level behavioral change outcomes

Changes in developmental levels. Children showed significant increases in VMA ($F[1,53]=34.18$, $p<0.001$; see Table 3 for more details), with an average gain of 10 months over a 6-month period, controlling for age at entry, months between IQ tests, total baseline ADOS-2 CSS, and baseline expressive language. Significant gains were also noted regarding NVMA ($F[1,53]=62.49$, $p<0.001$), with an average gain of 9 months over a 6-month period.

Higher baseline expressive language significantly predicted higher VMA and NVMA across both time points ($F[5,53]=7.96$, $p<0.001$ and $F[5,53]=2.80$, $p=0.03$ respectively). Lower baseline ADOS-2 CSS predicted higher VMA across time points ($F[1,53]=13.27$, $p=0.001$).

Changes in core autism symptoms. Significant decreases in social communication symptoms were noted on the BOSCC ($F[1,24]=9.82$, $p=0.005$) controlling for age at entry, months between BOSCC sessions, baseline expressive language level, and baseline NVRIQ. Children did not show

Table 3 Pre and post treatment patient level behavioral change outcomes.

Measure	Pre			Post			Cohen's d
	Mean	(SD)	*n*	Mean	(SD)	*n*	
Cognitive mental age							
Verbal	16.94	(10.99)	32	27.77[a]	(12.51)	32	−0.92
Non-verbal	21.66	(7.3)	32	30.66[a]	(8.13)	32	−1.17
ADOS-2 CSS							
SA	7.24	(2.06)	34	6.79	(1.95)	28	0.22
RRB	7.76	(1.69)	34	7.64	(1.75)	28	0.07
BOSCC							
SC	24.06	(7.79)	18	22.55[a]	(10.06)	22	0.17
RRB	7.89	(3.41)	18	7.39	(3.87)	22	0.14
VABS AE							
Communication	16.71	(8.13)	26	25.21[a]	(11.41)	24	−0.86
Daily living	17.80	(7.9)	28	26.71[a]	(12.95)	24	−0.85
Socialization	13.79	(6.57)	28	20.06[a]	(9.92)	24	−0.76
Motor	21.71	(4.47)	28	26.73[a]	(7.35)	24	−0.84
MONSI-CC							
Env. set-up	9.00	(1.87)	6	11.08[a]	(1.8)	6	−1.13
Child guided interactions	18.33	(2.42)	6	21.75[a]	(2.12)	6	−1.50
Active teaching and learning	26.00	(4.97)	6	30.08	(2.52)	6	−1.04
Opps. for social communication	3.67	(1.6)	6	3.67	(1.6)	6	−0.34
Natural reinforcement and scaffolding	13.25	(1.99)	6	13.25	(1.99)	6	−0.15

[a]Denotes significant change from pre-treatment to post-treatment changes when run with covariates in General Linear Mixed Models or paired-sample *t*-tests for MONSI-CC outcomes.

Note. ADOS-2 CSS, Autism Diagnostic Observation Schedule, 2nd Edition Calibrated Severity Score; SA, Social Affect; RRB, Restricted and Repetitive Behaviors; BOSCC, Brief Observation of Social Communication Change; SC, Social Communication; VABS AE, Vineland Adaptive Behavior Scales Age Equivalents; MONSI-CC, Measure of NDBI Strategy Implementation-Caregiver Change.

any significant changes in social communication symptoms ($F[1,51]=0.99$, $p=0.32$), when measured by the ADOS-2 CSS SA scores. When GLMM analyses were re-run with the subset of sample with *both* ADOS-2 *and* BOSCC scores available, results remained consistent (results available upon request). Lower baseline NVRIQ was a significant predictor of RRB, when measured by the BOSCC across both time points ($F[1,24]=4.97$, $p=0.04$). No other covariates were significant.

Changes in adaptive functioning. Children showed significant increases in AEs for communication abilities ($F[1,25]=26.32$, $p<0.001$), with an average gain of 9 months over a 7-month period, while controlling for age at entry, months between administration dates, baseline NVRIQ, and baseline CSS total. Significant increases were also noted in daily living skills ($F[1,27]=7.99$, $p=0.009$), social skills ($F[1,26]=4.99$, $p=0.034$), and motor skills ($F[1,27]=10.07$, $p=0.004$), with increases of 8, 5, and 4 months over a 7-month period respectively. Older children at entry showed higher levels of adaptive behavior regarding communication ($F[1,32]=13.40$, $p<0.01$), daily living ($F[1,33]=15.05$, $p<0.01$), and motor skills ($F[1,33]=6.34$, $p=0.02$) across both time points. More impairment in ASD symptoms corresponded with lower adaptive behaviors in communication ($F[1,32]=6.34$, $p=0.02$) and social skills ($F[1,33]=5.78$, $p=0.02$) across time points. More time between administrations ($F[1,32]=6.36$, $p=0.02$) and higher NVRIQ scores ($F[1,32]=4.79$, $p=0.04$) corresponded to higher adaptive behavior in communication skills across time points.

Changes in caregiver implementation of NDBI strategies. Caregivers showed significant increases in total use of NDBI strategies ($t[5]=-2.25$, $p=0.04$) on the MONSI-CC. All subdomain scores increased; however, only two subdomains (i.e., Environmental Set-up and Child Guided Interactions) showed significant change ($t[5]=-2.25$, $p=t0.04$ and $[5]=-2.37$, $p=0.03$) respectively.

4. Discussion

The current study provides initial evidence for the successful implementation of augmented NDBI in a community-based EI setting based on a novel treatment service model. This unique model delivers a comprehensive treatment package to families of children with ASD from a multidisciplinary team with extensive training in EBP in a community setting while maximizing caregiver involvement. Findings demonstrate initial feasibility of the model and provide preliminary support for effectiveness based on group-level improvements in developmental, adaptive functioning, and core autism symptoms in children with ASD and NDBI strategy implementation in their caregivers over the course of treatment.

Clinicians involved in the current program provided high ratings of feasibility and acceptability of the model. The strengths of the model identified by clinicians included increased caregiver involvement, high level of clinician training, and inclusion of EBP, which align with the initial vision of the program. These results demonstrate positive clinician attitudes toward EBP and buy-in to services they provide, a critical component of an effective treatment for children with ASD (Reaven, Blakeley-Smith, & Hepburn, 2014; Stahmer & Aarons, 2009). Multiple factors may have contributed to the high clinician satisfaction in this study. For example, clinicians were actively involved in the treatment development process and played key roles in designing and refining components of the model. Additionally, clinicians across disciplines entered the program with high levels of training, which may correspond to the increased familiarity and positive views of EBP. In other community-based EI programs, providers have reported lower knowledge base of EBP for ASD as well as interest in gaining more knowledge of and training in EBP (Stahmer et al., 2005). The multidisciplinary nature of the model, recognized by several clinicians as a strength, may have helped bolster a mutual respect for each discipline and sense of team when providing care for families. Overall, our findings support the idea that community-partnered participatory research allows for increased likelihood of sustained implementation of strategy use during the development of new treatment models.

Clinicians also identified barriers to more effective implementation of our community-based NDBI model at the system and family levels. These included relative inflexibility of program length, limited availability of slots for eligible children, and some families' minimal resources (e.g., limited finances and time). Creating a model that prioritizes caregiver involvement and endeavors to serve as many families as possible presents a double-edged sword. While caregiver empowerment and education have been shown to lead to positive child outcomes, some caregivers may not have the time or resources to completely participate to the full extent the program has to offer. The 6-month program length allows for more families to receive EBP per year; however, it does not address those families who may need extended treatment programs to fully generalize skills taught by the multidisciplinary team. Overall, the combination of strengths and barriers suggest that future efforts to implement evidence-based NDBIs in community settings should involve the systematic planning to establish and maintain organizational and administrative support for the clinicians and families in the program and flexibility in the length and dosage of intervention based on family needs.

Our program was utilized by families with varying racial, economic, and linguistic backgrounds. However, up to 80% of mothers had college or higher degrees, suggesting that maternal education for the current sample was higher than the general population. On average, families received approximately 10 h of intervention at our center per week, although those hours ranged widely from approximately 7 to 13 h per week. More than 60% of families utilized 75% of services offered through the model. This variability in total intervention hours may be a function of some families declining or not being eligible for optional child services and a delayed start in the provision of SW services. Although we were aware that many of the families who participated in our program received intervention services outside of our program, detailed information on the other services was not available. Future studies should explore the factors that contribute to the service utilization patterns and the relationship between the intensity of treatment and outcomes.

Children with ASD who participated in our model showed significant behavioral changes with small to large effect sizes, although due to the absence of a control group, these results need to be interpreted with caution. Children demonstrated large effect size increases regarding verbal and non-verbal abilities and adaptive communication, daily living, and motor skills. Medium effects were also noted for the improvement in socialization skill. Like other NDBI findings regarding changes in core symptoms of ASD (Vivanti et al., 2014), the current study found stability in these symptoms over time based on the ADOS-2 scores. However, though effects were small, statistically significant changes in social communication symptoms were noted when measured by the BOSCC, even after controlling for key child demographic factors. These findings are corroborated by other intervention studies that showed relatively larger changes in developmental skills compared to core autism symptom severity (e.g., Dawson et al., 2010), although a few studies indeed found significant treatment response in social communication symptoms (e.g., Estes et al., 2015). The results presented in this study used age equivalents and mental ages, similar to prior studies (Strain & Bovey, 2011), which are more sensitive to change compared to standard scores.

Finally, we demonstrated that caregivers significantly improved in their ability to incorporate NDBI strategies when interacting with their child. As caregivers were central recipients and collaborators in this model, improvement in caregiver implementation of NDBI strategies suggests that caregivers gained targeted skills over the course of parent-mediated intervention, though this was only based on a subset of the sample. We anticipate that positive increases in NDBI strategies are associated with positive increases in child developmental and adaptive skills; however, we were not able to examine moderation or mediation effects of caregiver behaviors on child outcomes due to small sample sizes. Similarly, we found that a few covariates in our models, such as age, non-verbal IQ, and language level at treatment entry, were significantly associated with outcome variables at both time points. Although we did not have power to examine how baseline child factors predict changes in skills, future studies with larger samples should examine these key developmental factors, such as expressive language and autism symptom severity, as potential mediators or moderators of treatment outcomes in young children with ASD.

Notwithstanding the strengths identified above, several limitations must be addressed. Despite positive clinician attitudes toward NDBI and high levels of training, we had limited capacity to monitor fidelity of clinician provision of treatment within the classroom setting. Although treatment fidelity guidelines exist for specific NDBIs, guidelines to track fidelity of generalized NDBI strategies implemented by multidisciplinary teams would be helpful for future studies with similar treatment models. We also obtained a 50% response rate from providers regarding their feedback on the feasibility and their acceptability of the model, which was lower than anticipated. The survey was sent to both current and previous clinicians who served at CADB. As such, we encourage future pilot and implementation studies to continuously monitor and incorporate stakeholder feedback in a more systematic and ongoing manner. Even though treatment end point outcomes were measured, we did not monitor treatment response continuously over the course of intervention as well as maintenance of skills at follow-up. Future studies should explore systematic ways to monitor progress over time which can inform treatment planning and adaptation of goals and strategies. Due to the mandate to serve all families and limited capacity to provide multiple treatments, we did not conduct a randomized-controlled trial to directly examine treatment-specific effects for our program in comparison with treatment-as-usual. Future studies may adopt similar techniques to Vivanti et al. (2014) by partnering with other community-based EI services to explore comparative effects. Finally, as described above, community-partnered participatory research increases the likelihood of adoption of strategies by end users, which include both clinicians and families. Thus, it will be imperative to maximize caregiver input when implementing additional changes to the model. Future efforts in the implementation of EBP in community settings should maximize caregiver input in the decision-making process.

5. Implications

The augmented model of NDBI implemented in a community setting presented in the current study shows strong acceptability and feasibility based on high clinician ratings and service utilization. Clinicians also noted several strengths of the model which align well with the indicators of high-quality NDBI programs identified in previous literature. Significant improvement in children's developmental and adaptive functioning as well as autism symptom levels and caregiver implementation of NDBI strategies over the course of treatment demonstrate promising evidence for the potential effectiveness of community implemented NDBI.

Acknowledgments

We would like to acknowledge Catherine Lord, who led the program development. We also would like to acknowledge Bethany Vibert, Jeannine Ederer, Tara Maloney, and research assistants at the Center for Autism and the Developing Brain (CADB) who assisted with treatment delivery and data collection. This study was funded by The Louis and Rachel Rudin Foundation (awarded to the Center for Autism and the Developing Brain).

References

Bayley, N. (2006). *Bayley-III: Bayley scales of infant and toddler development* (3rd ed.). San Antonio, TX: Pearson.

Bishop, S. L., Guthrie, W., Coffing, M., & Lord, C. (2011). Convergent validity of the Mullen scales of early learning and the differential ability scales in children with autism spectrum disorders. *American Journal on Intellectual and Developmental Disabilities, 116*(5), 331–343. https://doi.org/10.1352/1944-7558-116.5.331.

Bowen, D. J., Kreuter, M., Spring, B., Cofta-Woerpel, L., Linnan, L., Weiner, D., et al. (2009). How we design feasibility studies. *American Journal of Preventive Medicine, 36*, 452–457. https://doi.org/10.1016/j.amepre.2009.02.002.

Bruinsma, Y., Minjarez, M., Schreibman, L., & Stahmer, A. (2020). *Naturalistic developmental behavioral interventions for autism spectrum disorder.* Paul H. Brookes.

Dawson, G. (2008). Early behavioral intervention, brain plasticity, and the prevention of autism spectrum disorder. *Development and Psychopathology, 20*(3), 775–803. https://doi.org/10.1017/S0954579408000370.

Dawson, G., Rogers, S., Munson, J., Smith, M., Winter, J., Greenson, J., et al. (2010). Randomized, controlled trial of an intervention for toddlers with autism: The Early Start Denver Model. *Pediatrics, 125*(1), e17–e23.

Elliott, C. D. (2007). *Differential ability scales—Second edition (DAS-II)*. San Antonio, TX: Harcourt Assessment.

Estes, A., Munson, J., Rogers, S. J., Greenson, J., Winter, J., & Dawson, G. (2015). Long-term outcomes of early intervention in 6-year-old children with autism spectrum disorder. *Journal of the American Academy of Child & Adolescent Psychiatry, 54*(7), 580–587.

Gotham, K., Pickles, A., & Lord, C. (2009). Standardizing ADOS scores for a measure of severity in autism spectrum disorders. *Journal of Autism and Developmental Disorders, 39*(5), 693–705. https://doi.org/10.1007/s10803-008-0674-3.

Grzadzinski, R., Carr, T., Colombi, C., McGuire, K., Dufek, S., Pickles, A., et al. (2016). Measuring changes in social communication behaviors: Preliminary development of the brief observation of social communication change (BOSCC). *Journal of Autism and Developmental Disorders, 46*(7), 2464–2479. https://doi.org/10.1007/s10803-016-2782-9.

IDEA. (2004). *Individuals with disabilities education act, 20 U.S.C. § 1400*.

Kasari, C., Gulsrud, A. C., Wong, C., Kwon, S., & Locke, J. (2010). Randomized controlled caregiver mediated joint engagement intervention for toddlers with autism. *Journal of Autism and Developmental Disorders, 40*(9), 1045–1056. https://doi.org/10.1007/s10803-010-0955-5.

Kim, S. H., Grzadzinski, R., Martinez, K., & Lord, C. (2019). Measuring treatment response in children with autism spectrum disorder: Applications of the brief observation of social communication change to the autism diagnostic observation schedule. *Autism, 23*(5), 1176–1185. https://doi.org/10.1177/1362361318793253.

Krueger, C., & Tian, L. (2004). A comparison of the general linear mixed model and repeated measures ANOVA using a dataset with multiple missing data points. *Biological Research for Nursing, 6*(2), 151–157. https://doi.org/10.1177/1099800404267682.

Lord, C., Rutter, M., DiLavore, P. C., et al. (2012). *Autism diagnostic observation schedule: ADOS-2*. Los Angeles, CA: Western Psychological Services.

Mullen, E. M. (1995). *Mullen scales of early learning*. Circle Pines, MN: American Guidance Service Inc.

Nahmias, A. S., Pellecchia, M., Stahmer, A. C., & Mandell, D. S. (2019). Effectiveness of community-based early intervention for children with autism spectrum disorder: A meta-analysis. *Journal of Child Psychology and Psychiatry, 60*(11), 1200–1209. https://doi.org/10.1111/jcpp.13073.

Odom, S. L., Cox, A. W., & Brock, M. E. (2013). Implementation science, professional development, and autism spectrum disorders. *Exceptional Children, 79*(3), 233–251. https://doi.org/10.1177/001440291307900207.

Odom, S., Hume, K., Boyd, B., & Stabel, A. (2012). Moving beyond the intensive behavior treatment versus eclectic dichotomy: Evidence-based and individualized programs for learners with ASD. *Behavior Modification, 36*(3), 270–297. https://doi.org/10.1177/0145445512444595.

Proctor, E. K., Landsverk, J., Aarons, G., Chambers, D., Glisson, C., & Mittman, B. (2009). Implementation research in mental health services: An emerging science with conceptual, methodological, and training challenges. *Administration and Policy in Mental Health and Mental Health Services Research, 36*(1), 24–34. https://doi.org/10.1007/s10488-008-0197-4.

Proctor, E., Silmere, H., Raghavan, R., Hovmand, P., Aarons, G., Bunger, A., et al. (2011). Outcomes for implementation research: Conceptual distinctions, measurement challenges, and research agenda. *Administration and Policy in Mental Health and Mental Health Services Research, 38*(2), 65–76. https://doi.org/10.1007/s10488-010-0319-7.

Reaven, J., Blakeley-Smith, A., & Hepburn, S. (2014). *Bridging the research to practice gap in autism research: Implementing group CBT interventions for youth with ASD and anxiety in clinical practice*. https://doi.org/10.1007/978-3-319-06796-4_13.

Reed, P. (2015). Eclectic interventions. In *Interventions for autism* (pp. 223–260). John Wiley & Sons, Ltd. https://doi.org/10.1002/9781118897553.ch11.

Reichow, B. (2012). Overview of meta-analyses on early intensive behavioral intervention for young children with autism spectrum disorders. *Journal of Autism and Developmental Disorders, 42*(4), 512–520. https://doi.org/10.1007/s10803-011-1218-9.

Rispoli, K. M., Mathes, N. E., & Malcolm, A. L. (2019). Characterizing the parent role in school-based interventions for autism: A systematic literature review. *School Psychology, 34*, 444–457. https://doi.org/10.1037/spq0000283.

Rogers, S. J., & Dawson, G. (2009). *Early start Denver model for young children with autism.* New York, NY: Guilford Press.

Rogers, S. J., Dawson, G., & Vismara, L. (2012). *An early start for your child with autism.* New York: Guilford Press.

Schreibman, L., Dawson, G., Stahmer, A. C., Landa, R., Rogers, S. J., McGee, G. G., et al. (2015). Naturalistic developmental behavioral interventions: Empirically validated treatments for autism spectrum disorder. *Journal of Autism and Developmental Disorders, 45*(8), 2411–2428. https://doi.org/10.1007/s10803-015-2407-8.

Shire, S. Y., Chang, Y.-C., Shih, W., Bracaglia, S., Kodjoe, M., & Kasari, C. (2017). Hybrid implementation model of community-partnered early intervention for toddlers with autism: A randomized trial. *Journal of Child Psychology and Psychiatry, 58*(5), 612–622. https://doi.org/10.1111/jcpp.12672.

Sparrow, S. S., Balla, D., & Cicchetti, D. (2005). *Vineland adaptive behavior scales* (2nd ed.). Circle Pines, MN: AGS.

Stahmer, A. C., & Aarons, G. A. (2009). Attitudes toward adoption of evidence-based practices: A comparison of autism early intervention providers and children's mental health providers. *Psychological Services, 6*(3), 223–234. https://doi.org/10.1037/a0010738.

Stahmer, A. C., Collings, N. M., & Palinkas, L. A. (2005). Early intervention practices for children with autism: Descriptions from community providers. *Focus on Autism and Other Developmental Disabilities, 20*(2), 66–79. https://doi.org/10.1177/10883576050200020301.

Strain, P. S., & Bovey, E. H. (2011). Randomized, controlled trial of the LEAP model of early intervention for young children with autism spectrum disorders. *Topics in Early Childhood Special Education, 31*(3), 133–154.

Tiede, G., & Walton, K. M. (2019). Meta-analysis of naturalistic developmental behavioral interventions for young children with autism spectrum disorder. *Autism, 23*(8), 2080–2095. https://doi.org/10.1177/1362361319836371.

Vibert, B. A., Dufek, S., Klein, C. B., Choi, Y. B., Winter, J., Lord, C., et al. (2020). Quantifying caregiver change across early autism interventions using the measure of ndbi strategy implementation: Caregiver change (MONSI-CC). *Journal of Autism and Developmental Disorders, 50*(4), 1364–1379. https://doi.org/10.1007/s10803-019-04342-0.

Vivanti, G., Duncan, E., Dawson, G., & Rogers, S. J. (2017). *Implementing the group-based early start Denver model for preschoolers with autism, Springer International Publishing.* https://doi.org/10.1007/978-3-319-49691-7.

Vivanti, G., Paynter, J., Duncan, E., Fothergill, H., Dissanayake, C., Rogers, S. J., et al. (2014). Effectiveness and feasibility of the early start Denver model implemented in a group-based community childcare setting. *Journal of Autism and Developmental Disorders, 44*(12), 3140–3153. https://doi.org/10.1007/s10803-014-2168-9.

Zachor, D. A., Ben-Itzchak, E., Rabinovich, A. L., & Lahat, E. (2007). Change in autism core symptoms with intervention. *Research in Autism Spectrum Disorders, 1*(4), 304–317. https://doi.org/10.1016/j.rasd.2006.12.001.

Zwaigenbaum, L., Bauman, M. L., Choueiri, R., Kasari, C., Carter, A., Granpeesheh, D., et al. (2015). Early intervention for children with autism spectrum disorder under 3 years of age: Recommendations for practice and research. *Pediatrics, 136*(Suppl. 1), S60–S81. https://doi.org/10.1542/peds.2014-3667E.

CHAPTER THREE

Fathers, children, play and playfulness

Shelly J. Lane[a,b,*] and Jennifer St. George[c]

[a]Department of Occupational Therapy, Colorado State University, Fort Collins, CO, United States
[b]Department of Occupational Therapy, University of Newcastle, Newcastle, NSW, Australia
[c]Family Action Centre, University of Newcastle, Newcastle, NSW, Australia
*Corresponding author: e-mail address: shelly.lane@colostate.edu

Contents

1. Introduction	72
2. Defining play and playfulness	73
2.1 The benefits of play and playfulness for the child	77
2.2 Mothers, fathers and children at play	79
3. Focusing on fathers	82
3.1 Influence of paternal playfulness	84
3.2 Theories about father as playmate	85
3.3 Fathers' mental health	87
4. The father/child research project	90
4.1 Procedure	90
4.2 Measures	91
4.3 Our findings	94
5. Summary	97
6. Conclusion	98
Acknowledgments	98
References	98

Abstract

Is has become clear that fathers play a core role in the family; they are crucial for child development and family wellbeing. Father-child interaction is frequently around play, and this interaction serves to form an important bond between father and child that influences development throughout childhood. However, our understanding of how father-child play, child playfulness, and father playfulness interact to support development is limited. We know even less about this interaction for children with disabilities. In this paper we address play and playfulness in children, and parental playful interactions with their children. We examine fathers' playfulness and fathers as playmates, and present some preliminary research examining playfulness between fathers and their toddlers. Throughout we thread information on children with disabilities, first focusing on play and playfulness and later, on father-child play when children have disabilities.

International Review of Research in Developmental Disabilities, Volume 59
ISSN 2211-6095
https://doi.org/10.1016/bs.irrdd.2020.07.005

© 2020 Elsevier Inc.
All rights reserved.

1. Introduction

Over time we have come to recognize that fathers play an important role in family wellbeing and child care. While historically research did not give much credence to the contribution of the father to child development, it is now well recognized that fathers play a core role (Bentenuto & Venuti, 2019). In fact, Cabrera and colleagues (Cabrera, Fitzgerald, Bradley, & Roggman, 2014) suggest that fathering and mothering are equally crucial roles, sharing a great deal of similarities but also each having characteristics unique to mother or father. This overlapping yet also individual influence of mothers and fathers on child development is itself shaped by actions and beliefs of extended family members and the community at large (Lamb & Lewis, 2013). However, father–child engagement contributes to multiple aspects of child development both directly and indirectly (Lamb & Lewis, 2013), supporting development of language skills (Cabrera, Shannon, & Tamis-LaMonda, 2007; Lamb & Tamis-LeMonda, 2004; Tamis-LeMonda, Baumwell, & Cabrera, 2013) and social emotional skills (Tamis-LeMonda, Shannon, Cabrera, & Lamb, 2004). Further, a mutual father–child relationship has been shown to support the development of child self-regulation (Cabrera et al., 2007; Kochanska, Aksan, Prisco, & Adams, 2008; Kroll, 2017; Paquette, 2004b), and cognition (Cabrera et al., 2007). It has been suggested that fathers additionally serve a role in introducing children to the social world (Paquette, 2004a). Entire books have been written about the role of the father in the life of the child and reviewing all aspects of fathering is beyond the scope of this paper. Here we will focus on father–child play and playfulness in early childhood development. Cabrera and Roggman (2017) have suggested that studying playfulness in fathers, and the impact of playful interactions on the child, may add to our understanding of what is special about father play.

In this paper we begin by defining play and playfulness in children, and addressing the importance of both for child development, laying a foundation for looking at father–child interaction in play. We then take a look at maternal and paternal playful interactions with their children, identifying both similarities and differences. From there we focus on fathers, addressing fathers' playfulness and fathers as playmates. We look at the impact of fathers' mental health on father–child play interactions and present some preliminary work examining playfulness between fathers and their toddlers. Throughout all sections we thread information on children with disabilities, first focusing on play and playfulness and later on father–child play when children have disabilities.

2. Defining play and playfulness

Child's play is a fundamental occupation of childhood (Skard & Bundy, 2008) and well established to be vital for optimal childhood emotional, cognitive, social and physical development (Nijhof et al., 2018; Pellegrini & Smith, 1998; Roggman, Boyce, Cook, Christiansen, & Jones, 2004). In fact, Article 31 of the Convention on the Rights of the Child states that engaging in play and recreational activities is, is fact, a right of all children (United Nations [UN], 1989), a statement that is supported specifically for children with disabilities in Article 7 of the Convention of the Rights of Persons with Disabilities (UN, 2006). While play clearly differs across cultural contexts, it is present in all societies in which children are studied (Gosso & Carvalho, 2013). And yet, opportunities for and access to play is not universally available to all children. Poverty may impact access to play opportunities, living in isolated areas may do the same (Towler, 2017). Childhood disability may also prevent children from playing simply based on the nature of the disability and the challenge of making play accessible in all environments (Besio, Bulgarelli, & Stancheva-Popkostadinova, 2017; Lane & Mistrett, 1997; Towler, 2017). Additionally, for children with disabilities, play is often enfolded into therapeutic and learning interventions, where it becomes adult-initiated and controlled; more "play-like" than child play (Besio et al., 2017; Lane & Mistrett, 2002).

In working to understand play, why it is important, and why its absence should be of concern, we begin by endeavoring to define it; what is play? Reaching back to early work, Rubin, Fein, and Vandenberg (1983) indicated that researchers of the time had characterized play as having three dimensions: play as defined by the *context* likely to lead to behaviors associated with play; specific *behaviors or criteria* that reflect play; and the *disposition* to engage in play activities that distinguished it from other behaviors. These three dimensions, expanded on below, remain a useful way to begin to understand what play is, and why play is important.

Play as defined by *context* can be viewed from different perspectives. First, it is *culturally grounded* and defined based on what adults in a specific culture hold to encompass play (Rubin et al., 1983). Further, the cultural beliefs about play held by parents influence their support of and engagement in play with their child colleagues (Haight, Parke, & Black, 1997). Parents from some cultural backgrounds are comfortable in the role of playmate with their child, while others are not. Play is valued in some cultures, but this is not universally true (Gaskins, Haight, & Lancy, 2007; Haight et al., 1997). The time available for play influences the extent of play in different cultures. For instance, when children are expected to share the load of chores, less time is available for play, although often play can be intertwined with the work of chores (Besio et al., 2017). Second, the context of play can also be viewed by the physical and social environment in which it is to take place. Gosso and Carvalho (2013) suggest that it is the availability of time, space, objects, and people (both playmates and adult role models) that influence engagement in play across cultures. For instance, an environment with peers, play materials, toys, or and/or play structures invites a child to play. The nature of the play will differ depending on what the environment provides. Considering the child's age, the quantity of toys, and specific characteristics of play materials is important in supporting play (Dauch, Imwalle, Ocasio, & Metz, 2018). Providing children with a combination of new and familiar toys and limiting the number of toys available at any given time, allows children the opportunity to explore object affordances more thoroughly and play more deeply (Saracho & Spodek, 1998). Third, physical features of the play environment also influence how play unfolds (Dauch et al., 2018). Skard and Bundy (2008) indicated that the flexibility and safety of the play space influence engagement in play. In addition, physical features of the environment support a specific kind of play. Playgrounds and similar spaces tend to support engagement in free play; pretend play is best supported when children have the space they need to develop a play frame, choice about what to do, materials to support and invite pretence, and uninterrupted time to develop their play episodes (Robertson, Yim, & Paatsch, 2020).

Characteristics of, access to, and strategies for engagement with toys and play materials are each aspects of context that significantly influences the play of children with disabilities (Lane & Mistrett, 2002, 2008). For children with disabilities, physical play spaces are often barriers themselves, preventing children from accessing play spaces and opportunities (Lane & Mistrett, 2002, 2008) and the casual yet crucial ability to make friends and feel part of a peer group (Towler, 2017). While play objects and play materials may seem appealing, making them "work" (turning them on or off, access buttons, etc.) can be a challenge for children with disabilities. Further, the sensory features of some play materials may be overwhelming, making the play object or toy unenticing (Lane & Mistrett, 2002, 2008). Considering all aspects of context, and how they form barriers to or support for engagement in play is important in fulfilling the right of children to play.

The dimension of play as play *behaviors* reflects engaging in play as a natural activity associated with childhood. Theorists have endeavored to define actions and engagement that reflect play and its development over time. For instance, Parten's original definitions of a social play sequence (Parten, 1932) included a range of developmental behaviors beginning with unoccupied or unengaged behavior, and moving to solitary play; onlooker behavior where a child will watch others at play; parallel play in which children may play the same activity but do so side by side rather than in interaction; associative play in which children play with others for short periods of time; and lastly cooperative play during which interaction with other children around an activity is sustained. Piaget (1962) defined four stages of development that influence play: sensorimotor, during which children play using trial and error and base learning on experience; preoperational which occurs along with the development of language, memory and imagination do so as to support symbolic thinking; concrete operational where logic and method begin to infiltrate play actions; and formal operational, in which symbols can be used to represent abstract concepts. As an extension of these stages of development, Piaget identified observable and hierarchical categories of play, including functional play where the emphasis is on bodily movements and object manipulation, constructive play during which materials are used and combined in an organized way to make something, symbolic play which incorporates pretence and make-believe, and games with rules involving play with playmates in games that are guided by pre-established rules. Viewing play from the perspective of behavior categories has been suggested to make it more readily measurable and allow for closer examination of different forms of play (Rubin et al., 1983).

Play as *disposition*, the last of the perspectives on play, is also termed playfulness (Menashe-Grinberg & Atzaba-Poria, 2017; Morrison, Bundy, & Fisher, 1991; Neumann, 1971). Playfulness was initially described by Dewey (1933) as an attitude that emerged during play, reflecting the transaction between the child and the environment. In providing this definition, Dewey differentiates between play behavior and play as an attitude or disposition. This definition has largely remained stable since that time, although others have expanded on it to some extent. Playfulness is thus a process rather than a product (Barnett, 1991a; Rubin et al., 1983), and an attitude that influences how individuals approach an activity (Howard & McInnes, 2013). In this way, playfulness is considered an intrinsic characteristic that can enhance the quality and extent of play. As such, any activity can be perceived as play if one demonstrates the internal disposition of playfulness (Barnett, 1991a; Bundy, 1993). Playfulness is seen to be related to the player's capacity to enjoy and learn through play (Bundy, 1993) and considered to form an essential component of child development (Nijhof et al., 2018).

Features of playfulness include specific criteria that, when observed, allow the viewer to recognize that play is taking place. For instance, actively engaging, freely choosing what to do and how to do it, demonstrating intrinsic motivation, pretending, focusing on means rather than ends and displaying positive affect (e.g. Bundy, 1993; Rubin et al., 1983) all reflect aspects of playfulness. Bundy (1993) and Rubin et al. (1983) suggest that playfulness answers the question "what **can I do** with this object," supporting the characterization of playfulness as person-driven. This differentiates play, and playful interactions, from exploration which asks the question "what **can this object do**." Exploration is information gathering, familiarizing oneself with an object and laying a foundation for play. Playfulness shifts the person-object interaction from stimulus-driven to person-driven (Pelligrini & Bjorklund, 1998). Bundy suggested, based on the work of Neumann (1971) and Kooii and Vrijhof (1981), that playfulness was the outcome of a combination of three elements: intrinsic control, internal control, and freedom to suspend reality (Bundy, 1993). She suggested that each element existed on a continuum, and the sum of the degree to which each element was expressed lead to playful or non-playful interactions. She later added a fourth element to this conceptualization, suggesting that "framing" the play interaction, or being able to give, read, and respond to cues, was also core to playfulness. The construct of framing had been drawn from the work of Bateson (1972) who had indicated that communicating to others "this is play" and "this is how we interact in this situation" was crucial to setting up and continuing play (Bundy, 1997; Skard & Bundy, 2008). Thus, the more an individual feels free to suspend reality, has intrinsic motivation to engage, has internal control of the situation, and can give and receive cues about the play activity, the more playful is the interaction.

Playfulness has historically been considered a personality trait (Barnett, 1991b), and it has been associated with such characteristics as curiosity and creativity, being generally happy and expressing joy and humor, and also being physically active and verbal (Barnett, 1991b). These very characteristics used to capture playful dispositions can be highly challenging to display and recognize when children have disabilities. Children with disabilities can face challenges across many areas of development (e.g. language, social emotional maturation, sensory and motor development) that interfere with their ability to express joy, show curiosity, and engage physically in play. In order to convert disabilities into capabilities, and support all facets of play, additional physical and social supports are essential (Nussbaum, 2011).

2.1 The benefits of play and playfulness for the child

Play has long been established to provide benefits for child development. Pulling from the various theories on play and development we learn that play may be an important vehicle for learning to establish relationships, communicate and socialize, to understand emotions and conquer fears, display mastery of skills, and develop problem-solving and self-insight (Howard & McInnes, 2013). In fact, Nijhof et al. (2018) indicate that cognitive, social, emotional and physical development in children *rely* on engaging in play.

Children play at a level commensurate with their cognitive ability (Besio et al., 2017). And, while it is difficult to generalize about play across all levels of intellectual disability (ID), children with this diagnosis will likely show delays in accomplishment of the play stages described early, staying in exploratory play longer and developing symbolic play later, if at all. Play tends to remain at the solitary play level due to delayed and limited social skills often characterizing children with ID. There is some indication that, for children with ID, play is more repetitious and hampered by reductions in intrinsic motivation, perceptual delays, and learning delays. Delays in play such as these have been widely investigated and are clearly summarized in Besio et al. (2017). Interestingly, these authors also note that characteristics of play such as spontaneity and curiosity are not related to cognition, and thus may not be dampened by ID. Capitalizing on these abilities of children with ID requires access to opportunity and the context that supports such play.

Should we also care about *playfulness* in children? What benefits are associated with this attitude toward activity and engagement? Bundy indicates that playfulness is a flexible style or approach to task that supports creativity and problem solving Bundy (1993). She goes on to suggest that taking a playful approach to problem solving and task accomplishment is more important than the specific nature of the task itself. While all tasks may not be classified as play, any task can be approached in a playful manner. Bundy (1993) states "without playfulness, all activities become work" (pp. 217). The skill of not taking things too seriously, and the ability to approach tasks in a light-hearted manner, both aspects of playfulness, are excellent reasons to support the development of playfulness in all children. This disposition then, to make playful even relatively mundane tasks, may be a foundation for other skills.

In fact, while play has been linked with multiple aspects of development, as we noted at the outset of this paper, playfulness has been linked to other important skills and attributes. In the early work of Barnett, she indicated that playfulness linked to both positive and negative child characteristics (Barnett, 1991b). Greater playfulness was seen in children described as being bright, confident, active, cheerful, imaginative and curious. She indicated that playfulness might enhance creativity and problem-solving abilities (1991b) and help children with emotional regulation (1991a,b, 1998). Barnett also suggested that confidence was linked to all dimensions of playfulness and, as such, reflected emotional stability or self-awareness. Barnett indicated that playfulness was also linked to aggressiveness, impulsiveness and mischievousness. In examining the relationship between playfulness and these potentially negative behaviors, Barnett suggested that we take a different, more positive, perspective. She suggested that aggressiveness, impulsiveness and mischievousness could simply be viewed as typical, and even expected, aspects of physical aspects of play.

Based on shared characteristics between the constructs of playfulness and coping (e.g. both being self-directed, requiring active and flexible engagement and persistence), Saunders, Sayer, and Goodale (1999) examined this relationship in children, identifying a positive relationship between playfulness and what they termed as "adaptive coping," a finding supported in the later work of Bundy and colleagues (Bundy et al., 2008). The combination of playfulness and adaptive coping has been suggested to support the child in exploration of the world around them. And, as noted earlier, exploration is a foundation for play (Rubin et al., 1983). Along similar lines, Barnett indicated that playfulness helped children regulate distress, and regulate, express and understand their emotions (Barnett, 1991a,b, 1998).

In addition to the relationships described above, Barnett (2018) offered some interesting insights into perceptions of playfulness. She suggested that, in first and second grade, playful children are more desired by peers as friends and classmates and more socially adept; this was especially true for boys. Teachers however, saw playful boys as disruptive. Surprisingly, the social capital attributed to boys in grades one and two shifted in grade three. At this point teacher perspective seemed to have influenced student perspective such that by grade three playfulness in boys was not valued by peers, and instead it became associated with lower social status. The link to better social interactions, at least in early development, was also supported by Nijhof et al. (2018), indicating that playful activities offered children a safe opportunity to test out potential consequences of alternative scenarios, and develop flexibility in their behavioral, social and emotional repertoires.

Thus, children capable of engaging in more playful behaviors appear to also show many additional positive character attributes, including self-regulation, adaptive coping, social interaction skills, problem solving and creative thinking. These adaptive behaviors, where children learn to manage environmental demands and continue to meet their daily needs, are important to ongoing development. Children with disabilities have been noted to be at risk for reduced playfulness, potentially because there is a mismatch between a child's innate drive to play and their capability to independently engage in playful activities, something we should find problematic (Chiarello, Huntington, & Bundy, 2006; Lane & Mistrett, 1997, 2002). Often, well-intended interventions put what was intended to be play into the "play-like" realm identified by Besio et al. (2017) in which the core characteristics of intrinsic motivation, internal control, freedom to suspend reality and the ability to establish a flexible play frame are missing. Instead the interaction is focused on play as a tool for attaining therapy or education-oriented goals rather than focused on play and playfulness (Lane & Mistrett, 2002).

2.2 Mothers, fathers and children at play

There are many influences on a child's life that can affect their play activities and playfulness, but the role played by primary caregivers is crucial, especially in the early years (Lucassen et al., 2015). Children's playfulness and play skills are derived from the early play routines between mother and infant beginning in the infant's second month of life. These routines involve imitation, turn taking, manipulating a play activity to increase enjoyment, and determining the outcome of the game (Okimoto, Bundy, & Hanzlik, 2000). In many studies, a key focus is comparison between mother and father play behavior and comparison of parent effects on child outcomes. Some studies show that mother and father play interactions are similar, yet child outcomes differ. For example, Yago et al. (2014) found that while parents' play was similar as measured by the Nursing Child Assessment Teaching Scale, infants were more contingently responsive to fathers. Likewise, while parents' play may be similarly sensitive and challenging in a toddler–parent play situation, only fathers' play was a predictor of the child's later attachment representations (Ahnert et al., 2017; Grossmann et al., 2002).

Still other studies of mother- and father–child play show differences in parental behaviors. Mothers are often identified as establishing different forms of play interaction, involving more teaching, scaffolding, guiding, and exerting greater restraint (Ashbourne, Daly, & Brown, 2011; Menashe-Grinberg & Atzaba-Poria, 2017) while fathers are often described as being more likely to be playful, stimulating or challenging in their play with children (Cabrera & Roggman, 2017; Kazura, 2000; StGeorge, Wroe, & Cashin, 2018). As noted earlier, fathers allow their children to take the lead, playing more like a peer playmate, engaging in challenging play behaviors with their children, scaffolding and supporting children to accomplish something a bit more difficult (John, Halliburton, & Humphrey, 2013). Fathers encourage their child to take risks, engaging in "risky play," while at the same time as ensuring the child's safety (Paquette, 2004b). In addition, boisterous father-child interaction like rough-and-tumble play is common to father-child play and can have a positive influence on younger children who are rapidly developing emotionally and socially (Roggman, Boyce, Cook, Christiansen, & Jones, 2004). Fathers describe their way of engaging with their child in the context of play as 'being present' in the moment, and making a connection with their child (Ashbourne et al., 2011). These differences are reported to some extent in the literature on children with disabilities as well. In the Chiarello et al. (2006) study mentioned earlier, when investigators looked more closely at individual children, they identified that the degree of playfulness between mother–child and father–child interactions differed depending on child characteristics. Those children who were more playful with mothers tended to have greater motor challenges, while those more playful with fathers had stronger motor capabilities. This is consistent with the physicality of fathers during play and challenging play displayed by fathers.

Where mother and father play styles are different, some studies still show no difference in child outcomes. John et al. (2013) observed qualitatively different patterns of parent behaviors but similar child outcomes—fathers were more physical and challenging, and mothers were more structuring and guiding—but there were no differences in child responsivity to parents. Similarly, Kokkinaki and Vasdekis (2015) found stronger emotional matching and attunement in father–infant interaction than mother–infant, but no differences in child's interest in either parent.

For children with disabilities, mother and father interactions have both been shown to promote child play and playfulness. Chiarello et al. (2006) examined mother's and father's interactions with their child, their use of physical positioning and handling, and child motor behavior and playfulness in young children with motor delays. Outcomes indicated that neither mother nor father were overly directive in interactions with their child; both were supportive of play. Further, while mothers were seen as being somewhat more responsive during play, overall child playfulness did not differ whether the child engaged with mother or father. El-Ghoroury & Romanczyck (1999) found that mother-child and father-child play interactions with their child with autism were generally very similar, and that parents spent more time playing with their child with autism than with the child's siblings. The only difference between mother and father interaction approach was that mothers made more statements in verbal interactions than did fathers. Román-Oyola, Reynolds, Soto-Feliciano, Cabrera-Mercader, & Vega-Santana (2017) indicated that adult playfulness predicted emotional parental self-efficacy, or developing an emotional relationship, with their child with autism. In a more recent investigation of parent-child play with children with autism, Bentenuto and colleagues (Bentenuto, Perzolli, De Falco, & Venuti, 2020; Bentenuto & Venuit 2019) indicated that mothers and fathers were equally sensitive and emotionally available to their child during free play, and elicited a similar degree of emotional availability from their child. Both parents had some difficulty supporting ongoing engagement in play with their child but were generally non-intrusive in their interactions. Mothers seemed to prefer symbolic play while fathers preferred exploratory play, suggesting unique roles for each parent in child play, and a need to include both parents in intervention.

Overall then, parent-child play is an important aspect of development, across multiple domains. While mothers and fathers are both important playmates, differences are described both in their play/interaction style and, to some extent, in the impact of these interactions on child skills. Fathers engaging in playful interactions with their children support the development of adaptability, self-regulation (Roggman et al., 2004), and social competency in their child. These children may also be less likely to develop internalizing behaviors later in childhood (Cabrera & Mitchell, 2009; Jia, Kotila, & Schoppe-Sullivan, 2012). Playfulness in the guise of rough and tumble play enhances positive relationships within the dyad, which promotes the positive development of childhood skills related to social competency (Shannon, Tamis-LeMonda, London, & Cabrera, 2002; StGeorge & Freeman, 2017).

Similarly, these conclusions apply to some extent to father-child play when children have a disability. De Falco and colleagues (De Falco, Esposito, Venuti, & Bornstein, 2008) investigated father-child play when children had Down Syndrome, observing the difference between solitary and collaborative play as well as emotional availability. Outcomes indicated that children demonstrated higher levels of play when playing with their fathers (symbolic vs exploratory), which was enhanced by greater emotional availability in the father-child dyadic interaction. Father-child attunement was also strong during play interactions, suggesting that fathers were able to adjust their play interactions to meet the capabilities and interests of their child.

More generally, and for both parents, play and playful interactions between parent and child requires both parties to participate. Howard and McInnes (2013) indicate that a positive relationship with parents and caregivers is essential to the development of attachment, and thus crucial to the child's ability to feel safe as they explore their world. Adults need to be able to communicate, to "talk" and "listen" to their child verbally and non-verbally, and within this interaction allow the child to control the communication. As noted earlier, the giving and reading of cues is part of the framing dimension of playfulness; the cycle of giving and reading cues contributes to the ability to maintain the engagement in play (Bundy, 1997). This reciprocal interaction in support of play and playfulness unfolds naturally when children are typically developing. However, it can present challenges for children with disabilities. A child's ability to respond to parent stimulation is dependent on their physical, cognitive, and social-emotional characteristics. When children with disability are less able to respond to parental communication and cues for play with the expected and anticipated "typical" pleasure, reciprocity or communication, the parental response may be flattened, and the engagement in play cut short.

3. Focusing on fathers

Up to this point we have established that
- Child play and playfulness are important features of child development;
- The engagement in play affords children the opportunity to develop skills across all domains of development;
- Playfulness is a way of approaching tasks, that involves characteristics such as choice, intrinsic motivation, freedom to pretend, and the ability to give and read cues;
- Mothers and fathers offer children the opportunity to benefit from play, with somewhat different styles and somewhat different outcomes.

We now turn our focus to fathers, to explore in greater depth father-child play and playfulness. As has been noted, both mothers and fathers can be playful in interactions with their children (Menashe-Grinberg & Atzaba-Poria, 2017). However, fathers engage in play more than any other form of care for their child (Cabrera & Roggman, 2017; Mehall, Spinrad, Eisenberg, & Gaertner, 2009; Paquette, 2004a). Fathers are described as having a unique style of play that can be seen in early father–infant interactions. It has been called stimulating and arousing, and may disrupt the child's state (Yogman, 1981). Fathers have been shown to allow their child take the lead, and to scaffold play to a higher level, challenging and motivating more complex behaviors (John et al., 2013). In addition, in engaging in play with fathers, children develop the skills needed to cope with anxiety (Bögels & Phares, 2008). These attributes or positive influences have been primarily studied in fathers of typically developing children. However, to a more limited extent, they can be extended to our understanding of father-child play with children with disabilities. In fact, while fathers of children with autism report being involved with child-care routines, they indicate they spend the majority of their time with their child in play and leisure activities (Potter, 2017). Similarly, in a study of parents of children with intellectual disabilities, mothers and fathers both perceived play as an important role for fathers to take (Simmerman, Blacher, & Baker, 2001). Fathers have been called the primary playmate for infants and toddlers, much as mothers fulfil the role of primary caregiver (John et al., 2013; Roggman et al., 2004). Indeed, fathers appear to be playing whether they are engaged in child-care activities or leisure interactions (Coyl-Shepherd & Hanlon, 2013).

There has been interest in looking at father-child play when children have autism and investigators suggests that fathers endeavor to engage their child in play. While play may have an overarching theme of teaching through play, or using play as a vehicle for learning (Mitchell & Lashewicz, 2015), fathers report playing or spending leisure time with their child several times a week (Potter, 2017), and fathers suggest playing to their child with autism more often than do fathers of typically developing children (Pisula, 2008). These findings reinforce that play is a very important father-child activity. Including play as a component of leisure activity, Mitchell and Lashewicz (2015) found that, while leisure activities with their child required a great deal of effort, fathers took the initiative to make such opportunities available and meaningful for their child with autism. Interestingly these investigators also suggested that this engagement in leisure had a positive impact on the father as well, providing an avenue for fathers to interact with their children.

Play with children with autism may still involve rough and tumble play, and in fact fathers suggested that this was often the best way to get their child to smile and laugh (Vacca, 2013). Fathers may view their child's play as different from that of typical children, but can accept this, and often use their child's interests to engage in fun (Bonsall, 2018; Mitchell & Lashewicz, 2015). Investigators such as Potter (2017), and Mitchell and Lashewicz (2015) suggest that we view the play of children with autism not as deficient but instead simply as different. Fathers who can embrace this difference appear to have found a way to connect with their child in a manner that puts fun and joy into the interaction (Bonsall, 2018; Mitchell & Lashewicz, 2015).

Fathers of children with cognitive disabilities also take on a role of playmate to interact with their child (De Falco et al., 2008; Simmerman et al., 2001), although the father-child role also incorporates other aspects of parenting. Fathers have been shown to adjust their playful interactions in a manner consistent with the child's ability (De Falco et al., 2008), supporting both play and interaction.

3.1 Influence of paternal playfulness

Given this apparent paternal propensity to play, there is a surprising lack of research concerning men's playfulness as a psychological or cognitive trait or attribute. Adult playfulness generally has been investigated less than the playfulness of the child, and rarely in relationship to parent-child interactions. In seeking to define playfulness in adults, Proyer, Brauer, & Wolf (2019) suggested a model that included other-directedness, intellectual features such as liking to play, lightheartedness, and whimsicality, or the ability to find something amusing in odd or grotesque situations. They developed an assessment tool capturing these features of adult playfulness and found links between playfulness and psychological functioning and well-being. However, there were no gender or age-related differences, reinforcing the similarities between men and women.

Playfulness in adults is said to be associated with adaptability, learning, growth and an ability to view things as challenges rather than threats, however there is limited research to support these suggestions (Van Vleet & Feeney, 2015). The limited research that is available indicates that playful adults show greater willingness to try new approaches, are more comfortable with the unexpected, and overall show greater adaptability (Shen, 2010; Shen, Chick, & Pitas, 2017). Playful adults often engage in novel tasks or in novel situations, allowing themselves to practice variations of skills.

While this provides the opportunity to practice, it has the added benefit of experience with uncertainty and problem solving, both attributes of adaptability (Shen et al., 2017). Playfulness in adults has also been shown to support better coping and potentially enhance resilience (Magnuson & Barnett, 2013). Whether adult playfulness has a positive influence on that of the child remains unclear. Shen et al. (2017) examined the relationship between adult playfulness and playfulness of young adult children, and father, investigators indicated found that only mothers' playfulness was linked to that of the young adult. These investigators suggested this was due to the stronger role that is still played by mothers in child rearing. Additional research in this area is needed.

Other characterizations of adult playfulness posit it as imaginary, creative, unconventional, and enjoyable. This specific construct of playfulness (in both fathers and mothers) has been linked to children's vocabulary, emotion regulation and absence of negativity; however, several of these associations are mediated by additional parenting behaviors such as sensitivity (Lovas, 2005; Menashe-Grinberg & Atzaba-Poria, 2017) or closeness (Shorer, Swissa, Levavi, & Swissa, 2019). Overall, the limited available evidence points to fathers' playful co-occupations influencing childhood language, social competence, and resilience development.

3.2 Theories about father as playmate

In view of the fact that fathers are often nominated as playmates for their children, several domains of research have sought to clarify the biological and sociological roots of these observations.

3.2.1 Biological influences on fathering

Within biological studies, findings tend to converge on hormones playing a part in men's attitude to parenting. For example, testosterone levels decline when men become fathers, and influence paternal behaviors across the short and long-term (Gettler, McDade, Agustin, & Kuzawa, 2011; Gettler, McDade, Feranil, & Kuzawa, 2011; van der Pol et al., 2019), although more in-depth research is required (Meijer et al., 2019). Oxytocin, a hormone central to parenting, is found to be related to different behaviors in mothers compared to fathers. In mothers, oxytocin is associated with sensitive caregiving and affectionate physical contact, while in fathers, oxytocin levels are associated with sensitive caregiving and stimulatory physical touch (Apter-Levi, Zagoory-Sharon, & Feldman, 2014; Rilling, 2013). Fathering can also be observed in patterns of brain network activation. Preliminary investigations indicated that, when interacting with their own infant, mothers showed greater activation of emotional-motivational regions, while fathers showed greater activation in social cognitive regions (Atzil, Hendler, Zagoory-Sharon, Winetraub, & Feldman, 2012). The activity of different hormones and different networks are posited as reasons for differences in the way that paternal relationship and parenting styles manifest. For a thorough discussion, see Abraham and Feldman (2018).

3.2.2 An evolutionary perspective

From an evolutionary perspective, fathers' physical and psychological differences from mothers are considered to be biologically based, yet culturally influenced. In this view, fathers facilitate the child's experiential knowledge and growth of confidence. They introduce the child to novelty and risk, encouraging initiative and perseverance, metaphorically "opening their child to the world" (Bowlby, 1988; Paquette, 2004a).

Two aspects of fathering that may serve this particular function of "opening the child to the world" are the arousing style of fathers' behavior and fathers' propensity to engage in vigorous physical play. Fathers' play often involves bursts of high energy that increase as playtime extends (Feldman, 2003). Blocking play moves, sudden changes of routine that provoke surprise, humorous interchanges or pretending to fight, bring surprise and complexity to the child; this paternal behavior has been documented in numerous studies (Grossmann et al., 2002; Keltner, Capps, Kring, Young, & Heerey, 2001; Yogman, Kindlon, & Earls, 1995). The stimulation and challenge invoke aspects of the child's wider social and experiential milieu and help the child towards successful independence. Additionally, the physicality that characterizes much of father-child play is understood to strengthen the child's physiology and guide the child towards physical self-control and skilful manipulation of strength (Fry, 2014).

3.2.3 Fathers and attachment

Within attachment theory, fathers' play has come to represent a site of interaction that fosters the child's bond with the father. The bond is developed as fathers, through play rather than through sensitive responding to distress, provide a secure base for their child's exploration of the world around it (Grossmann & Grossmann, 2019). Fathers provide this secure base by being sensitive to the child's fear and caution at the same time as providing stimulation and challenge. These attributes encourage the child's physical exploration of objects and the environment, as well stretching its psychological capabilities such as attention and perseverance (StGeorge et al., 2018). In families where the child has a disability, fathers' involvement and the quality of his relationship with the child are linked to better child outcomes, such as behavior (Climie & Mitchell, 2017), and play quality (de Falco et al., 2008). The evidence supporting this interpretation of fathers' play style as the site and mechanism for a child's secure attachment relationship is robustly supported by research over the last 30 years (Grossmann & Grossmann, 2019).

3.3 Fathers' mental health

Not unlike mothers, a father's parenting, including his play and playfulness, is vulnerable to a number of factors, including his mental health. Indicators of poor mental health in fathers include depression, anxiety and stress, including parenting stress. And, while there is no evidence to link father's mental ill-health directly to child play and playfulness per se, we can draw conclusions based on what we do know.

Depression is distinctively characterized by low positive affect and anhedonia, while anxiety has physiological hyperarousal as a unique feature. Both depression and anxiety have general distress as a common factor, which can include symptoms of irritability and nervous tension (Nieuwenhuijsen, de Boer, Verbeek, Blonk, & van Dijk, 2003). Unsurprisingly then, there is emerging evidence of the negative impact of paternal mental health on children's development during toddlerhood (e.g. Aktar, Majdandzic, de Vente, & Bogels, 2014; Cabrera & Mitchell, 2009; Price-Robertson, 2015), and this impact is likely to impact the quality of father's play and subsequently children's play development and the expression of playfulness (Roggman et al., 2004). However, it is worth noting that Ahnert et al. (2017) found paternal play quality to be independent of fathers' personality and perceived parenting stress.

3.3.1 Depression

Studies of paternal depression have largely focused on paternal depression during infancy and its impact on development and behavior. Paternal depression appears to have a negative impact on child development and behavior that is both separate from and different to the influence of maternal depression (e.g. Fletcher, Freeman, Garfield, & Vimpani, 2011; Sethna, Murray, Netsi, Psychogiou, & Ramchandani, 2015; Sethna, Murray, Edmonson, Iles, & Ramchandani, 2017). However, the effect is reported to be small, and potentially mediated by several factors including child and father age, and sample race/ethnicity (Wilson & Durbin, 2010). For preschool and school-aged children multiple mediating variables have been identified between paternal postnatal depression and child psychological concerns. Notable variables include maternal depression and couple conflict (Gutierrez-Galvo, Stein, Hanington, Heron, & Ramchandani, 2015). Relative to father-child play, evidence indicates that depressed fathers are less responsive in free-play activities, less likely to engage in activities such as singing or outdoor play, and less likely to touch their infants. The interactions of depressed fathers were also found to be less intrusive and more withdrawn (Sethna, Murray, Edmondson, Iles, & Ramchandani, 2017). Paternal depression therefore has the potential to negatively impact their behavior, and thus their playfulness. The presence of paternal depression has been associated with sub-optimal parent-child relations and with reduced paternal sensitivity to child cues (Price-Robertson, 2015). When fathers are depressed, infants smile and laugh less (Ramchandani et al., 2011), and children experience both internalizing (e.g. emotional) and externalizing (e.g. conduct- and hyperactivity-related behavior) problems in infancy and early childhood (Price-Robertson, 2015), even when the presence of paternal depression is relatively short-lived. For example, paternal depression during only the pregnancy and perinatal periods has been associated with child psychiatric and oppositional defiant/conduct disorders that can last into middle childhood (Ramchandani et al., 2011).

3.3.2 Anxiety
Anxious behaviors may also play a role in fathers' interactions with their children. A consistent relationship has been found between a father's anxiety and the exhibition of avoidant behavior in infants, most likely a behavior learned through social referencing (Aktar et al., 2014). Fathers' anxiety is linked to fathers being more controlling (Teetsel, Ginsburg, & Drake, 2014), overinvolved and less challenging (Moller, Majdandzic, & Bogels, 2015). Inference can be drawn about links between paternal anxiety and father-child playfulness given the impacts presented here. Playfulness is not supported by avoidance of interaction, or parental control of interaction. More research in this area is very much needed.

3.3.3 Parenting stress
Another form of stress affecting many parents is directly related to their feelings about their child, about their own capabilities, and about the support available to them (Abidin, Jenkins, & McGaughey, 1992). Abidin's Parenting Stress Model (1992) suggests that high levels of parenting stress, in conjunction with difficult child behaviors, may lead to an increase in

negative parenting behaviors (such as physical discipline). Displays of negative parenting behaviors have, in turn, been evidenced to influence children's social development and behavior. For example, a father's parenting stress decreases his involvement in care and play (Ahnert et al., 2017), and may also increase his involvement with discipline, with an associated increase in child internalizing and externalizing behaviors (Cabrera & Mitchell, 2009; Giallo, Cooklin, Zerman, & Vittorino, 2013; Gulenc, Butler, Sarkadi, & Hiscock, 2018). It is notable that the deleterious relationship between parenting stress and child behavior is not consistently identified, and the reported negative impact may in fact be mediated by such things as partner relationship characteristics and satisfaction (Cabrera & Mitchell, 2009), or whether fathers are resident or non-resident (Lee, Pace, Lee, & Knauer, 2018).

3.3.4 Father mental health and child disability

The broad topic of paternal mental health when children have disabilities is complex and likely involves a number of influential variables. It is beyond the scope of this paper to summarize the vast literature on parental mental health when a child has a disability, but here we will touch on some points of interest. Following Rafferty, Tidman, and Ekas's (2020) lead, it is likely best to examine these variables by looking at a bi-directional relationship between parent (father) and child, and assuming that parenting is the outcome of influences at the person, family and cultural level. Both fathers and mothers of children with autism experience high degrees of stress, and the extent of stress may not differ between parents (May, Fletcher, Dempsey, & Newman, 2015; McStay, Dissanayake, Scheeren, Koot, & Begeer, 2014). Parenting stress when a child has autism may be related to the child behaviors often associated with autism, as well as the relationship between mother and father. The impact of high levels of parenting stress can be seen in several parenting behaviors, such as involvement, communication and limit setting (Cousino & Hazen, 2013; Hartley, Mihaila, Otalora-Fadner, & Bussanich, 2014; Osborne & Reed, 2010).

Similarly depression is influenced by multiple factors, and has been show to differ depending on the child disability; fathers of children and adolescents with autism experience more symptoms of depression than do fathers of children and adolescents with Down Syndrome or Fragile X Syndrome, and their symptoms of depression are more often within a range of clinical significance (Hartley, Seltzer, Head, & Abbeduto, 2012; Sanders & Morgan, 1997). Parenting stress related to having a child with autism, for both mothers and fathers, has been shown to be high and, in some studies, linked to co-parenting quality (May et al., 2015; McStay et al., 2014). Interestingly, for fathers, their sense of parenting competency and stress was strongly related to the quality of the co-parenting relationship. However, for mothers the sense of parenting competency was related to parenting stress (May et al., 2015).

It is not difficult to extrapolate from the impact of mental health disorders such as depression, anxiety, and stress on parenting broadly to the impact on parent-child play and playfulness. However, little insight has been offered specifically to the relationship between paternal mental health and children's playfulness. We examined the relationship between paternal mental health (i.e. depression, anxiety and stress) and children's playfulness as part of the Father-Child Play Project, hypothesizing that children of fathers showing greater depression, anxiety or stress would display less playfulness.

4. The father/child research project

Father/toddler pairs from a community population (non-clinical) taking part in an ongoing study examining father/child play participated in this study. Pairs were recruited via snowball and volunteer sampling techniques, based on the following criteria: (1) English as a first language; (2) father was the biological parent (3) father living with both the child and partner; (4) father and child were absent of major physical or mental health conditions likely to inhibit participation in play. Data from 63 father/toddler pairs was available for analysis. All fathers were either married or in defacto relationships, 76% had completed the equivalent of junior college or university, and were 90% were currently employed. Fathers ranged in age from 25-49 (M = 32 years, SD = 4.7 years; Table 1). Most fathers indicated their care role with their child was substantial, although less than that of the mother (57%); 30% of fathers indicated the child-care role was equally shared. Children ranged in age from 12 to 24 months (M = 19 months, SD = 3 months), 29 boys and 34 girls. All children were typically developing, and fathers had no acknowledged concerns for their own physical health.

4.1 Procedure

Father/toddler pairs attended one play session conducted in a comfortable room setting at the University. Fathers were invited to play with their child in four play segments, each 7-min long. Play segments included (1) 2-bag play—father/child pairs were given a bag of colored wooden blocks and a bag containing two hand puppets (a tiger and a monkey) and asked to play

Table 1 Participant demographics.

	Mean [SD]
Father age years	34.1 [4.7]
Father work hours (mean [SD])	36 [11]
Child age months (mean [SD])	20 [3.1]
Birth order (N, %)	
First born	48 (76%)
Second born	11 (18%)
Third born	3 (5%)
Attend daycare (N, %)	
Yes	41 (65%)
No	20 (32%)

with both as they wished; (2) risky play—in which the dyad was given a small slide and asked to play with it as they normally would at home; (3) rough and tumble play—in which the dyad was asked to play physically, as they would at home; and (4) free play—in which they were asked to play as they would at home; some pairs had toys to play with and others did not. The procedure for the 2-bag play segment was adapted from the assessment protocol described by McCabe, Rebello-Britto, Hernandez, and Brooks-Gunn (2004). All other play segments were conducted using the same instructions across dyads, as noted above. The order of play segments was controlled such that all participants began with 2-bag play and finished with free play; the order of risky play and rough and tumble play were determined randomly. Only risky play and rough and tumble play were examined in the current study. Play segments generally took place on a $2\,m^2$ rug; at times father or child moved from the rug but were still in range of the cameras. The videotaping procedure has been previously described (StGeorge, Fletcher, & Palazzi, 2016). Fathers also completed online questionnaires concerning their mental health, their parenting, and their child's development.

4.2 Measures

4.2.1 Fathers' mental health

To investigate paternal mental health, we used the Depression Anxiety Stress Scale 42 (DASS-42) and the Parenting Stress Index Fourth Edition—Short

Form (PSI-4-SF). The DASS-42 (Lovibond & Lovibond, 1995) is a self-report assessment widely used in parenting research (e.g. Giallo et al., 2013). It is comprised of three subscales reflecting (a) depression, (b) anxiety, and (c) stress and yields standard scores for each of the three scales. It has been shown to have acceptable to excellent internal consistency and concurrent validity (Antony, Bieing, Cox, Enns, & Swinson, 1998). In the current study, Cronbach's alpha for the total stress scale was 0.927.

The PSI-4-SF (Abidin, 2012) measures parenting stress across three subscales: (a) Parental Distress (PD)—stress directly associated with the role of parenting, (b) Difficult Child (DC)—the parent's perceptions of the child's temperament, and (c) Parent-Child Dysfunctional Interaction (P-CDI). Scores for each subscale and a Total Stress score are generated (Abidin, 2012). The PSI-4-SF correlates highly with the PSI-4, full form version (Total Stress, at $r = 0.99$; PD, $r = 0.99$; PCD, $r = 0.98$; and DC, $r = 0.97$; Abidin, 2012). Test-retest reliability of the original PSI-SF produced a coefficient for the Total Stress scale of $r = 0.84$. In the current study, Cronbach's alpha for the Parenting Total Stress scale was 0.907.

4.2.2 Child playfulness

Child playfulness was scored on video recordings of play segments, using the Test of Playfulness Version 4 (ToP V4) (Bundy, 2010). ToP items are divided into three subscales: (a) extent—proportion of time observed, rated from "rarely or never" to "almost always," (b) intensity—the degree to which the behavior was observed, rated from low to high intensity, and (c) skilfulness—the ease of performance of each item, rated from "unskilled" to "highly skilled." Subscale scores are summed to provide a single playfulness score. The ToP is designed to score playfulness as observed through free play, ideally in more than one environment. A 15-min observation period is optimal (Brentnall, Bundy, & Kay, 2008). We combined two 7-min play periods (risky play and rough and tumble play) in this study, amounting to approximately 15 min of play observation. Items are scored using a three-point Likert scale, with higher scores reflecting greater playfulness. Prior research has established the ToP to be a valid measure of playfulness as a unitary construct, reflecting a range of playfulness levels (Bundy, 2001). Raw scores were subjected to Rasch analysis (Winsteps Version 4.0.1; Linacre, 2017) to generate interval level scores. ToP V4 was determined to be valid within acceptable limits; 94% of the items conformed to the expectations of the Rasch model. Authors deemed this acceptable although slightly lower than the desired 95% (Bundy, 2010).

In this study, the ToP was scored by two trained and calibrated researchers. Inter-rater reliability was established as follows: videos were divided into blocks, each containing 10–12 videos. Two calibrated researchers completed the first block to establish inter-rater reliability. Researchers each scored half of each remaining blocks, with 20% of each block scored by both researchers. Using a two-way random-effects model intra-class correlations (ICC), jointly scored videos had an $r = 0.926$ with a 95% confidence interval from 0.719 to 0.995 ($F(3,21) = 13.568$, $P < 0.000$). Final scores for dually rated videos reflected the average score for both raters.

4.2.3 Fathers' support of playfulness

Support of playfulness is an emerging area of investigation, and as such there are few instruments available that examine parent support of child playfulness. The Parent/Caregiver Support of Young Children's Playfulness scale (PSYCP) was co-developed by Waldman-Levi and the author of the ToP (Bundy, Nelson, Metzger, & Bingaman, 2001; Bundy & Waldman-Levi, 2016). It was designed to assess how parents and caregivers support playfulness and was driven by literature regarding child's play and playfulness (Skard & Bundy, 2008), and adult playfulness (Barnett, 2007). Items are designed to parallel those on the ToP. For instance, a ToP item reads "Is actively engaged [in play]" and the parallel item on the PSYCP indicates "Parent is actively supporting of the child's engagement in free play." Similarly, the ToP item "Tries to overcome barriers or obstacles to persist with an activity." is paralleled in the PSYCP by "Parent helps the child overcome barriers or obstacles in order to persist with the activity." PSYCP items are scored on two four-point scales; *quality* of the behavior observed (PSYCPq), and the *frequency* (PSYCPf) of the observed behavior occurred. The PSYCP is a criterion-referenced observation tool, with reliability and validity testing on parents in populations of typically developing children and children diagnosed with Autism Spectrum Disorder in process (Waldman-Levi & Bundy, 2016). Using the ToP and the PSYCP jointly provides a comprehensive perspective of the dyadic playful interaction. While the PSYCP is new to research, it was developed and underpinned by the same concepts as the ToP.

4.2.4 Rough and tumble play quality

Using the Rough and Tumble Play Quality (RTPQ) observational tool that had been previously developed (Fletcher, StGeorge, & Freeman, 2013), two researchers independently coded the Rough and Tumble play segment in which dyads engaged. The 16-item RTPQ rates the quality of father-child verbal and non-verbal interactions across paternal warmth, control, dominance, sensitivity, physical engagement and playfulness, using dyadic (father and child) information, on a five-point Likert scale ranging from "poor" to "excellent." Minimum and maximum scores range from 16 to 80. The measure has demonstrated convergent validity with fathers' report of their positive parenting involvement ($r = 0.41$, $P = 0.04$), and has high internal consistency (Cronbach's $\alpha = 0.95$; Fletcher et al., 2013). For this study, one researcher coded all recorded RTP sessions, with 30% of recordings being randomly selected for coding by a second researcher to establish interrater reliability. For the videos that were scored by two coders, the average of the RTP-Q ratings was calculated and used in analyses. There was a high reliability between coders (ICC$=0.96$) and high internal consistency ($\alpha = 0.96$).

4.3 Our findings

Children's standardized ToP scores fell within a typical range, and generally fit the Rasch model (Table 2). They were not associated with any demographic variables such as child age, gender, and daycare attendance, nor fathers' age or work hours.

Examining relationships among father and child variables (Table 2), we found that child playfulness (ToP) was positively associated with fathers' support of playfulness, but only for the subscale of playfulness quality (PSYCPq; $r = 0.27$, $P < 0.05$). Furthermore, child playfulness was moderately associated with the RTPQ measuring father-child rough and tumble play quality ($r = 0.43$, $P < 0.01$).

Fathers' total parenting stress scores ranged from 38 to 101; no fathers scored above the 85th percentile, which indicates a clinical score of concern. All fathers' DASS stress scores were within normal range, 0–28, with no fathers scoring in the range for clinical concern. While there were links between parenting stress scores and DASS scores, there was no association between child playfulness scores and fathers' parenting stress scores or the depression, stress and anxiety scales. Similarly, we found no associations between any father stress scores and RTPQ score.

However, there was an association between the subscale frequency of fathers' support of playfulness (PSYCPf) and his scores for the Parent-Child Dysfunctional Interaction and Difficult Child (P-DC) subscales of the PSI; the higher the PSI subscale score, the higher the fathers' PSYCPf score. This indicates that play support frequency was higher among fathers who rated their interactions with their child as not meeting their expectations and their child as more difficult to manage.

Table 2 Mean scores (standard deviations) on various questionnaires used in this study, and correlations among scales.

	M [SD]	1	2	3	4	5	6	7	8	9	10	11	12
1. ToP raw	46.5 [8.3]												
2. ToP std	0.45 [1.6]	0.32*											
3. PSYCPtot	95.3 [10.8]	0.12	0.18										
4. PSYCPf	46.0 [5.6]	0.04	0.03	0.72**									
5. PSYCPq	49.3 [7.9]	0.19	0.27*	0.87**	0.29*								
6. RTPQ	55.4 [12.9]	0.43**	0.17	0.19	0.07	0.22							
7. PSI-PD	26.4 [7.3]	0.05	−0.01	−0.01	0.05	0.05	0.10						
8. PSI-PCDI	18.1 [4.8]	0.00	−0.09	0.01	0.37**	0.25	−0.07	0.49**					
9. PSI-DC	22.8 [6.0]	0.04	−0.08	0.07	0.28*	0.10	0.04	0.36**	0.782**				
10. PSI-Total	67.3 [14.9]	0.04	−0.06	0.03	0.25	0.14	0.05	0.79**	0.87**	0.83**			
11. DASS-D	3.5 [4.4]	0.08	0.17	0.07	0.14	0.00	0.08	0.56**	0.31*	0.27*	0.48**		
12. DASS-A	2.8 [2.8]	0.02	0.08	0.06	0.16	0.03	0.04	0.22	0.10	0.07	0.16	0.37**	
13. DASS-S	8.7 [6.5]	0.19	0.16	0.07	0.15	−0.01	0.07	0.49**	0.26*	0.15	0.38**	0.71**	0.60**

* $P < 0.05$ level (two-tailed). ** $P < 0.01$ level (two-tailed).
ToP, test of playfulness; PSCYP, parent/caregiver support of young children's playfulness (tot, total; f, frequency; q, quality); RTPQ, rough and tumble play quality; PSI parenting stress index (PD, parental distress; PCDI, parent child dysfunctional interaction; DC, difficult child); DASS, depression, anxiety and stress scales (D, depression; A, anxiety; S, stress).

These findings only partially supported our hypotheses that fathers' mental health would influence his child's playfulness. Our results indicated that children's playfulness was associated with the *quality* of fathers' support of playfulness support, but not with the frequency. Thus, it is more the character of playfulness support than how often it occurs that appears to support child playfulness. We also found that child playfulness was associated with fathers' quality of rough and tumble play. Both of these scales represent a quality of father-child interaction, e.g., low or high warmth or reciprocity and this suggests that this relational aspect is more important to the child than the frequency of paternal support. This seems an instantiation of the broader acceptance that even though fathers spend less time with their children than mothers, their effect on the child is meaningful (Lewis & Lamb, 2003; McWayne, Downer, Campos, & Harris, 2013).

Our results also indicated that fathers' perceptions of his child's behavior (through the PSI subscales) were associated with the frequency of his support of playfulness (PSYCPf). Since these are correlational, concurrent measures, it may be plausible to consider that fathers increase their frequency of play support when they perceive problems within their child, in order to facilitate the child's positive development and playful attitude. On the other hand, perhaps fathers' frequency of support engenders poorer perceptions of his child. Additional research will be necessary to clarify this relationship. Scores on the parenting stress subscales were not related to the quality of fathers' rough and tumble play with their children.

Our findings tend to parallel that of Cabrera and Mitchell (2009), wherein fathers' parenting stress did not directly associate with child behavior but does associate with parenting behaviors. We suggest that our findings may be due, in part, to the characteristics of our sample. This group of fathers had many individual protective factors that together contribute to family resiliency. Protective factors serve to guide individuals to view adverse events in a way that avoids negative outcomes. In contrast, risk factors increase the likelihood of a negative outcome (Benzies & Mychasiuk, 2009). The majority of our participants were married to the child's mother, employed, well educated, and earning an income that provided well for their family. While quality of marriage was not assessed in the current study, other investigators have indicated that a strong marriage contributes to lower occurrences of depression and stress, thus conferring another protective factor not accounted for in this study. We suggest that in looking at the relationship between father mental health and child-care and play, future investigations consider how the broader context of family protective factors contributes to this interaction.

Children in this study were typically developing and fell within a typical range for playfulness. Like the fathers, the children in this study appear to be supported by several protective barriers, including living with both their mother and father in stable, high income earning households (Benzies & Mychasiuk, 2009). The children's typical levels of playfulness may be related to their parents' capabilities. Competence in structuring the child's play environment to suit their cognitive abilities, a feature consistent with our population, is found in parents who had a better understanding of general child development (Marjanovič-Umek and Fekonja-Peklaj, 2017). In addition, fathers with higher levels of education tend to interact more with their children (Cabrera et al., 2007). Playing with more competent partners, fathers in this case, exposes children to opportunities that enable them to play at a higher level (Marjanovič-Umek & Fekonja-Peklaj, 2017).

5. Summary

In this paper we have touched on several aspects of fathers, children, play and playfulness. We have identified that there is support for the following:

- Child play and playfulness is influenced by parental involvement;
- Fathers may be overall less involved than mothers in child care tasks, yet their interactions have strong influences on both typically developing children and children with a disability;
- Mothers and fathers' parenting characteristics overlap, and are also distinct relative to their styles, with fathers' interactional style often observed to be around play and to be characterized as more boisterous, stimulating and physical;
- Child behavior and disability broadly and specifically influences parent-child interactions, including those linked to play and playfulness;
- Fathers' mental health, including parenting stress, is linked to parenting behaviors and subsequently to child behavior; the causal direction is not yet clear;
- Scientific perspectives provide a rationale for fathers' behaviors; there is biological evidence of parenting, and father differences, at both neuroendocrine and brain network activation levels. These processes are explained through an evolutionary-psychological perspective that posits the fathering role as one that introduces the child to a broader environment of social interaction, challenge and consequences.

6. Conclusion

While the importance of the mother in child-care and wellbeing is well established, the importance of father remains an emerging topic. In spite of literature dating back nearly two decades documenting the importance of fathers to such things as child cognition, language, and emotional regulation, there is still much to learn about the role and contribution of the father to child development and wellbeing. Here we have focused on father-child play and playfulness, both because play is a foundation for child development and because paternal interactions with their infants and children are often around play. Father-child play and playful interactions are themselves complex, and the quality and quantity of these interactions are influenced by multiple variables; child characteristics inclusive of ability and disability, family dynamics, parenting relationships and interactions, work/life balance, and community influences, will impact father-child relationships and interactions, including those related to play. Having now established fathers as core to child health and development, there remains much to learn.

Acknowledgments

We would like to sincerely thank the honors students who worked with us on the data used in this paper: Elizabeth Dorn, Karina Hogan, Ellen McBriarty. In addition, we extend our thanks to the families who participated in the research described in this paper.

References

Abidin, R. R. (2012). *Parenting stress index* (4th Ed.). Lutz, FL: PAR.

Abidin, R. R., Jenkins, C. L., & McGaughey, M. C. (1992). The relationship of early family variables to children's subsequent behavioral adjustment. *Journal of Clinical Child Psychology, 21*(1), 60–69. https://doi.org/10.1207/s15374424jccp2101_9.

Abraham, E., & Feldman, R. (2018). The neurobiology of human allomaternal care; implications for fathering, coparenting, and children's social development. *Physiology and Behavior, 193*, 25–34. https://doi.org/10.1016/j.physbeh.2017.12.034.

Ahnert, L., Teufl, L., Ruiz, N., Piskernik, B., Supper, B., Remiorz, S., et al. (2017). Father–child play during the preschool years and child internalizing behaviors: Between robustness and vulnerability. *Infant Mental Health Journal, 38*(6), 743–756. https://doi.org/10.1002/imhj.21679.

Aktar, E., Majdandzic, M., de Vente, W., & Bogels, S. M. (2014). Parental social anxiety disorder prospectively predicts toddlers' fear/avoidance in a social referencing paradigm. *Journal of Child Psychology & Psychiatry & Allied Disciplines, 55*(1), 77–87. https://doi.org/10.1111/jcpp.12121.

Antony, M. M., Bieing, P. J., Cox, B. J., Enns, M. W., & Swinson, R. P. (1998). The psychometric properties of the 42-item and 21-item depression anxiety stress scales in clinical groups and a community sample. *Psychological Assessment, 10*(2), 176–181. https://doi.org/10.1037/1040-3590.10.2.176.

Apter-Levi, Y., Zagoory-Sharon, O., & Feldman, R. (2014). Oxytocin and vasopressin support distinct configurations of social synchrony. *Brain Research, 1580,* 124–132.

Ashbourne, L. M., Daly, K. J., & Brown, J. L. (2011). Responsiveness in father–child relation-ships: The experience of fathers. *Fathering, 9*(1), 69–86.

Atzil, S., Hendler, T., Zagoory-Sharon, O., Winetraub, Y., & Feldman, R. (2012). Synchrony and specificity in the maternal and the paternal brain: relations to oxytocin and vasopressin. *Journal of the American Academy of Child & Adolescent Psychiatry, 51*(8), 798–811.

Barnett, L. A. (1991a). The playful child: Measurement of a disposition to play. *Play & Culture, 4,* 51–74.

Barnett, L. A. (1991b). Characterizing playfulness: Correlates with individual attributes and personality traits. *Play & Culture, 4,* 371–393.

Barnett, L. A. (1998). The adaptive powers of being playful. In M. Duncan, G. Chick, & A. Aycock (Eds.), *Vol. 1. Play and cultural studies* (pp. 97–120). Greenwhich, CT: Ablex Publishing Corp.

Barnett, L. A. (2007). The nature of playfulness in young adults. *Personality and Individual Differences, 43*(4), 949–958.

Barnett, L. A. (2018). The education of playful boys: class clowns in the classroom. *Frontiers in Psychology, 9*(MAR), 1–18. https://doi.org/10.3389/fpsyg.2018.00232.

Bateson, G. (1972). Toward a theory of play and fantasy. In G. Bateson (Ed.), *Steps to an ecology of the mind* (pp. 14–20). New York, NY: Bantam.

Bentenuto, A., Perzolli, S., de Falco, S., & Venuti, P. (2020). The emotional availability in mother-child and father-child interactions in families with children with Autism Spectrum Disorder. *Research in Autism Spectrum Disorders, 75,* 101569. https://doi.org/10.1016/j.rasd.2020.101569.

Bentenuto, A., & Venuti, P. (2019). From supporting to co-parenting: The new roles of fathers. *Parenting, 19*(1–2), 30–33. https://doi.org/10.1080/15295192.2019.1555423.

Benzies, K., & Mychasiuk, R. (2009). Fostering family resiliency: A review of the key protective factors. *Child & Family Social Work, 14*(1), 103–114. https://doi.org/10.1111/j.1365-2206.2008.00586.x.

Besio, S., Bulgarelli, D., & Stancheva-Popkostadinova, V. (2017). Why play and which play for children with disabilities? In S. Besio, D. Bulgarelli, & V. Stancheva-Popkostadinova (Eds.), *Play development in children with disabilities* (pp. 1–8). Warsaw/Berlin: DeGruyter Open Ltd.

Bögels, S. M., & Phares, V. (2008). Fathers' role in the etiology, prevention and treatment of child anxiety: A review and a new model. *Clinical Psychology Review, 28,* 539–558. https://doi.org/10.1016/j.cpr.2007.07.011.

Bonsall, A. (2018). Narrative transitions in views and behaviors of fathers parenting children with disabilities. *Journal of Family Studies, 24*(2), 95–108. https://doi.org/10.1080/13229400.2015.1106336.

Bowlby, J. (1988). *A secure base: Parent-child attachment and healthy human development.* New York, NY: Basic Books.

Brentnall, J., Bundy, A. C., & Kay, F. C. S. (2008). The effect of the length of observation on test of playfulness scores. *OTJR: Occupation, Participation, Health, 28*(3), 133–140. https://doi.org/10.3928/15394492-20080601-02.

Bundy, A. C. (1993). Assessment of play and leisure: Delineation of the problem. *American Journal of Occupational Therapy, 47,* 217–222.

Bundy, A. C. (1997). Play and playfulness: What to look for. In L. D. Parham & L. S. Fazio (Eds.), *Play in occupational therapy for children* (pp. 56–62). St. Louis: Mosby.

Bundy, A. C. (2001). Measuring play performance. In M. Law, C. Baum, & W. Dunn (Eds.), *Measuring occupational performance: Supporting best practice in occupational therapy* (pp. 89–102). Thorofare, NJ: SLACK Incorporated.

Bundy, A. (2010). *Test of playfulness (ToP): Version 4.2 manual.* Unpublished Manual.

Bundy, A. C., Luckett, T., Naughton, G. A, Tranter, P. J., Wyver, S. R., Ragen, J., Singleton, E., & Spies, G. (2008). A playful interaction: Occupational therapy for 'all' children on the school ground. American Journal of Occupational Therapy, 62(5), 522–527.

Bundy, A. C., Nelson, L., Metzger, M., & Bingaman, K. (2001). Validity and reliability of a test of playfulness. *OTJR: Occupation, Participation, and Health, 21,* 276–292.

Bundy, A., & Waldman-Levy, A. (2016). *Parent/Caregiver's support of young children's playfulness (PSYCP, 6th ed.).* Unpublished.

Cabrera, N., Fitzgerald, H., Bradley, R., & Roggman, L. (2014). The ecology of father-child relationships: An expanded model. *Journal of Family Theory & Review, 6*(4), 336–354. https://doi.org/10.1111/jftr.12054.

Cabrera, N., & Mitchell, S. (2009). An exploratory study of fathers' parenting stress and toddlers' social development in low-income African American families. *Fathering, 7*(3), 201–225. https://doi.org/10.3149/fth.0703.201.

Cabrera, N. J., & Roggman, L. (2017). Father play: Is it special? *Infant Mental Health Journal, 38*(6), 706–708. https://doi.org/10.1002/imhj.21680.

Cabrera, N., Shannon, J. D., & Tamis-LaMonda, C. (2007). Fathers' influence on their children's cognitive and emotional development: From toddlers to pre-k. *Applied Development Science, 11*(4), 208–213. https://doi.org/10.1080/10888690701762100.

Chiarello, L. A., Huntington, A., & Bundy, A. (2006). A comparison of motor behaviors, interaction, and playfulness during mother-child and father-child play with children with motor delay. *Physical and Occupational Therapy in Pediatrics, 26*(1–2), 129–151. https://doi.org/10.1300/J006v26n01_09.

Climie, E. A., & Mitchell, K. (2017). Parent-child relationship and behavior problems in children with ADHD. *International Journal of Developmental Disabilities, 63*(1/2), 27–35.

Cousino, M. K., & Hazen, R. A. (2013). Parenting stress among caregivers of children with chronic illness: a systematic review. *Journal of Pediatric Psychology, 38*(8), 809–828. https://doi.org/10.1093/jpepsy/jst049.

Coyl-Shepherd, D. D., & Hanlon, C. (2013). Family play and leisure activities: Correlates of parents' and children's socio-emotional well-being. *International Journal of Play, 2*(3), 254–272. https://doi.org/10.1080/21594937.2013.855376.

Dauch, C., Imwalle, M., Ocasio, B., & Metz, A. E. (2018). The influence of the number of toys in the environment on toddlers' play. *Infant Behavior and Development, 50,* 78–87.

De Falco, S., Esposito, G., Venuti, P., & Bornstein, M. H. (2008). Fathers' play with the Down syndrome children. *Journal of Intellectual Disability Research, 52*(6), 490–502.

Dewey, J. (1933). *How we think.* Buffalo, NY: Prometheus Books.

El-Ghoroury, N. H., & Romanczyk, R. G. (1999). Play interactions of family members towards children with autism. *Journal of Autism & Developmental Disorders, 29*(3), 249–258.

Feldman, R. (2003). Infant-mother and infant-father synchrony: The coregulation of positive arousal. *Infant Mental Health Journal, 24*(1), 1–23.

Fletcher, R., StGeorge, J., & Freeman, E. (2013). Rough and tumble play quality: Theoretical foundations for a new measure of father–child interaction. *Early Child Development and Care, 183*(6), 746–759.

Fletcher, R. J., Freeman, E., Garfield, C., & Vimpani, G. (2011). The effects of early paternal depression on children's development. *Medical Journal of Australia, 195*(11/12), 685–689. https://doi.org/10.5694/mja11.10192.doi:10.1080/03004430.2012.723439.

Fry, D. P. (2014). Environment of evolutionary adaptedness, rough-and-tumble play, tand the selection of restraint in human aggression. In D. Narvaez, K. Valentino, A. Fuentes, J. J. McKenna, & P. Gray (Eds.), *Ancestral landscapes in human evolution: Culture, childrearing and social wellbeing* (pp. 169–188). Oxford, UK: Oxford University Press.

Gaskins, S., Haight, W., & Lancy, D. F. (2007). The cultural construction of play. In A. Goncu & S. Gaskins (Eds.), *Play and development: Evolutionary, sociocultural and functions perspectives* (pp. 179–202). Mahwah, NJ: LEA.

Gettler, L. T., McDade, T. W., Agustin, S. S., & Kuzawa, C. W. (2011). Short-term changes in fathers' hormones during father-child play: Impacts of paternal attitudes and experience. *Hormones and Behavior*, *60*(5), 599–606. https://doi.org/10.1016/j.yhbeh.2011.08.009.

Gettler, L. T., McDade, T. W., Feranil, A. B., & Kuzawa, C. W. (2011). Longitudinal evidence that fatherhood decreases testosterone in human males. *Proceedings of the National Academy of Sciences*, *108*(39), 16194–16199. https://doi.org/10.1073/pnas.1105403108.

Giallo, R., Cooklin, A., Zerman, N., & Vittorino, R. (2013). Psychological distress of fathers attending an Australian early parenting service for early parenting difficulties. *Clinical Psychologist*, *17*(2), 46–55. https://doi.org/10.1111/j.1742-9552.2012.00044.x.

Gosso, Y., & Carvalho, A. M. A (2013). *Play and cultural context*. In P. K. Smith (Ed.), Encyclopedia on early childhood development. Retrieved from http://www.child-encyclopedia.com/play/according-experts/play-and-cultural-context.

Grossmann, K., & Grossmann, K. E. (2019). Essentials when studying child-father attachment: A fundamental view on safe haven and secure base phenomena. *Attachment & Human Development*, 1–6. https://doi.org/10.1080/14616734.2019.1589056.

Grossmann, K., Grossmann, K. E., Fremmer-Bombik, E., Kindler, H., Scheuerer-Englisch, H., & Zimmermann, P. (2002). The uniqueness of the child-father attachment relationship: Fathers' sensitive and challenging play as a pivotal variable in a 16-year longitudinal study. *Social Development*, *11*(3), 301–337. https://doi.org/10.1111/1467-9507.00202.

Gulenc, A., Butler, E., Sarkadi, A., & Hiscock, H. (2018). Paternal psychological distress, parenting, and child behaviour: A population based, cross-sectional study. *Child Care Health and Development*, *44*, 892–900. https://doi.org/10.1111/cch12607.

Gutierrez-Galvo, L., Stein, A., Hanington, L., Heron, J., & Ramchandani, P. (2015). Paternal depression in the postnatal period and child development: Mediators and moderators. *Pediatrics*, *135*(2), e339–e347. https://doi.org/10.1542/peds.2014-2411.

Haight, W. L., Parke, R. D., & Black, J. E. (1997). Mothers' and fathers' beliefs about and spontaneous participation in their toddlers' pretend play. *Merrill-Palmer Quarterly*, *43*(2), 271–290.

Hartley, S. L., Mihaila, I., Otalora-Fadner, H. S., & Bussanich, P. M. (2014). Division of labor in families of children and adolescents with autism spectrum disorder. *Family Relations*, *63*(5), 627–638. https://doi.org/10.1111/fare.12093.

Hartley, S. L., Seltzer, M. M., Head, L., & Abbeduto, L. (2012). Psychological well-being in fathers of adolescents and young adults with Down syndrome, Fragile X syndrome, and autism. *Family Relations*, *61*, 327–342. https://doi.org/10.1111/j.1740-3729.2011.00693.x.

Howard, J., & McInnes, K. (2013). The essence of play: A practice companion for professionals working with children and young people. Retrieved from http://ebookcentral.proquest.com.

Jia, R., Kotila, L. E., & Schoppe-Sullivan, S. J. (2012). Transactional relations between father involvement and preschoolers' socioemotional adjustment. *Journal of Family Psychology*, *26*(6), 848–857.

John, A., Halliburton, A., & Humphrey, J. (2013). Child-mother and child-father play interaction patterns with preschoolers. *Early Child Development and Care*, *183*(3–4), 483–497. https://doi.org/10.1080/03004430.2012.711595.

Kazura, K. (2000). Fathers' qualitative and quantitative involvement: An investigation of attachment, play, and social interactions. *Journal of Men's Studies*, *9*(1), 41–57. https://doi.org/10.3149/jms.0901.41.

Keltner, D., Capps, L., Kring, A. M., Young, R. C., & Heerey, E. A. (2001). Just teasing: A conceptual analysis and empirical review. *Psychological Bulletin, 127*(2), 229–248. https://doi.org/10.1037/0033-2909.127.2.229.

Kochanska, G., Aksan, N., Prisco, T. R., & Adams, E. E. (2008). Mother–child and father–child mutually responsive orientation in the first 2 years and children's outcomes at preschool age: Mechanisms of influence. *Child Development, 79,* 30–44.

Kokkinaki, T., & Vasdekis, V. G. S. (2015). Comparing emotional coordination in early spontaneous mother-infant and father-infant interactions. *European Journal of Developmental Psychology, 12*(1), 69–84.

Kooii, R. V., & Vrijhof, H.J. (1981). Play and development. *Topics in Learning Disabilities, 1,* 57–67.

Kroll, L. R. (2017). Early childhood curriculum development: the role of play in building self-regulatory capacity in young children. *Early Child Development and Care, 187*(5-6), 854–868. https://doi.org/10.1080/03004430.2016.1223063.

Lamb, M. E., & Lewis, C. (2013). Father-child relationships. In N. J. Cabrera & C. S. Tamis-LeMonda (Eds.), *Handbook of father involvement: Multidisciplinary perspectives* (2nd ed., pp. 119–134). Taylor & Francis Group.

Lamb, M. E., & Tamis-LeMonda, C. S. (2004). The role of the father: An introduction. In M. E. Lamb (Ed.), *The role of the father in child development* (4th ed., pp. 1–31). New York, NY: Wiley.

Lane, S. J., & Mistrett, S. G. (1997). Can and should technology be used as a tool for early intervention? In J. Angelo & S. J. Lane (Eds.), *Assistive technology for rehabilitation therapists* (pp. 191–210). Philadelphia, PA: F. A. Davis.

Lane, S. J., & Mistrett, S. G. (2002). Let's Play!: Assistive technology interventions for play. *Young Exceptional Children, 5*(2), 19–27.

Lane, S. J., & Mistrett, S. (2008). Facilitating play. In L. D. Parham & L. S. Fazio (Eds.), *Play in occupational therapy for children* (2nd ed., pp. 72–95). St. Louis, MO: Mosby Publishers.

Lee, S. J., Pace, G. T., Lee, J. T., & Knauer, H. (2018). The association of fathers' parental warmth and parenting stress to child behavior problems. *Children and Youth Services Review, 91,* 1–10. https://doi.org/10.1016/j.childyouth.2018.05.020.

Lewis, C., & Lamb, M. E. (2003). Fathers' influences on children's development: The evidence from two-parent families. *European Journal of Psychology of Education, 18,* 211–228.

Linacre, J. M. (2017). *Winsteps® Rasch measurement computer program.* Beaverton, Oregon: Winsteps.com.

Lovas, G. S. (2005). Gender and patterns of emotional availability in mother–toddler and father–toddler dyads. *Infant Mental Health Journal, 26*(4), 327–353. https://doi.org/10.1002/imhj.20056.

Lovibond, S. H., & Lovibond, P. F. (1995). *Manual for the depression anxiety stress scales* (2nd ed.). Sydney: Psychology Foundation.

Lucassen, N., Kok, R., Bakermans-Kranenburg, M. J., Van Ijzendoorn, M. H., Jaddoe, V. W. V., Hofman, A., et al. (2015). Executive functions in early childhood: The role of maternal and paternal parenting practices. *British Journal of Developmental Psychology, 33*(4), 489–505.

Magnuson, C. D., & Barnett, L. A. (2013). The playful advantage: How playfulness enhances coping with stress. *Leisure Sciences, 35,* 129–144. https://doi.org/10.1080/01490400.2013.761905.

Marjanovic-Umek, L., & Fekonja-Peklaj, U. (2017). The roles of child gender and parental knowledge of child development in parent-child interactive play. *Sex Roles, 77,* 496–509. https://doi.org/10.1007/s11199-016-0734-7.

May, C., Fletcher, R., Dempsey, I., & Newman, L. (2015). Modeling relations among coparenting quality, autism-specific parenting self-efficacy, and parenting stress in mothers and fathers of children with ASD. *Parenting, 15,* 119–133. https://doi.org/10.1080/15295192.2015.1020145.

McCabe, L. A., Rebello-Britto, P., Hernandez, M., & Brooks-Gunn, J. (2004). Games children play: Observing young children's self-regulation across laboratory, home and school settings. In R. P. D. Delcarmen-Wiggins & A. Carter (Eds.), *Handbook of Infant, Toddler, and Preschool Mental Health* (pp. 491–521). New York: Oxford University Press.

McStay, R. L., Dissanayake, C., Scheeren, A., Koot, H. M., & Begeer, S. (2014). Parenting stress and autism: The role of age, sutism severity, quality of life and problem behavior of children and adolescents with autism. *Autism, 18*(5), 502–510.

McWayne, C., Downer, J. T., Campos, R., & Harris, R. D. (2013). Father involvement during early childhood and its association with children's early learning: A meta-analysis. *Early Education & Development, 24*(6), 898–922. https://doi.org/10.1177/1362361313485163.

Mehall, K. G., Spinrad, T. L., Eisenberg, N., & Gaertner, B. M. (2009). Examining the relations of infant temperament and couples' marital satisfaction to mother and father involvement: A longitudinal study. *Fathering, 7*(1), 23. https://doi.org/10.3149/fth.0701.23.

Meijer, W. M., van Ijzendoorn, M. H., & Bakermans-Kranenburg, M. J. (2019). Challenging the challenge hypothesis on testosterone in fathers: Limited meta-analytic support. *Psychoneuroendocrinology, 110*, 104435. https://doi.org/10.1016/j.psyneuen.2019.104435.

Menashe-Grinberg, A., & Atzaba-Poria, N. (2017). Mother–child and father–child play interaction: The importance of parental playfulness as a moderator of the links between parental behavior and child negativity. *Infant Mental Health Journal, 38*(6), 772–784. https://doi.org/10.1002/imhj.21678.

Mitchell, J., & Lashewicz, B. (2015). More than a pal: The generative leisure work of fathers raising children with Autism spectrum disorder. *Fathering, 13*(2), 130–145.

Moller, E. L., Majdandžić, M., & Bogels, S. M. (2015). Parental anxiety, parenting behavior, and infant anxiety: Differential associations for fathers and mothers. *Journal of Child and Family Studies, 24*(9), 2626–2637.

Morrison, C. D., Bundy, A. C., & Fisher, A. G. (1991). The contribution of motor skills and playfulness to the play performance of preschoolers. *American Journal of Occupational Therapy, 45*(8), 687–694.

Neumann, E. A. (1971). *The elements of play*. New York, NY: MSS Information.

Nieuwenhuijsen, K., De Boer, A. G. E. M., Verbeek, J. H. A. M., Blonk, R. W. B., & Van Dijk, F. J. H. (2003). The depression anxiety stress scales (DASS): Detecting anxiety disorder and depression in employees absent from work because of mental health problems. *Occupational and Environmental Medicine, 60*(Suppl. 1), 77–82. https://doi.org/10.1136/oem.60.suppl_1.i77.

Nijhof, S. L., Vinkers, C. H., van Geelen, S. M., Duijff, S. N., Achterberg, E. J. M., van der Net, J., et al. (2018). Healthy play, better coping: The importance of play for the development of children in health and disease. *Neuroscience and Biobehavioral Reviews, 95*(July), 421–429. https://doi.org/10.1016/j.neubiorev.2018.09.024.

Nussbaum, M. (2011). *Creating capabilities*. Cambridge, MA: Harvard University Press.

Okimoto, A. M., Bundy, A., & Hanzlik, J. (2000). Playfulness in children with and without disability: Measurement and intervention. *American Journal of Occupational Therapy, 54*(1), 73–82.

Osborne, L. A., & Reed, P. (2010). Stress and self-perceived parenting behaviors of parents of children with autistic spectrum conditions. *Research in Autism Spectrum Disorders, 4*(3), 405–414. https://doi.org/10.1016/j.rasd.2009.10.011.

Paquette, D. (2004a). Theorizing the father-child relationship: Mechanisms and developmental outcomes. *Human Development, 47*(4), 193–219. https://doi.org/10.1159/000078723.

Paquette, D. (2004b). Dichotomizing paternal and maternal functions as a means to better understand their primary contributions. *Human Development, 47*(4), 237–238. https://doi.org/10.1159/000078726.

Parten, M. B. (1932). Social participation among pre-school children. *Journal of Abnormal and Social Psychology, 27*, 243–269.

Pellegrini, A., & Smith, P. K. (1998). The development of play during childhood: Forms and possible functions. *Child Psychology & Psychiatry Review, 3*(2), 51–57.

Pelligrini, A., & Bjorklund, D. F. (1998). *Applied child study: A developmental approach.* Mahwah, NJ: Lawrence Erlbbaum Associates, Inc. Publishers.

Piaget, J. (1962). *Play, dreams and imitation.* New York, NY: W.W. Norton & CO, Inc.

Pisula, E. (2008). Interactions of fathers and their children with autism. *Polish Psychological Bulletin, 39*(1), 35–41. https://doi.org/10.2478/v10059-008-0005-8.

Potter, C. A. (2017). Father involvement in the care, play, and education of children with autism. *Journal of Intellectual and Developmental Disability, 42*(4), 375–384. https://doi.org/10.3109/13668250.2016.1245851.

Price-Robertson, R. (2015). Fatherhood and mental illness: A review of key issues (CFCA30). Retrieved from https://aifs.gov.au/cfca/publications/fatherhood-and-mental-illness.

Proyer, R. T., Brauer, K., & Wolf, A. (2019). Assessing other-directed lighthearted, intellectual, and whimsical playfulness in adults: Development and initial validation of the OLIW-S using self- and peer-ratings. *European Journal of Psychological Assessment.* https://doi.org/10.1027/1015-5759/a000531. July 2.

Rafferty, D., Tidman, L., & Ekas, N. V. (2020). Parenting experiences of fathers of children with autism spectrum disorder with or without intellectual disability. *Journal of Intellectual Disability Research, 64*(6), 463–474.

Ramchandani, P. G., Psychogiou, L., Vlachos, H., Iles, J., Sethna, V., Netsi, E., et al. (2011). Paternal depression: An examination of its links with father, child and family functioning in the postnatal period. *Depression and Anxiety, 28*(6), 471–477. https://doi.org/10.1002/da.20814.

Rilling, J. K. (2013). The neural and hormonal bases of human prenatal care. *Neuropsychologia, 51*(4), 731–747.

Robertson, N., Yim, B., & Paatsch, L. (2020). Connections between children's involvement in dramatic play the the quality of early childhood environments. *Early child Development and Care, 190*(3), 376–389. https://doi.org/10.1080/03004430.2018.1473389.

Roggman, L., Boyce, L., Cook, G., Christiansen, K., & Jones, D. (2004). Playing with daddy: Social toy play, early head start, and developmental outcomes. *Fathering, 2*(1), 83–108. https://doi.org/10.3149/fth.0201.83.

Román-Oyola, R., Reynolds, S., Soto-feliciano, I., Cabrera-mercader, L., & Vega-Santana, J. (2017). Child's Sensory Profile and adult playfulness as predictors of parental self-efficacy. *American Journal of Occupational Therapy, 71*(2017), 7102220010. https://doi.org/10.5014/ajot.2017.021097.

Rubin, K. H, Fein, G., & Vandenberg, B. (1983). Play. In M. Hetherington (Ed.), *Vol. 4. Handbook of child psychology* (pp. 694–774).

Sanders, J. L., & Morgan, S. B. (1997). Family stress and adjustment as perceived by parents of children with autism or Down syndrome: Implications for intervention. *Child and Family Behavior Therapy, 19*, 15–32.

Saracho, O. N., & Spodek, B. (1998). *Multiple perspectives on play in early childhood education.* Albany, NY: SUNY Press.

Saunders, I., Sayer, M., & Goodale, A. (1999). The relationship between playfulness and coping in preschool children: A pilot study. *American Journal of Occupational Therapy, 53*(2), 221–226.

Sethna, V., Murray, L., Edmondson, O., Iles, J., & Ramchandani, P. G. (2017). Depression and playfulness in fathers and young infants: A matched design comparison study. *Journal of Affective Disorders, 229*, 364–370. https://doi.org/10.1016/j.jad.2017.12.107.

Sethna, V., Murray, L., Netsi, E., Psychogiou, L., & Ramchandani, P. G. (2015). Paternal depression in the postnatal period and early father–infant interactions. *Parenting Science and Practice, 15*(1), 1–8. https://doi.org/10.1080/15295192.2015.992732.

Shannon, J., Tamis-LeMonda, C. S., London, K., & Cabrera, N. J. (2002). Beyond rough and tumble.pdf. *Parenting: Science and Practice, 2*(2), 77–104.

Shen, X. (2010). *Adult playfulness as a personality trait: Its conceptualization, measurement, and relationship to psychological well-being (Doctoral dissertation).* Pennsylvania State University Library Catalog (OCLC No. 859524715).

Shen, X., Chick, G., & Pitas, N. A. (2017). From playful parents to adaptable children: a structural equation model of the relationships between playfulness and adaptability among young adults and their parents. *International Journal of Play, 6*(3), 244–254. https://doi.org/10.1080/21594937.2017.1382983.

Shorer, M., Swissa, O., Levavi, P., & Swissa, A. (2019). Parental playfulness and children's emotional regulation: The mediating role of parents' emotional regulation and the parent-child relationship. *Early Child Development and Care.* https://doi.org/10.1080/03004430.2019.1612385.

Simmerman, S., Blacher, J., & Baker, B. L. (2001). Fathers' and mothers' perceptions of father involvement in families with young children with a disability. *Journal of Intellectual and Developmental Disability, 26*(4), 325–338. https://doi.org/10.1080/1366825012008733 5.

Skard, G., & Bundy, A. C. (2008). Test of Playfulness. In L. D. Parham & L. S. Fazio (Eds.), *Play in occupational therapy for children* (2nd ed., pp. 71–93). St. Louis, MO: Mosby.

StGeorge, J., Fletcher, R., & Palazzi, K. (2016). Comparing fathers' physical and toy play and links to child behaviour: An exploratory study. *Infant and Child Development, 26*(1), 1–22. https://doi.org/10.1002/icd.1958.

StGeorge, J., & Freeman, E. (2017). Measurement of father–child rough-and-tumble play and its relations to child behavior. *Infant Mental Health Journal, 38*(6), 709–725. https://doi.org/10.1002/imhj.21676.

StGeorge, J., Wroe, J. K., & Cashin, M. E. (2018). The concept and measurement of fathers' stimulating play: a review. *Attachment & Human Development, 20*(6), 634–658. https://doi.org/10.1080/14616734.2018.1465106.

Tamis-LeMonda, C. S., Baumwell, L., & Cabrera, N. J. (2013). Father's role in language development. In N. J. Cabrera & C. S. Tamis-LeMonda (Eds.), *Handbook of father involvement: Multidisciplinary perspectives* (2nd ed., pp. 135–150). Taylor & Francis Group.

Tamis-LeMonda, C. S., Shannon, J. D., Cabrera, N. J., & Lamb, M. E. (2004). Fathers and mothers at play with their 2- and 3-year-olds: Contributions to language and cognitive development. *Child Development, 75*(6), 1806–1820. https://doi.org/10.1111/j.1467-8624.2004.00818.x.

Teetsel, R. N., Ginsburg, G. S., & Drake, K. L. (2014). Anxiety-promoting parenting behaviors: a comparison of anxious mothers and fathers. *Child Psychiatry and Human Development, 45*(2), 133–142.

The United Nations. (1989). Convention on the Rights of the Child. *Treaty Series, 1577,* 3.

The United Nations. (2006). Convention on the Rights of Persons with Disabilities. *Treaty Series, 2515,* 3.

Towler, K. (2017). Children's right to play, whoever they are, wherever they are. The play rights of children and young people with disabilities. In S. Besio, D. Bulgarelli, & V. Stancheva-Popkostadinova (Eds.), *Play development in children with disabilities* (pp. 53–57). Warsaw/Berlin: DeGruyter Open Ltd.

Vacca, J. J. (2013). The parenting process from the father's perspective: analysis of perceptions of fathers about raising their child with autism spectrum disorder. *Best Practices in Mental Health, 9,* 79–93.

van der Pol, L. D., Groeneveld, M. G., van Berkel, S. R., Endendijk, J. J., Hallers-Haalboom, E. T., & Mesman, J. (2019). Fathers: The interplay between testosterone levels and self-control in relation to parenting quality. *Hormones and Behavior, 112,* 100–106. https://doi.org/10.1016/j.yhbeh.2019.04.003.

Van Vleet, M., & Feeney, B. C. (2015). Play behavior and playfulness in adulthood. *Social and Personality Psychology Compas, 9*(11), 630–643. https://doi.org/10.1111/spc3.12205.

Waldman-Levi, A., & Bundy, A. (2016). A glimpse into co-occupations: Parent/caregiver's support of young children's playfulness scale. *Occupational Therapy in Mental Health, 32*(3), 217–227. https://doi.org/10.1080/0164212X.2015.1116420.

Wilson, S., & Durbin, C. E. (2010). Effects of paternal depression on fathers' parenting behaviors: A meta-analytic review. *Clinical Psychology Review, 30*(2), 167–180. https://doi.org/10.1016/j.cpr.2009.10.007.

Yago, S., Hirose, T., Okamitsu, M., Okabayashi, Y., Hiroi, K., Nozomi, N., et al. (2014). Differences and similarities between fathre-infant interaction and mother-infant interaction. *Journal of Medical and Dental Sciences, 61*(1), 7–16.

Yogman, M. W. (1981). Games fathers and mothers play with their infants. *Infant Mental Health Journal, 2*, 241–248.

Yogman, M. W., Kindlon, D., & Earls, F. (1995). Father involvement and cognitive/behavioral outcomes of preterm infants. *Journal of the American Academy of Child and Adolescent Psychiatry, 34*(1), 58–66.

CHAPTER FOUR

Feasibility and acceptability of an online response inhibition cognitive training program for youth with Williams syndrome

Natalie G. Brei[a],*, Ana-Maria Raicu[b], Han Joo Lee[c], and Bonita P. Klein-Tasman[c]

[a]Catholic Social Services of Southern Nebraska, Lincoln, NE, United States
[b]Michigan State University, East Lansing, MI, United States
[c]University of Wisconsin-Milwaukee, Milwaukee, WI, United States
*Corresponding author: e-mail address: nbrei@cssisus.org

Contents

1. Introduction	108
1.1 Inhibitory control and Williams syndrome	108
1.2 Cognitive training and internet-based intervention	109
1.3 The potential of online interventions for WS	110
1.4 The need for studies of feasibility and acceptability	111
1.5 Summary and rationale	112
1.6 Study aims	112
2. Method	112
2.1 Participants	112
2.2 Measures	113
2.3 Procedure	114
3. Results	119
3.1 Attendance and program completion	119
3.2 TEI-SF	119
3.3 TAQ	120
3.4 ATQ	122
4. Discussion	126
4.1 Feasibility and acceptability of specific study features	127
4.2 Innovation, limitations, and future directions	128
5. Conclusion	129
Acknowledgments	129
Source of funding	130
Conflict of interest	130
References	130
Further reading	134

International Review of Research in Developmental Disabilities, Volume 59
ISSN 2211-6095
https://doi.org/10.1016/bs.irrdd.2020.09.002

© 2020 Elsevier Inc.
All rights reserved.

Abstract

Williams syndrome (WS) is a genetic neurodevelopmental disorder often accompanied by inhibitory difficulties. Online cognitive training programs show promise for improving cognitive functions. No such interventions have been developed for individuals with WS, but to explore the practicality of large-scale online cognitive training for this population, we must first investigate whether families of those with WS find these programs feasible and acceptable.

Twenty individuals aged 10–17 years with WS, along with parents, participated in a pilot online cognitive training program supervised in real time using videoconference software. We evaluated the feasibility and acceptability of this response inhibition training using three parent questionnaires.

Descriptive data are reported for the measures of feasibility and acceptability. Overall, the online procedures received a positive reaction from families. Parents were likely to recommend the study to others. They indicated training was ethical and acceptable despite feeling neutral about effectiveness. The frequency and duration of sessions were acceptable to families (two 20-to-30-min sessions per week; 10 sessions total). Families provided feedback and offered suggestions for improvement, such as more flexibility in scheduling and decreasing time spent in review of procedures.

1. Introduction

Williams syndrome (WS) is a genetic neurodevelopmental disorder caused by a microdeletion on chromosome 7q11.23 (Hillier et al., 2003), with prevalence estimates of about 1 in every 7500 births (Stromme, Bjornstad, & Ramstad, 2002). Most individuals with WS display mild to moderate intellectual disability and personal strengths in expressive vocabulary and auditory short-term memory (Mervis & Klein-Tasman, 2000). People with Williams syndrome are often "overfriendly" and often show significant attention deficits, high impulsivity, and non–social anxiety (Leyfer, Woodruff-Borden, Klein–Tasman, Fricke, & Mervis, 2006; Mervis & Klein–Tasman, 2000; Rhodes, Riby, Matthews, & Coghill, 2011).

1.1 Inhibitory control and Williams syndrome

Problems with executive function, especially 'response inhibition' (RI), are increasingly seen as a contributing factor to the observed behavioral phenotype in WS (Frigerio et al., 2006; Gothelf et al., 2008; Horn, Dolan, Elliott, Deakin, & Woodruff, 2003a; Mobbs et al., 2007; Porter, Coltheart, & Langdon, 2007). RI allows us to stop a movement or inhibit a stimulus-response association, and challenges with RI translate into difficulties stopping unwanted behavior and have been linked with impulsivity and attention problems (Horn et al., 2003; Mobbs et al., 2007). About 64% of those with WS meet criteria for ADHD (Leyfer et al., 2006) and show similar executive function characteristics as those with ADHD, including difficulties with impulsivity, inhibition of responses, concentration, and error recovery (Greer, Riby, Hamiliton, & Riby, 2013; Rhodes et al., 2011; Rhodes, Riby, Park, Fraser, & Campbell, 2010).

The hypersociability that is characteristic of those with WS involves excessive use of social engagement techniques (Reilly, Losh, Bellugi, & Wulfeck, 2004). Research suggests that impaired RI influences social disinhibition in WS and contributes to the overall behavioral phenotype (Carney, Brown, & Henry, 2013). The social disinhibition in WS may create social vulnerability related to overly friendly behavior (Fisher, Moskowitz, & Hodapp, 2013). Additionally, anxiety is highly comorbid in those with WS and is thought to be linked to executive functioning and poor inhibitory control (Derakshan, Smyth, & Eysenck, 2009; Woodruff-Borden, Kistler, Henderson, Crawford, & Mervis, 2010). The interplay of anxiety and inhibition in WS has yet to be fully understood, especially in WS, but it is possible that anxiety impairs the executive functions by making it difficult to shift away from a threat and inhibit an overly fearful response.

Based on this cluster of difficulties, poor inhibition may contribute to challenges with psychosocial functioning across many settings for those with WS. Although some research indicates spared inhibitory function in WS (Capitão et al., 2011; Costanzo et al., 2013), there is support for the position that impaired executive functions and social inhibition in WS make inhibitory control a potential target for improvement.

1.2 Cognitive training and internet-based intervention

Cognitive training involves methods that target improvement in brain processes such as memory, executive skills, and attention. Cognitive training has shown positive to largely promising results in other adult and child populations for a wide variety of cognitive skills (Amir et al., 2009; Cicerone et al., 2000; Karch et al., 2013; Klonoff et al., 2007). Notably, positive results were seen even in early studies designed to build inhibition skills, including in children with ADHD and other disabilities (Baer & Nietzel, 1991; Duckworth, Ragland, Sommerfeld, & Wyne, 1974). Expanding the intervention research that targets functions such as response inhibition for those with WS is an important next step, given that inhibition is crucial for academic and social success, particularly when social vulnerability is high (see Jawaid et al., 2012). Cognitive training may be helpful in targeting compromised processes in the WS brain (Greer et al., 2013); however, little is known about the feasibility or potential efficacy of delivering these online interventions to youth with this complex developmental disorder.

Recently, cognitive training has taken the exciting leap into online, computer-based delivery. The first FDA-approved, digital game-based treatment for ADHD was released earlier this year (EndeavorRx; 2020 Akili Interactive Labs, Inc). Further, telehealth delivery of services has exploded in the wake of the COVID-19 pandemic restrictions enforced in 2020, making online cognitive training programs even more relevant. Internet-based delivery of intervention increases efficiency and dissemination efforts by overcoming barriers including access, cost, time, and geographical location (Ybarra & Eaton, 2005). With regard to cognitive training programs specifically, positive results across age and population type are noted for an impressive spread of cognitive functions, most notably executive function, response control, and impulsiveness (Gagnon & Belleville, 2012; Slate, Meyer, Burns, & Montgomery, 1998).

It is important to consider that improvement sometimes does not generalize to untrained tasks (Simons et al., 2016). It is acknowledged that the literature does contain null results (Enge et al., 2014; Kable et al., 2017). Nevertheless, there is indication of promise for computer-based cognitive training, with documentation of a transfer to untrained skills (Loosli, Buschkuehl, Perrig, & Jaeggi, 2012; Thorell, Lindqvist, Nutley, Bohlin, & Klingberg, 2009; Walton et al., 2015). Further, some authors have reported therapeutic effects on everyday functioning in children with anxiety (Lee, Goetz, Turkel, & Siwiec, 2015). In recent research, Kühn et al. (2017) specifically examined effects of game-based inhibition training in older adults and found that cortical growth in areas associated with RI was directly related to time spent playing the inhibition game as well as improvement on a computer-based measure of inhibition.

1.3 The potential of online interventions for WS

Given the promising effects of online cognitive training programs noted above, there is now a strong basis for extending such training to targeted clinical populations. Online cognitive training for individuals with WS would be an innovative way to improve skills and decrease impairment in everyday life. Large-scale research targeting such populations is nearly impossible due to logistic barriers, but online-delivered programs could be an acceptable and feasible solution. For one, they would be easier to disseminate to a clinical population spread across the country or the world. In addition, such a program could be cost-effective in using free or inexpensive video conferencing tools and requiring less staff and space than traditional intervention programs. Further, children and adolescents may be more drawn to a computerized task that could be made game-like or competitive in nature. This could boost adherence, acceptability, and even enjoyment. If acceptable to families, internet-based delivery options could open doors to intervention beyond RI training.

1.4 The need for studies of feasibility and acceptability

With this vision of improved functioning in WS and enabling greater access via online delivery of interventions, we have begun testing the very first internet-delivered cognitive training for individuals with WS: a program targeting response inhibition in WS youth. We acknowledge that any potential intervention must be accompanied by investigation of specific factors that influence improvement in RI as a result of cognitive training, such as adherence or the feasibility and acceptability of the training program (Owen et al., 2010). Studies of feasibility are a necessary step in refining interventions to improve acceptability and the likelihood of effectiveness, and they are an important prerequisite to larger studies of efficacy (Bowen et al., 2009; Fletcher et al., 2016). To improve adherence and recognize the full potential of an intervention, feasibility and acceptability studies of online training, not just for the WS population but for the general population, are of critical importance (Kaltenthaler et al., 2008). For studies involving youth, understanding parental acceptance, adherence, and engagement is pivotal to intervention development prior to designing larger study trials (Haine-Schlagel & Walsh, 2015).

Feasibility or acceptability assessments have been included in studies of many computerized or internet-based interventions, including programs targeting coping with traumatic stress, anxiety, or depression, building manualized therapy skills, and boosting adherence (Botella, Serrano, Baños, & Garcia-Palacios, 2015; Kassam-Adams et al., 2016; Khanna & Kendall, 2010; Rathus, Campbell, Miller, & Smith, 2015; Spirito et al., 2015; Wenze, Armey, & Miller, 2014). Some computer-based treatment has assessed satisfaction or sought program evaluation from participants, finding positive ratings and high levels of satisfaction and acceptability, including in children with ASD and intellectual disability (Benyakorn et al., 2018; Botella et al., 2015). Other researchers first assessed usability of an intervention before piloting with a small sample, allowing for tailoring of the program and collection of favorable ratings of usability and acceptability (Stark et al., 2016). These studies provide examples and guidance for evaluating feasibility of internet-delivered interventions.

1.5 Summary and rationale

Response inhibition difficulties seem to underlie a cluster of symptoms in WS, and these are manifested through disinhibited behavior, high rates of ADHD, and trouble with shifting or disengaging from threats. While some emerging computer-based interventions target response inhibition, there is little research on either computer-based intervention for WS *or* on response inhibition in WS. To help those with WS benefit from the newly-emerging computer-based intervention programs that target cognitive processes, we must first determine whether it is feasible and acceptable to apply internet-based, self-administered cognitive training to this population.

1.6 Study aims

This purpose of this study is to examine the feasibility and acceptability of online cognitive training targeting response inhibition improvement in youth with Williams syndrome. The larger pilot study (Brei, 2017) included a cognitive assessment, evaluation of RI functioning and changes in RI, the cognitive training program itself, and parent report of therapeutic effects on everyday functioning, but these results lie beyond the current paper's scope. The current study provides quantitative and qualitative information derived from parent report measures to inform future computer-based cognitive training endeavors for those with WS and possibly for other populations with genetic or developmental differences.

2. Method

2.1 Participants

Participants were 20 children and adolescents with WS (8 females), aged 10–17 years, and 20 parents (one 'primary' caregiver alongside each child). The youth had all been genetically diagnosed with Williams syndrome previously, the first and main language spoken in the home was English, and families possessed a computer with internet access as well as a second electronic device capable of video conferencing. Exclusion criteria were: legal adult, previous inhibition training, and comorbid diagnosis of ASD due to possible interference with interpretation of results. No minimum IQ was required, as we sought to use a representative sample of IQ in children with WS. Fliers announcing the larger pilot study were mailed to families seen by the principal investigators in prior studies of WS. Fliers were also distributed by the Williams Syndrome Association via email to attendees of the Williams Syndrome Conference and to families near several Midwestern metro areas. A description of the study was posted on the Williams syndrome Research Registry. The broader pilot study was submitted to the online registry of Clinical Trials. Interested families were instructed to contact the principal investigators to complete a screening form and arrange participation. See Table 1 for a characterization of the sample.

This research was conducted with the understanding and written consent of each participant and his or her parent, according to ethical principles outlined by the Institutional Review Board. This research was independently reviewed and approved for ethical soundness by the Institutional Review Board within the Human Research Protection Program at the institution conducting this research. Families were compensated with a total of $40 per child upon completion.

2.2 Measures

Treatment evaluation inventory-short form (TEI-SF; Kelley, Heffer, Gresham, & Elliott, 1989). This is a Likert scale with 8 statements related to treatment acceptability, child consent, discomfort, and overall reaction. Parents rate from "strongly disagree" to "strongly agree." Higher scores indicate greater

Table 1 Demographics.
Participant demographics

Population	20 children/adolescents with Williams syndrome, and primary caregivers
Gender	12 males, 8 females
Age	Mean: 14 years, SD: 1.9 years, Range: 10–17 years
Intelligence quotient	Mean standard score: 67; SD: 16; Range: 44–97
ADHD comorbidity	$n = 16$ (80%): 13 Inattentive type; 3 combined type

agreement. This measure has good psychometric properties. It was administered via online parent self-report immediately after the training program was complete.

Treatment acceptability questionnaire (TAQ; Hunsley, 1992). The TAQ is 7-point Likert scale consisting of 6 questions related to acceptability, effectiveness, and ethics of the treatment and the knowledge and trustworthiness of the providers. Higher scores indicate a more positive rating. This measure was administered via online parent self-report immediately after the training program was complete. While the TEI-SF focuses more on treatment procedures and likability, the TAQ incorporates feedback derived from interactions with the study staff and feelings of ethicality.

After treatment questionnaire (ATQ; Brei & Klein-Tasman, 2016). This is a study-specific measure of feasibility and acceptability created by the principal investigators. It consists of 22 questions about technological preferences, program flow, session length and number, and level of staff involvement. It includes open-ended questions to gain parent feedback. See Table 2 for further description of items included in these three measures.

2.3 Procedure

While the present study focuses on the feasibility and acceptability of internet delivery of the cognitive training intervention, the larger study's phases are briefly described here to demonstrate the steps involved in this program's development and to help readers understand participants' experience, which informed questionnaire responses. All phases of the study were delivered online except the initial in-person meeting. See Fig. 1 for study flow.

Part I: Baseline (2 h total). Study staff met with participants in person to administer a standardized measure of cognitive functioning and a diagnostic interview. Study staff assisted parents in computer setup for the study either in person or via videoconferencing equipment. Participants then met with staff from home via videoconferencing equipment to complete an online, computerized RI assessment lasting about 1 h (see Table 2 for a description of the experimental tasks). Parents also completed an online questionnaire battery (six brief standardized measures) about child mood, behavior, attention, and anxiety. After Baseline, participants were randomly assigned to the Treatment or Waitlist Crossover condition of the cognitive training program, stratifying by intellectual functioning.

Special adaptations for acceptability in WS. To facilitate the acceptability of the RI assessment for participants with WS and their parents, the computerized RI assessment was first introduced to one volunteer child with WS

Table 2 Description of measures.

Measure	Items/description
Feasibility and acceptability	
Treatment evaluation inventory—Short form (TEI-SF; Kelley et al., 1989)	Parents rate on a Likert scale their responses to items assessing the following: acceptability of the program, willingness to use this procedure to target behavior change, acceptability without child consent, likability of procedures, expectations of discomfort, likelihood of improvement, parent-enforced use of the program, overall reaction to the program
Treatment acceptability questionnaire (TAQ; Hunsley, 1992)	Parents rate on a Likert scale their responses to items assessing the following: level of acceptability, degree of ethicality, level of effectiveness, perceptions of side effects, degree of provider knowledge, degree of provider trustworthiness
ATQ (Study-specific questionnaire created by principal investigators)	Parents rate on a Likert scale their responses to items and provide optional comments for the following: phone or email preference, comfort using the study's videoconference tool, alternative videoconference preferences, problems, and comments, ease and independence in computer setup, staff assistance with technology and training, session number, length, and effectiveness, ideas for improving study or staff, more rigorous sessions and child fatigue, likelihood of participation if session frequency or length increased, particular likes or dislikes, staff correspondence and involvement, supervision vs. independent completion, suggestions for improving clarity, likelihood of recommending to others and why
Training and evaluation	Experimental Tasks used for RI assessment and training measures

Continued

Table 2 Description of measures.—cont'd

Measure	Items/description
Go/No-Go task (Lee, 2014)	The 8-min computerized Go/No-Go task adapted for this study consists of 75% go trials requiring a button press after each stimulus (alphabet letter) and 25% no-go trials. It assesses response time and inhibition after the discriminatory stimulus (the letter 'X')
Motor stroop task (Lee, 2014)	The 10-min computerized Motor Stroop Task adapted for this study requires participants to press a particular button depending on which side of the screen the stimulus appears
Stop-signal task (Lee, 2014)	The 10-min computerized Stop Signal Task adapted for this study instructs participants to press computer keys indicating whether an arrow on the screen points left or right. Participants were to inhibit the response if the stop signal (audible beep) followed the appearance of the stimulus
Response inhibition training program (Lee, 2014)	Computerized training program developed for this study is a game-like computer program tapping into motor inhibition and interference control within an engaging story line. An introduction and 'practice level' is administered prior to training. Participants complete three 5-min "levels" per session, and levels incorporate various demands on inhibitory requirement and include feedback. Inhibitory demands become more challenging as participants progress. Adaptations were designed with consideration of the lowered IQ present in WS and the potential for frustration stemming from inability to meet passing criterion. All participants received approximately the same 'dosage' of training

Note: The larger pilot study included baseline assessment of cognitive ability, executive functioning, and comorbidities. Additionally, at each time point, parents completed six online questionnaires pertaining to everyday functioning in areas of attention, anxiety, affect, question-asking frequency, and emotion regulation.

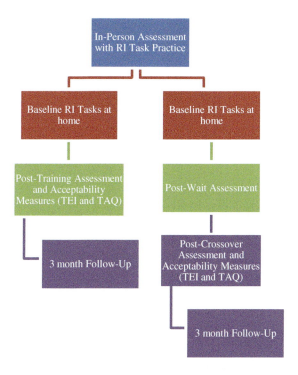

Fig. 1 Study flow chart. This displays the sequence of training procedures and questionnaire administration. In-person assessment and RI task practice were followed by baseline assessment and training/wait, crossover, and Follow-up. The feasibility and acceptability measures were completed immediately after the training and at Follow-up. *Notes*: The Response Inhibition (RI) Task and Parent Questionnaires were administered at each time point. The feasibility and acceptability measures (Treatment Evaluation Inventory-Short Form and Treatment Acceptability Questionnaire; TEI-SF and TAQ) were completed immediately after the Post-Training/Crossover assessment. The After Treatment Questionnaire (ATQ) was completed at Follow-up.

and adjusted based on staff observations and volunteer feedback. Given that intellectual functioning in this population falls in the mildly to moderately delayed range, adaptations to increase participant understanding and acceptance included the addition of detailed instructions presented visually with accompanying audio, teaching of correct responding using the computer keyboard and mouse, and the addition of practice trials. Study participants were then administered this standardized 5-min 'practice' to ensure that instructions were understood. In allowing for a supervised, standardized practice for all participants, we hoped to improve treatment acceptability by increasing familiarity with the task demands and reducing frustration, misunderstanding, or forgetting. All participants were supervised until they demonstrated an understanding of the goal of the task, and behavioral observations (including mood and practice progression) were recorded for each child.

Part II: Treatment or waitlist crossover (6–7 h total). The game-like cognitive training program utilized in this phase was developed for a recent series of clinical trials studies and showed promise for improving RI in individuals with disorders characterized by poor RI (Lee, Espil, Bauer, Siwiec, & Woods, 2018). See Table 2 for a description of the training program.

Participants in the Treatment condition completed ten 20- to 30-min sessions of training (about two per week) over the course of about 5 weeks. Time spent training was 15 min total, with practice, pauses, and review built into the session. They were then administered the 1-h RI assessment tasks that had been administered at Baseline. The Waitlist Crossover group waited during those 5 weeks, were administered the RI assessment tasks, completed crossover training, and then were administered the RI assessment tasks once again. Parents repeated the questionnaires about child psychosocial functioning and attention after the wait and after training.

The first two training sessions were supervised by study staff via videoconferencing equipment, and all videoconferencing activity was securely recorded to ensure proper administration. Parents supervised the child at all times but were instructed not to assist the child during the RI assessment or training game. Brief breaks that did not interfere with administration were allowed. For cases in which participants did not respond to a program-generated email prompt to complete a training session, study staff reached out to families via phone to troubleshoot barriers.

Adaptations to improve acceptability for WS. The cognitive training game was adapted from the original version used in clinical trials. It was tailored specifically for youth with WS based on the volunteer participant's feedback and on typical levels of cognitive functioning and ADHD comorbidity in WS. The main adaptation involved adjusting passing criteria to provide more positive feedback for smaller gains, considering the lower IQ present in WS and the potential for frustration if passing criteria were too difficult. Additionally, before each of the ten training sessions, there was a brief review and practice of the training game procedures.

Part III: Follow-up (45 min). Three months after completion of training, each participant completed the Follow-up assessment in which they were again administered the computerized RI assessment tasks after a brief review.

Parents again completed the questionnaire battery on child functioning. The Follow-up session occurred as the final phase of the study for all participants.

Assessment of feasibility and acceptability. The TEI-SF and TAQ parent report measures were administered online to parents immediately upon their child's completion of the training, before Follow-up. At Follow-up, the final feasibility and acceptability questionnaire specific to this study, the After Treatment Questionnaire (ATQ), was sent to parents to complete online anonymously, with the option for open-ended comments (refer to Table 2).

3. Results

Results focus on descriptive data from the responses on each of the parent-reported feasibility and acceptability measures. Responses are reported as positive if the parent indicated a more positive than neutral response on each scale. Only one family dropped out of treatment before the completion of the study, just before Follow-up.

3.1 Attendance and program completion

Out of 20 participant families, there was a 100% completion rate for the 10-session training program. There were 19 families who completed the entire program, including the 10 training sessions plus the RI assessment at each time point; one participant did not complete the 3-month follow up RI assessment. Feasibility and acceptability questionnaire completion was similarly high, with 85% and 90% of parents completing the TEI-SF and TAQ measures, respectively, immediately after training had ended, and 70% of parents completing the ATQ at the Follow-up assessment.

3.2 TEI-SF

Results from the Treatment Evaluation Inventory ($n = 17$), on a 0–4 acceptability scale, indicate that parents had a favorable response to the intervention. The majority of parents (71%) agreed or strongly agreed that they liked the procedures ($M = 2.76$, $SD = 0.75$, where 0 is "strongly disagree" and 4 is "strongly agree"), and most (76%) had a positive reaction to training ($M = 2.88$; $SD = 0.93$). 41% of parents agreed or strongly agreed that this intervention was an acceptable way of treating the presenting issues, while 47% reported feeling neutral ($M = 2.47$; $SD = 0.94$). Only a smaller subset

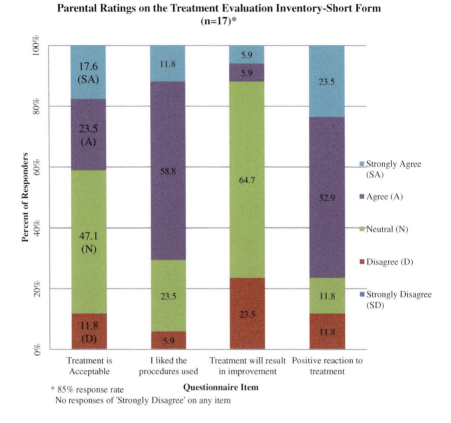

Fig. 2 Parental ratings on TEI-SF. This displays key parental responses on items of the treatment evaluation inventory-short form, including responses about acceptability, procedures, perception of improvement, and reaction to training.

(12%) thought the training would likely result in permanent improvement; the majority felt neutral (M = 1.94; SD = 0.75). See Fig. 2 for more details about particular item responses.

3.3 TAQ

Results from the Treatment Acceptability Questionnaire, a 1–7 acceptability scale, ($n = 18$) indicate a positive response with regard to acceptability, with 72% of the respondents finding the intervention at least slightly acceptable (39% reported the training was "very acceptable") (M = 5.44, SD = 1.50, where 1 is "very unacceptable" and 7 is "very acceptable"). The strong majority of parents reported that the intervention was very

Feasibility of online cognitive training for WS

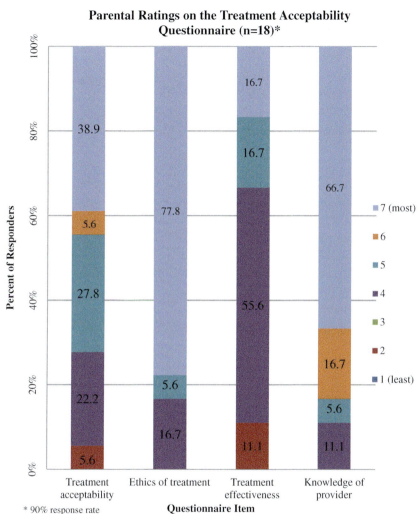

Fig. 3 Parental ratings on TAQ. This displays key parental responses on items of the Treatment Acceptability Questionnaire, including responses about acceptability, ethics, effectiveness, and provider knowledge.

ethical (M = 6.34; SD = 1.20) and the providers were very knowledgeable (M = 6.34; SD = 1.04) and trustworthy (M = 6.61; SD = 0.85). On average, parents were neutral regarding its effectiveness (M = 4.44; SD = 1.42). See Fig. 3, which displays all parental responses to items.

3.4 ATQ

The After Treatment Questionnaire ($n = 14$) provided anonymous parental perceptions and feedback informing both feasibility and acceptability, the training process, use of technology, email vs. phone communication, staff involvement, training program difficulty, and participant comfort with various procedures. It allowed parents to provide feedback and suggestions for modification and improvement.

Positive feedback. Parents were enthusiastic about the engaging nature of the 10-session training program. Many reported being pleased with the playful, game-like nature of the training tasks and commented on the engaging graphics. They also noted that staff engagement with the child (e.g, regular encouragement and social reinforcement) boosted the child's enjoyment and engagement during study procedures. They were positive about the study framework and design. They reported feeling comfortable with the videoconferencing tools used and with the use of video throughout the session for supervision and interaction. They appreciated having staff walk them through program installation and setup. Most preferred email communication from staff, which was the primary modality used, as opposed to phone calls. They affirmed the level of staff involvement/supervision provided, and most believed it necessary and helpful to have constant staff supervision during the first two sessions. Parents noted that it was helpful to have flexibility about the time of day their child completed unsupervised training sessions. Some reported feeling excited at seeing their child's improvement during the study. Encouragingly, most parents indicated that they were likely to recommend the study to another family.

Suggestions for modification and improvement. Parents offered several ways to modify the training program for future use. Some were in favor of expanding video conferencing options to include those which were already downloaded or embedded on their device. They also asked for greater flexibility in scheduling the supervised training sessions. Some parents commented that the review and practice of training game procedures before each session should be briefer. A few parents described that more rigorous sessions would be manageable and may result in greater improvement. Some reported issues with videoconferencing (e.g., audio/video lag) or difficulty with computer setup. They felt that limiting the number of parent questionnaires during the study would be helpful, and they suggested having a shorter RI assessment, as this step was repeated multiple times. Parents also offered ideas for making the procedures even more child-friendly, in particular connecting with the child through informal conversation at the start of any supervised session. Most parents would not have supported more rigorous (longer, more frequent, or more intense) sessions, as they felt their child would have been too fatigued, although over half would still have been willing to participate. See Table 3 for results from the ATQ and participant responses to the open-ended questions.

Table 3 Results from after treatment questionnaire ($n = 14$)[a].

Relevant question	Percent	Relevant responses in open-ended comment space
Preferred email	71	
Comfortable using study video chat	100	• Video chatting was a very easy and smooth way for us to use and communicate. We did not encounter problems
Prefer alternative video chat options	36	• We did not have any issues but another method would be fine
Audio/video problems	36	• We had a few sound glitches but they were solved pretty quickly • There was a bit of a delay, and often there was a background hum
Easy setup	50	• In scheduling, include a few day and evening times to have us pick from • No surprises. Everything was outlined and explained in detail
Difficult setup	29	• Positioning camera to pick up correct video [was hard]
Prefer study staff help with setup	79	• Everything was outlined and explained in detail
Prefer staff supervision	86	• Spend a bit more time chatting with the child before jumping in
Would not support more sessions	64	• There were more than enough sessions • I think the number was about right. It took a bit to become comfortable with it • I think it may have been a little more effective with a few more sessions

Continued

Table 3 Results from after treatment questionnaire ($n = 14$)[a].—cont'd

Relevant question	Percent	Relevant responses in open-ended comment space
Would not support longer sessions	71	• They were long enough. For my son it seemed to tax his attending skills • I think shorter sessions are definitely better. Frustration levels peak if any longer • I don't think my son would have been as cooperative • They were long enough to be productive, but any longer and his attention would have been lost. It was very hard to keep him on task
Would still participate if more or longer sessions	57	• It would be interesting to see 3×/3wk results • I thought the 20 min sessions were a good length. Maybe add another session or two
Believed child would fatigue with more rigorous sessions	86	• [It was] too repetitive, easy to get bored and/or frustrated • It wasn't difficult to comply, and if it can help other Williams Syndrome families with children with attention issues, it's very worthwhile! • My son got bored with it but to me (not as video game savvy!) • I would say 10–12 sessions of equal or shorter duration. Twice per week worked well
Assistance was helpful (vs. doing all sessions alone)	50	• [Research staff] were very friendly and professional • [My child] responds well to positive reinforcement so that was something she hoped would happen during the testing. That cheering on from the staff is a wonderful thing

Table 3 Results from after treatment questionnaire $(n = 14)^a$.—cont'd

Relevant question	Percent	Relevant responses in open-ended comment space
Overall: Would recommend this study	86	• It surprised me that [my child] learned to inhibit his response. I didn't expect an effect • We enjoyed it. I was impressed with the improvements [my child] made. It opened my eyes to see how much she wanted to know her scores. Even though she was frustrated when she missed a cue or made a mistake, she was happy in the end • I would recommend this study because it allowed us to add input to a good cause. It was easy to do and the time commitment was flexible and convenient • It was fun for my daughter to play, and our family is always eager to help researchers • She got a kick out of the noises and music in the game—who thought of that one? • I thought it was explained well. I didn't realize I would be repeating the parent surveys so many times–that's the only thing that surprised me a bit, but it wasn't a problem • We wouldn't recommend this study, because we haven't noticed improvements • I would be eager to see findings from a larger number of participants. I am also curious as to how shorter attention spans influence tasks. Also curious about how you tease out attending difficulties vs. impulse control. I think my son knew what to do and thought about controlling the impulse but his mind would wander during the activities • If it could help you learn how to help our kids I'd recommend it

[a]70% response rate.

Note: This table includes *all* participant responses providing specific information in the comments.

4. Discussion

These results use quantitative and qualitative data to describe the acceptability and feasibility of an online intervention aimed at improving response inhibition in children and adolescents with Williams syndrome. That a study is *feasible* means it involves procedures that assist researchers in developing formal interventions and can include investigation of constructs such as acceptability, implementation, practicality, and adaptation, to name a few (Bowen et al., 2009). Describing *acceptability* involves examining possible consumers' perceptions of study procedures and involves constructs such as attitude toward treatment, ethicality, and perceptions of effectiveness (Kazdin, 1980; Sekhon, Cartwright, & Francis, 2017). In this study, *feasibility* reflected the investigators' ability to deliver the program as intended through the use of videoconference-based supervision, online software for RI assessments and the training game, and online questionnaires and interviews to record parental assessment of child functioning at various time points. *Acceptability* referred to the degree to which parents reported the study procedures were acceptable, understandable, ethical, and helpful.

Encouraging feedback about the training program's acceptability and procedures was obtained. In particular, parents were likely to recommend the study to others. This overall inclination to endorse the treatment to others is promising for future success of online cognitive interventions, as it indicates parents felt the program would be worthwhile to other families. This likelihood of recommendation was present despite neutral feelings as to whether the training would result in lasting improvement. Low expectations of treatment effectiveness may indicate the need for study staff to have placed more emphasis on possible results, as perceived effectiveness of an intervention is important in establishing its acceptability (Sekhon et al., 2017). Timely completion within the prescribed schedule ($2 \times$/week for 5 weeks), the ability of WS participants to grasp procedures and complete the tasks, and positive parent feedback about time spent on the procedures all support the study's feasibility. Very low dropout levels and perceptions of ethicality in this study support its acceptability (Sekhon et al., 2017).

There was a high level of completion of study procedures, with 100% of participants completing the training program itself and only one participant failing to complete the final follow-up assessment of RI. This gives a general indication of study feasibility, along with parent feedback about the ease of delivery and completion through online videoconference and training game software. The high completion rate is also likely related to frequent, active email or phone check-ins by study personnel to remind families to complete sessions if a session had not yet been completed as expected during the week. With a low attrition level for the program overall, the absence of some parents' completion of the final measures is not believed to reflect a lack of engagement in treatment or a problem with acceptability. Further, most parents were enthusiastic about participation, which implies there was not an unwillingness to complete the feasibility and acceptability measures.

Almost 90% of parents would recommend this study to others, which is promising given that this study was the first of its kind in this population and has much potential for refinement. With these encouraging results, it is hoped that researchers will continue to explore and improve online training programs for future use with children with Williams syndrome.

4.1 Feasibility and acceptability of specific study features

Computer-based delivery and videoconferencing software. The majority of parents thought computer setup was easy, and about half appreciated help with setup, but some parents did consider this step to be difficult. It may be helpful to create a walk-through installation video that parents can view, as this step became time-consuming to troubleshoot via videoconference. For consistency, our study's procedures allowed only one option for videoconferencing software. However, given that about one-third of parents would have preferred using an alternative or more familiar videoconferencing tool than the one used in this study, it seems that families would be more comfortable if conferencing were offered via the software they already have installed on their electronic device.

Training schedule. A large majority of parents believed their child would have fatigued if sessions had been more rigorous. It is possible that more rigorous sessions themselves would not cause fatigue if the child were not required to complete the online RI assessment three to four times depending on treatment group. While most parents did not believe more or longer sessions would have made training more effective in improving skills, they were not averse to participating in a study involving more or longer sessions. This indicates that many parents are willing and open to explore the possibilities in order to further the research that may benefit their child.

Staff involvement. Stark et al. (2016) suggest that treatments may be enhanced if providers regularly monitor progress and check in with the family. With all parents reporting that study personnel involvement was sufficient, it would be interesting to explore how much researcher supervision and assistance is actually necessary for families to remain satisfied. This could help put the training in families' hands and increase dissemination all the more.

4.2 Innovation, limitations, and future directions

This examination of feasibility and acceptability of an online cognitive training program was the first study of its kind in the child and adolescent Williams syndrome population. Such a technology-based and internet-delivered cognitive training program for clinical populations is relatively new. This study helps promote research in this area, which may help to improve cost-effectiveness and dissemination to populations with rare conditions through easier access to home-based delivery. Further, this study demonstrates that cognitive training programs can be adapted in a feasible and acceptable way for individuals with WS and their families—and potentially to others with developmental conditions or similar IQ. Because every assessment in the current study was supervised and observed live via videoconferencing software, staff were able provide encouragement to participants and families, improve understanding and motivation, assist with technical problems, make general observations, and collect feedback to make adjustments, all which likely influenced the acceptability of the procedures and inform future research.

The limitations of this small-sample study are acknowledged, as is the difficulty of gathering a substantial number of children with a rare genetic condition. However, as noted by Bowen et al. (2009) and Fletcher et al. (2016), it is helpful to begin with a limited number of participants in order to gain candid feedback and inform establishment of a feasible delivery method. It is noted that this sample consisted of families who possessed adequate technological resources, which may not reflect the general population. Additionally, no guidelines exist for study procedures in those with genetic or neurodevelopmental conditions, such as optimal training length or spacing of cognitive training sessions. Future endeavors may aim to determine the optimal amount, quality, and intensity of training and explore whether a condensed time frame improves acceptability. Researchers may find Ritterband et al.' (2003) steps for developing web-based interventions as a helpful resource.

Limitations of the feasibility and acceptability measures include that formal, written feedback was only collected after children completed training, which omits feedback from parents and children who dropped out of the study ($n = 1$) or did not complete all parent measures, as described in Results. Because parental feedback was kept anonymous to encourage transparency, it was not possible to determine whether demographic characteristics or comorbidities influenced perceptions of acceptability.

Formal feedback was only obtained from parents and not from participants themselves. Parental feedback about feasibility and acceptability of interventions is a necessary focus, as parent support of an intervention is critical to the use of that intervention for a child (Stahmer & Pellecchia, 2015). Further, parent participation affects child attendance and engagement in treatments (Haine-Schlagel & Walsh, 2015). Staff observations about participant engagement indicated that children were generally accepting, willing, and even excited to play the training game, and several parents noted their child's reactions on the ATQ. At the same time, children and adolescents with WS could likely provide feedback to developmentally appropriate questions about the ethics and acceptability of such programs and their level of willingness to participate. Future studies should provide a wider range of technology and videoconferencing options, examine the role of parental involvement in the intervention and results, include formal, written participant feedback from youth, and track changes in parental perception of treatment acceptability over time.

5. Conclusion

This study helps to establish the feasibility and acceptability of an online cognitive inhibition training program for children and families with Williams syndrome. Though parents did not anticipate lasting cognitive or behavioral changes, feedback from parents was largely positive and provided information about expanding accessibility and flexibility of treatments for their children. It is hoped that these results will prompt researchers to develop, improve, and disseminate online interventions for children with WS and other developmental disabilities.

Acknowledgments

The authors wish to thank the participants and families who made this project possible, the undergraduate and graduate research assistants at UW-Milwaukee, in particular Kristin Basche, who aided in data collection and study maintenance, and Carolyn Mervis, PhD at the University of Louisville for participant referrals. This work was funded by a generous grant from the Williams Syndrome Association awarded to Klein-Tasman, B.P. (WS#0110).

Source of funding

Funding was provided through a grant from the Williams Syndrome Association (WSA #0110), undergraduate research support from the UWM Office of Undergraduate Research and a Distinguished Dissertation Fellowship from the UWM Graduate School.

Conflict of interest

No conflict of interest has been declared.

References

Amir, N., Beard, C., Taylor, C. T., Klumpp, H., Elias, J., Burns, M., et al. (2009). Attention training in individuals with generalized social phobia: A randomized controlled trial. *Journal of Consulting and Clinical Psychology*, 77(5), 961–973. https://doi.org/10.1037/a0016685.

Baer, R. A., & Nietzel, M. T. (1991). Cognitive and behavioral treatment of impulsivity in children: A meta-analytic review of the outcome literature. *Journal of Clinical Child Psychology*, 20(4), 400–412. https://doi.org/10.1207/s15374424jccp2004_9.

Benyakorn, S., Calub, C. A., Riley, S. J., Schneider, A., Iosif, A. M., Solomon, M., et al. (2018). Computerized cognitive training in children with autism and intellectual disabilities: Feasibility and satisfaction study. *JMIR Mental Health*, 5(2), e40. https://doi.org/10.2196/mental.9564.

Botella, C., Serrano, B., Baños, R. M., & Garcia-Palacios, A. (2015). Virtual reality exposure-based therapy for the treatment of post-traumatic stress disorder: A review of its efficacy, the adequacy of the treatment protocol, and its acceptability. *Neuropsychiatric Disease and Treatment*, 11, 2533–2545. https://doi.org/10.2147/NDT.S89542.

Bowen, D. J., Kreuter, M., Spring, B., Cofta-Woerpel, L., Linnan, L., Weiner, D., et al. (2009). How we design feasibility studies. *American Journal of Preventive Medicine*, 36(5), 452–457. https://doi.org/10.1016/j.amepre.2009.02.002.

Brei, N. (2017). *Effects of online response inhibition training in children with Williams syndrome: A pilot study*. Theses and Dissertations. 1589. https://dc.uwm.edu/etd/1589.

Brei, N., & Klein-Tasman, B. P. (2016). *After-treatment questionnaire*. Unpublished questionnaire.

Capitão, L., Sampaio, A., Férnandez, M., Sousa, N., Pinheiro, A., & Gonçalves, Ó. F. (2011). Williams syndrome hypersociability: A neuropsychological study of the amygdala and prefrontal cortex hypotheses. *Research in Developmental Disabilities*, 32(3), 1169–1179. https://doi.org/10.1016/j.ridd.2011.01.006.

Carney, D. P., Brown, J. H., & Henry, L. A. (2013). Executive function in Williams and Down syndromes. *Research in Developmental Disabilities*, 34(1), 46–55. https://doi.org/10.1016/j.ridd.2012.07.013.

Cicerone, K. D., Dahlberg, C., Kalmar, K., Langenbahn, D. M., Malec, J. F., Bergquist, T. F., et al. (2000). Evidence-based cognitive rehabilitation: Recommendations for clinical practice. *Archives of Physical Medicine and Rehabilitation*, 81(12), 1596–1615. https://doi.org/10.1053/apmr.2000.19240.

Costanzo, F., Varuzza, C., Menghini, D., Addona, F., Gianesini, T., & Vicari, S. (2013). Executive functions in intellectual disabilities: A comparison between Williams syndrome and Down syndrome. *Research in Developmental Disabilities*, 34(5), 1770–1780. https://doi.org/10.1016/j.ridd.2013.01.024.

Derakshan, N., Smyth, S., & Eysenck, M. W. (2009). Effects of state anxiety on performance using a task-switching paradigm: An investigation of attentional control theory. *Psychonomic Bulletin & Review*, 16(6), 1112–1117. https://doi.org/10.3758/PBR.16.6.1112.

Duckworth, S. V., Ragland, G. G., Sommerfeld, R. E., & Wyne, M. D. (1974). Modification of conceptual impulsivity in retarded children. *American Journal of Mental Deficiency, 79*(1), 59–63.

Enge, S., Behnke, A., Fleischhauer, M., Küttler, L., Kliegel, M., & Strobel, A. (2014). No evidence for true training and transfer effects after inhibitory control training in young healthy adults. *Journal of Experimental Psychology: Learning, Memory, and Cognition, 40*(4), 987–1001. https://doi.org/10.1037/a0036165.

Fisher, M., Moskowitz, A., & Hodapp, R. (2013). Differences in social vulnerability among individuals with autism spectrum disorder, Williams syndrome, and Down syndrome. *Research in Autism Spectrum Disorders, 7*(8), 931–937. https://doi.org/10.1016/j.rasd.2013.04.009.

Fletcher, A., Jamal, F., Moore, G., Evans, R. E., Murphy, S., & Bonell, C. (2016). Realist complex intervention science: Applying realist principles across all phases of the Medical Research Council framework for developing and evaluating complex interventions. *Evaluation (London), 22*(3), 286–303. https://doi.org/10.1177/1356389016652743.

Frigerio, E., Burt, D. M., Gagliardi, C., Cioffi, G., Martelli, S., Perrett, D. I., et al. (2006). Is everybody always my friend? Perception of approachability in Williams syndrome. *Neuropsychologia, 44*(2), 254–259.

Gagnon, L. G., & Belleville, S. (2012). Training of attentional control in mild cognitive impairment with executive deficits: Results from a double-blind randomised controlled study. *Neuropsychological Rehabilitation, 22*(6), 809–835. https://doi.org/10.1080/09602011.2012.691044.

Gothelf, D., Searcy, Y. M., Reilly, J., Lai, P. T., Lanre-Amos, T., Millis, D., et al. (2008). Association between cerebral shape and social use of language in Williams syndrome. *American Journal of Medical Genetics Part A, 146A*(21), 2753–2761. https://doi.org/10.1002/ajmg.a.32507.

Greer, J., Riby, D. M., Hamiliton, C., & Riby, L. M. (2013). Attentional lapse and inhibition control in adults with Williams syndrome. *Research in Developmental Disabilities, 34*(11), 4170–4177. https://doi.org/10.1016/j.ridd.2013.08.041.

Haine-Schlagel, R., & Walsh, N. E. (2015). A review of parent participation engagement in child and family mental health treatment. *Clinical Child and Family Psychology Review, 18*(2), 133–150. https://doi.org/10.1007/s10567-015-0182-x.

Hillier, L. W., Fulton, R. S., Fulton, L. A., Graves, T. A., Pepin, K. H., Wagner-McPherson, C., et al. (2003). The DNA sequence of human chromosome 7. *Nature, 424*(6945), 157–164. https://doi.org/10.1038/nature01782.

Horn, N. R., Dolan, M., Elliott, R., Deakin, J. F. W., & Woodruff, P. W. R. (2003). Response inhibition and impulsivity: An fMRI study. *Neuropsychologia, 41*(14), 1959–1966.

Hunsley, J. (1992). Development of the treatment acceptability questionnaire. *Journal of Psychopathology and Behavioral Assessment, 14*(1), 55–64. https://doi.org/10.1007/BF00960091.

Jawaid, A., Riby, D. M., Owens, J., White, S. W., Tarar, T., & Schulz, P. E. (2012). 'Too withdrawn' or 'too friendly': Considering social vulnerability in two neuro-developmental disorders. *Journal of Intellectual Disability Research, 56*(4), 335–350. https://doi.org/10.1111/j.1365-2788.2011.01452.x.

Kable, J., Caulfield, M. K., Falcone, M., McConnell, M., Bernardo, L., & Lerman, C. (2017). No effect of commercial cognitive training on brain activity, choice behavior, or cognitive performance. *The Journal of Neuroscience, 37*(31), 7390–7402. https://doi.org/10.1523/JNEUROSCI.2832-16.2017.

Kaltenthaler, E., Sutcliffe, P., Parry, G., Beverley, C., Rees, A., & Ferriter, M. (2008). The acceptability to patients of computerized cognitive behavior therapy for depression: A systematic review. *Psychological Medicine, 38*, 1521–1530. https://doi.org/10.1017/S0033291707002607.

Karch, D., Albers, L., Renner, G., Lichtenauer, N., von Kries, R., & Roseveare, D. (2013). The efficacy of cognitive training programs in children and adolescents: A meta-analysis. *Deutsches Ärzteblatt International*, *110*(39), 643–652.

Kassam-Adams, N., Marsac, M. L., Kohser, K. L., Kenardy, J., March, S., & Winston, F. K. (2016). Pilot randomized controlled trial of a novel web-based intervention to prevent posttraumatic stress in children following medical events. *Journal of Pediatric Psychology*, *41*(1), 138–148. https://doi.org/10.1093/jpepsy/jsv057.

Kazdin, A. E. (1980). Acceptability of alternative treatments for deviant child behavior. *Journal of Applied Behavior Analysis*, *13*, 259–273. https://doi.org/10.1901/jaba.1980. 13-259.

Kelley, M., Heffer, R., Gresham, F., & Elliott, S. (1989). Development of a modified treatment evaluation inventory. *Journal of Psychopathology and Behavioral Assessment*, *11*, 235–247. https://doi.org/10.1007/BF00960495.

Khanna, M. S., & Kendall, P. C. (2010). Computer-assisted cognitive behavioral therapy for child anxiety: Results of a randomized clinical trial. *Journal of Consulting and Clinical Psychology*, *78*(5), 737–745. https://doi.org/10.1037/a0019739.

Klonoff, P. S., Talley, M. C., Dawson, L. K., Myles, S. M., Watt, L. M., Gehrels, J., et al. (2007). The relationship of cognitive retraining to neurological patients' work and school status. *Brain Injury*, *21*(11), 1097–1107. https://doi.org/10.1080/02699050701687342.

Kühn, S., Lorenz, R. C., Weichenberger, M., Becker, M., Haesner, M., & Gallinat, J. (2017). Taking control! Structural and behavioural plasticity in response to game-based inhibition training in older adults. *NeuroImage*, *156*, 199–206. https://doi. org/10.1016/j.neuroimage.2017.05.026.

Lee, H. (2014). *Go/no-go task, motor stroop task, stop signal task, and "Rainbow tower defense game" response inhibition training program, adapted for children with Williams syndrome. Unpublished measure.*

Lee, H. J., Espil, F. M., Bauer, C. C., Siwiec, S. G., & Woods, D. W. (2018). Computerized response inhibition training for children with trichotillomania. *Psychiatry Research*, *262*, 20–27. https://doi.org/10.1016/j.psychres.2017.12.070.

Lee, H., Goetz, A. R., Turkel, J. E., & Siwiec, S. G. (2015). Computerized attention retraining for individuals with elevated health anxiety. *Anxiety, Stress & Coping: An International Journal*, *28*(2), 226–237. https://doi.org/10.1080/10615806.2014.918964.

Leyfer, O. T., Woodruff-Borden, J., Klein-Tasman, B. P., Fricke, J. S., & Mervis, C. B. (2006). Prevalence of psychiatric disorders in 4 to 16-year-olds with Williams syndrome. *American Journal of Medical Genetics. Part B, Neuropsychiatric Genetics: The Official Publication of the International Society of Psychiatric Genetics*, *141B*(6), 615–622. https://doi.org/10. 1002/ajmg.b.30344.

Loosli, S. V., Buschkuehl, M., Perrig, W. J., & Jaeggi, S. M. (2012). Working memory training improves reading processes in typically developing children. *Child Neuropsychology*, *18*(1), 62–78. https://doi.org/10.1080/09297049.2011.575772.

Mervis, C. B., & Klein-Tasman, B. P. (2000). Williams syndrome: Cognition, personality, and adaptive behavior. *Mental Retardation and Developmental Disabilities Research Reviews*, *6*(2), 148–158. https://doi.org/10.1002/1098-2779(2000)6:2<148::AID-MRDD10> 3.0.CO;2-T.

Mobbs, D., Eckert, M. A., Mills, D., Korenberg, J., Bellugi, U., Galaburda, A. M., et al. (2007). Frontostriatal dysfunction during response inhibition in Williams syndrome. *Biological Psychiatry*, *62*(3), 256–261. https://doi.org/10.1016/j.biopsych.2006.05.041.

Owen, A. M., Hampshire, A., Grahn, J. A., Stenton, R., Dajani, S., Burns, A. S., et al. (2010). Putting brain training to the test. *Nature*, *465*(7299), 775–778. https://doi. org/10.1038/nature09042.

Porter, M. A., Coltheart, M., & Langdon, R. (2007). The neuropsychological basis of hypersociability in Williams and Down syndrome. *Neuropsychologia*, *45*(12), 2839–2849. https://doi.org/10.1016/j.neuropsychologia.2007.05.006.

Rathus, J., Campbell, B., Miller, A., & Smith, H. (2015). Treatment acceptability study of walking the middle path, a new DBT skills module for adolescents and their families. *American Journal of Psychotherapy*, *69*(2), 163–178. https://doi.org/10.1176/appi. psychotherapy.2015.69.2.163.

Reilly, J., Losh, M., Bellugi, U., & Wulfeck, B. (2004). "Frog, where are you?" narratives in children with specific language impairment, early focal brain injury, and Williams syndrome. *Brain and Language*, *88*(2), 229–247. https://doi.org/10.1016/S0093-934X(03) 00101-9.

Rhodes, S. M., Riby, D. M., Matthews, K., & Coghill, D. R. (2011). Attention-deficit/ hyperactivity disorder and Williams syndrome: Shared behavioral and neuropsychological profiles. *Journal of Clinical and Experimental Neuropsychology*, *33*(1), 147–156. https:// doi.org/10.1080/13803395.2010.495057.

Rhodes, S. M., Riby, D. M., Park, J., Fraser, E., & Campbell, L. E. (2010). Executive neuropsychological functioning in individuals with Williams syndrome. *Neuropsychologia*, *48*(5), 1216–1226. https://doi.org/10.1016/j.neuropsychologia.2009.12.021.

Ritterband, L. M., Gonder-Frederick, L. A., Cox, D. J., Clifton, A. D., West, R. W., & Borowitz, S. M. (2003). Internet interventions: In review, in use, and into the future. *Professional Psychology: Research and Practice*, *34*(5), 527–534. https://doi.org/10. 1037/0735-7028.34.5.527.

Sekhon, M., Cartwright, M., & Francis, J. J. (2017). Acceptability of healthcare interventions: An overview of reviews and development of a theoretical framework. *BMC Health Services Research*, *17*(1), 88. https://doi.org/10.1186/s12913-017-2031-8.

Simons, D. J., Boot, W. R., Charness, N., Gathercole, S. E., Chabris, C. F., Hambrick, D. Z., et al. (2016). Do "brain-training" programs work? *Psychological Science in the Public Interest*, *17*(3), 103–186. https://doi.org/10.1177/1529100616661983.

Slate, S. E., Meyer, T. L., Burns, W. J., & Montgomery, D. D. (1998). Computerized cognitive training for severely emotionally disturbed children with ADHD. *Behavior Modification*, *22*(3), 415–437. https://doi.org/10.1177/01454455980223012.

Spirito, A., Wolff, J. C., Seaboyer, L. M., Hunt, J., Esposito-Smythers, C., Nuget, N., et al. (2015). Concurrent treatment for adolescent and parent depressed mood and suicidality: Feasibility, acceptability, and preliminary findings. *Journal of Child and Adolescent Psychopharmacology*, *25*(2), 131–139. https://doi.org/10.1089/cap.2013.0130.

Stahmer, A., & Pellecchia, M. (2015). Moving towards a more ecologically valid model of parent-implemented interventions in autism. *Autism*, *19*(3), 259–261.

Stark, L. J., Opipari-Arrigan, L., Filigno, S. S., Simon, S. L., Leonard, A., Mogayzel, P. J., et al. (2016). Web-based intervention for nutritional management in cystic fibrosis: Development, usability, and pilot trial. *Journal of Pediatric Psychology*, *41*(5), 510–521. https://doi.org/10.1093/jpepsy/jsv108.

Stromme, P., Bjornstad, P. G., & Ramstad, K. (2002). Prevalence estimation of Williams syndrome. *Journal of Child Neurology*, *17*(4), 269–271. https://doi.org/10. 1177/088307380201700406.

Thorell, L. B., Lindqvist, S., Nutley, S. B., Bohlin, G., & Klingberg, T. (2009). Training and transfer effects of executive functions in preschool children. *Developmental Science*, *12*(1), 103–113. https://doi.org/10.1111/j.1467-7687.2008.00745.x.

Walton, C., Kavanagh, A., Downey, L., Lomas, J., Camfield, D., & Stough, C. (2015). Online cognitive training in healthy older adults: A preliminary study on the effects of single versus multi-domain training. *Translational Neuroscience*, *6*, 13–19. https://doi. org/10.1515/tnsci-2015-0003.

Wenze, S., Armey, M. F., & Miller, I. W. (2014). Feasibility and acceptability of a mobile intervention to improve treatment adherence in bipolar disorder: A pilot study. *Behavior Modification*, *38*(4), 497–515. https://doi.org/10.1177/0145445513518421.

Woodruff-Borden, J., Kistler, D. J., Henderson, D. R., Crawford, N. A., & Mervis, C. B. (2010). Longitudinal course of anxiety in children and adolescents with Williams syndrome. *American Journal of Medical Genetics. Part C, Seminars in Medical Genetics*, *154C*(2), 277–290. https://doi.org/10.1002/ajmg.c.30259.

Ybarra, M. L., & Eaton, W. W. (2005). Internet-based mental health interventions. *Mental Health Services Research*, *7*(2), 75–87. https://doi.org/10.1007/s11020-005-3779-8.

Further reading

Herrera, C., Chambon, C., Michel, B. F., Paban, V., & Alescio-Lautier, B. (2012). Positive effects of computer-based cognitive training in adults with mild cognitive impairment. *Neuropsychologia*, *50*(8), 1871–1881. https://doi.org/10.1016/j.neuropsychologia.2012.04.012.

Little, K., Riby, D. M., Janes, E., Clark, F., Fleck, R., & Rodgers, J. (2013). Heterogeneity of social approach behaviour in Williams syndrome: The role of response inhibition. *Research in Developmental Disabilities*, *34*(3), 959–967. https://doi.org/10.1016/j.ridd.2012.11.020.

Nigg, J. T. (2001). Is ADHD a disinhibitory disorder? *Psychological Bulletin*, *127*(5), 571–598. https://doi.org/10.1037/0033-2909.127.5.571.

Shahar, N., & Meiran, N. (2015). Learning to control actions: Transfer effects following a procedural cognitive control computerized training. *PLoS One*, *10*(3). https://doi.org/10.1371/journal.pone.0119992.

CHAPTER FIVE

The effect of parent personality on the acquisition and use of mindfulness skills during an MBSR intervention

Catherine M. Sanner*, Hadley A. McGregor, Amanda E. Preston, and Cameron L. Neece

Department of Psychology, Loma Linda University, Loma Linda, CA, United States
*Corresponding author: e-mail address: csanner@llu.edu

Contents

1. Current study	139
2. Method	140
2.1 Participants	140
2.2 Procedures	141
2.3 Measures	143
2.4 Data analytic plan	145
3. Results	147
3.1 Specific aim 1	147
3.2 Specific aim 2	148
4. Discussion	153
4.1 Limitations	156
4.2 Clinical implications and future directions	157
Conflict of interest	158
References	158

Abstract

Mindfulness based stress reduction (MBSR) has been shown to reduce stress among parents of children with DD, who often experience higher levels of stress than parents of typically developing (TD) children. The current study examined how parent personality impacted parents' learning and acquisition of mindfulness skills. Participants included 50 parents who participated in a waitlist-control trial examining the efficacy of MBSR for parents of children with DD. Results showed that Openness predicted increases in the trajectory of use of mindfulness over the course of the MBSR intervention. Openness also predicted increases in specific facets of mindfulness (i.e. Observe and Non-reactivity), while Conscientiousness predicted increases in Acting with Awareness specifically, from pre to post intervention. This study highlighted

International Review of Research in Developmental Disabilities, Volume 59
ISSN 2211-6095
https://doi.org/10.1016/bs.irrdd.2020.09.004

© 2020 Elsevier Inc.
All rights reserved.

135

> Openness and Conscientiousness as important personality traits with regard to how parents of children with DD learn and acquire mindfulness skills. Clinical implications and future directions are discussed.

Research has shown that parents of children with developmental delay (DD) report higher levels of stress when compared to parents of typically developing (TD) children (Abbeduto, Weissman, & Short-Meyerson, 1999; Baker, Blacher, Crnic, & Edelbrock, 2002). This is important as increased levels of parenting stress has been associated with decreased parental physical health (Johnson, Frenn, Feetham, & Simpson, 2011), higher levels of parental depression (Feldman et al., 2007; Hastings, Daley, Burns, & Beck, 2006), poorer parent well-being (Gerstein, Crnic, Blacher, & Baker, 2009), as well as less effective parenting (Crnic, Gaze, & Hoffman, 2005). It has also been shown to be related to negative child outcomes such as greater levels of behavioral problems (Baker et al., 2003; Neece, Green, & Baker, 2012; Orsmond, Seltzer, Krauss, & Hong, 2003) and the development of internalizing problems and psychological disorders among children with DD (Baker et al., 2002; Baker, Neece, Fenning, Crnic, & Blacher, 2010). These findings underscore the importance of providing greater supports for this vulnerable population.

Mindfulness based stress reduction (MBSR) is an empirically supported stress-reduction intervention with over three decades of research highlighting its effectiveness in reducing stress and anxiety, as well as promoting overall well-being in a variety of populations (Grossman, Niemann, Schmidt, & Walach, 2004). MBSR typically includes formal mindful meditation instruction and practices to help integrate mindfulness into everyday life and to increase coping and decrease physiological and emotional reactivity (Bazzano et al., 2015). Previous studies have shown that parents and caregivers of children with DD who engage in MBSR exhibit reductions in parenting stress (Bazzano et al., 2015; Beer, Ward, & Moar, 2013; Neece, 2014), as well as increases in the five core facets of mindfulness (Roberts & Neece, 2015).

Mindfulness has been operationalized as containing five core facets which are used to assess the general propensity to be mindful in everyday life (Baer, Smith, Hopkins, Krietemeyer, & Toney, 2006). According to Baer's model, mindfulness is a capacity to react non-judgmentally (taking a non-evaluative stance in regard to the inner experience), observe (noticing experiences), act with awareness (purposefully attending to moment-to-moment behaviors), describe (labeling experiences with words), and respond non-reactively (in regard to the inner experience) (Baer et al., 2006; Cash & Whittingham, 2010). Research has shown that increases in these five facets have been linked to reductions in stress (Brown, Bravo, Roos, & Pearson, 2015; Bullis, Bøe, Asnaani, & Hofmann, 2014). Additionally, increases in these facets in parents have also been shown to be related to reductions of internalizing and externalizing problems in TD children (Han et al., 2019). These findings highlight the beneficial nature of the five facets of mindfulness for both parent stress, as well as child behavior problems. Although research has shown that engaging in MBSR is associated with an increase in these five facets (Carmody & Baer, 2008; Roberts & Neece, 2015), research on person-specific factors that may influence the use or tendency to engage in MBSR is scarce.

Given the positive benefits of mindfulness practice and the fact that increased use of mindfulness is associated with improved outcomes (de Vibe et al., 2015), it is important that we understand the individual differences that are associated with increased use. Research has shown that there is a relationship among various personality traits and mindfulness practice (Brown & Ryan, 2003; Feltman, Robinson, & Ode, 2009; Latzman & Masuda, 2013; van den Hurk et al., 2011). One of the most common conceptualizations of personality is from the Big Five Inventory (BFI; McCrae & Costa, 2013), which posits that personality encompasses five different traits including neuroticism, openness, conscientiousness, extraversion, and agreeableness. Across numerous studies, neuroticism has been shown to have a strong inverse relationship with the use of mindfulness (Latzman & Masuda, 2013; van den Hurk et al., 2011). Conversely, openness (Baer et al., 2006; Latzman & Masuda, 2013), agreeableness (Giluk, 2009), and extraversion have all been shown to be positively correlated with mindfulness practice (van den Hurk et al., 2011). The literature on the relationship between conscientiousness and mindfulness is not as clear and the results of various studies indicate mixed findings (Giluk, 2009; Latzman & Masuda, 2013; van den Hurk et al., 2011).

The relationship between each of these five personality traits and mindfulness practice has been examined cross-sectionally within several populations, but few studies have looked at the personality traits within the context of an MBSR intervention. A few studies have found neuroticism to be a moderator of treatment effects in an MBSR intervention (de Vibe et al., 2015; Jagielski et al., 2020; Nyklíček & Irrmischer, 2017). In each of these studies, participants who were high in neuroticism saw greater improvements in well-being following an MBSR intervention.

Researchers attributed this finding due to the fact that individuals who are high in neuroticism tend to report higher instances of negative mood and therefore have more to benefit from learning mindfulness techniques. Findings on conscientiousness were mixed across different samples. For medical and psychology students, greater conscientiousness was associated with greater decreases in stress following an MBSR intervention (de Vibe et al., 2015); while for women with cancer diagnoses, lower levels of conscientiousness was related to lower levels of distress after intervention (Jagielski et al., 2020). These differences in effects of conscientiousness on stress outcomes in various populations may be attributed to different types of stress and stressors present and how they relate to personality. Specifically, in a study including women with cancer diagnoses, women who were low in conscientiousness were more likely to experience distress so they had more to gain from the MBSR intervention (Jagielski et al., 2020). In a study with medical and psychology students, researchers posited that students high in conscientiousness were likely to have higher levels of stress related to graduate school and studying, and therefore had more variability to improve from (de Vibe et al., 2015). Given that parents of children with DD have high levels of stress that tend to be chronic across the lifespan (Miodrag & Hodapp, 2010), it is possible that the personality facets associated with parenting stress are different and may have a unique impact on how parents learn mindfulness.

Although these studies examine the relation between personality and MBSR intervention outcomes, they do not address how personality may affect the learning and use of mindfulness skills. A greater understanding of the personality factors that affect the learning and use of mindfulness may help to better inform which individuals may benefit the most from MBSR. One study by Barkan et al. (2016) looked at personality and learning of mindfulness in an MBSR intervention with a population of older adults. The authors found that openness predicted use of meditation techniques both during and following an MBSR intervention whereas agreeableness was more associated with the use of these techniques during the intervention. Despite the numerous studies that have examined outcomes associated with MBSR, very few studies have looked at how personality factors affect the learning of mindfulness (Barkan et al., 2016).

In addition to use of mindfulness skills, personality affects the degree to which an individual engages with the different facets of mindfulness (Spinhoven, Huijbers, Zheng, Ormel, & Speckens, 2017; van den Hurk et al., 2011). The Describe facet is important to many mindfulness techniques and it involves developing an ability to identify and label inner and outer experiences (Baer et al., 2006). Research suggests that this skill may be linked to ability to attend to the present moment (Baer, Smith, & Allen, 2004) which would likely lead to better self-regulation (Shapiro, Carlson, Astin, & Freedman, 2006). Given these possible connections (van den Hurk et al., 2011), studies have found that the Describing facet is associated with openness (Spinhoven et al., 2017; van den Hurk et al., 2011), extraversion, and conscientiousness (van den Hurk et al., 2011). Openness to experience may also influence how willing participants are to engage in mindfulness activities and it has been linked to the observing facet of mindfulness (Spinhoven et al., 2017). Individuals who are more open are often labeled as curious and insightful (McCrae & Costa Jr., 2013) and therefore may be more likely to notice their surroundings and experiences. The facets of non-judgment, non-reactivity, and acceptance are also key aspects of mindfulness and have been linked inversely to neuroticism (Spinhoven et al., 2017; van den Hurk et al., 2011). Researchers suggest that the strong, negative relationship between neuroticism and these facets may be because each of these facets are related to self-regulatory skills that may be difficult for individuals who are high in neuroticism. Given the relationships among the personality traits and five facets of mindfulness, it is important to understand how we can best increase use of the five facets in individuals with varying personality profiles.

1. Current study

Research has shown that engaging in MBSR and continued use is associated with an increase in acting with awareness, responding non-judgmentally, non-reactivity, observing, and describing (Carmody & Baer, 2008; Roberts & Neece, 2015). Increased use of the five facets of mindfulness in parenting have been shown to be related to reductions in parenting stress and improvements in parent well-being (Corthorn, 2018). However, to our knowledge, no studies have looked at how parents learn mindfulness through MBSR and improve in the five facets of mindfulness or how factors such as personality may affect this process. Given the role of mindfulness practice in decreasing stress as the result of an MBSR intervention, it is important that we understand how differences in parents' personality may alter responsiveness to intervention. Personality may have a different relation with mindfulness based on types of stress typical in different populations (de Vibe et al., 2015; Jagielski et al., 2020), and it is possible that personality affects parents of children with DD differently, as they typically experience high levels of stress that are chronic across the lifespan (Miodrag & Hodapp, 2010). The current study aimed to explore the relations between personality and both use of mindfulness and increases in the five facets of mindfulness over the course of an MBSR intervention. Specifically, we addressed the following aims: (1) To examine personality traits as predictors of changes in the frequency of parents' use of mindfulness over the course of the MBSR intervention, (2) to examine personality as a predictor of changes in specific facets of mindfulness over the course of the MBSR intervention. For Aim 1 we hypothesized that parents who had higher levels of extroversion, conscientiousness, agreeableness, and openness to experiences would predict increases in parents' use of mindfulness. We also hypothesized that parents with higher levels of neuroticism would predict decreases in parents' use of mindfulness. For Aim 2, we hypothesized that personality traits that are significantly related to individual facets of mindfulness will lead to significant changes in parents' use of mindfulness.

2. Method

This method for the Mindful Awareness for Parenting Stress (MAPS) study has been used in the following manuscripts (Chan & Neece, 2018; Neece, 2014; Roberts & Neece, 2015; Sanner & Neece, 2017).

2.1 Participants

In the current study, we used data from the MAPS study. Eligible participants included parents who had a child between 2.5 and 5 years of age who had been diagnosed with a DD, either by the Inland Regional Center or by independent assessment. Parents also had to report at least 10 child behavior problems on the Eyberg Child Behavior Inventory (Robinson, Eyberg, & Ross, 1980). Also, the parent could not be engaged in any form of psychological treatment at the time he or she was referred to participate in the study. Finally, children with extreme physical disabilities or intellectual impairments were excluded from the study, as this impaired their ability to participate in a parent–child interaction task that was part of the larger study.

For this study, we included data from 50 participants from the MAPS study. Most of the parents who participated were female (96%), many were married (76%), and the mean age was 37.11 years ($SD = 6.53$). Half of the parents identified as Hispanic (50%). Parents reported diverse family income ranging from $0 to over $95,000 a year, with 36% of families earning less than $35,000 per year. There were varying levels of education attainment but 52% of parents did not receive formal education past a high school diploma or an equivalent degree. The children in these families were predominantly male (70%) with a mean age of 4.28 years $(SD=0.97)$. Autism Spectrum Disorder (62%) was the most common child diagnosis and the remaining children had various other developmental delays (38%). Additional demographic data are summarized in Table 1, and means and standard deviations of all study variables are included in Table 2.

2.2 Procedures

Procedures were approved by the Institutional Review Board at Loma Linda University. In the current study, we used data from a larger randomized control trial examining the efficacy of Mindfulness-Based Stress Reduction in reducing parenting stress and child behavior problems among families of children with DD (Chan & Neece, 2018; Neece, 2014). We recruited most of the participants through the Inland Regional Center, which is a government agency that provides services for individuals with DD; additional

Table 1 Characteristics of participants in MBSR intervention.

N = 50	N	%	M (SD)
Parent demographics			
Age			37.11 (6.53)
Gender (Female)	48	96	
Race (Hispanic)	25	50	
Married	38	76	
Family Income (<$35,000)	18	36	
Parent formal education			
≤ High school diploma/GED	26	52	
College or professional degree	24	48	
Child demographics			
Age			4.28 (0.97)
Gender (male)	35	70	
Diagnosis (ASD)	31	62	

Table 2 Means and standard deviations of personality and mindfulness variables.

Study variables	M	SD
BFI openness	3.31	0.66
BFI agreeableness	3.84	0.59
BFI neuroticism	2.69	0.76
BFI conscientiousness	3.57	0.65
BFI extraversion	3.34	0.87
SUDS (use of mindfulness) pre-Tx	3.19	3.11
SUDS (use of mindfulness) post-Tx	6.54	1.87
FFMQ observe pre-Tx	23.92	5.71
FFMQ non-judgment pre-Tx	23.00	7.13
FFMQ acting with awareness pre-Tx	23.20	6.46
FFMQ non-reactivity pre-Tx	19.19	4.21
FFMQ describe pre-Tx	26.47	6.59

Note. BFI, Big Five personality inventory; SUDS, subjective units of distress; FFMQ, five facets of mindfulness questionnaire; pre-Tx, pre-treatment; post-Tx, post-treatment.

recruitment was done through the local newspaper, local elementary schools, and community disability groups. To ensure that families met the specified eligibility criteria, research staff first did a phone screening with all parents who had contacted the MAPS Laboratory and expressed interest in participating in the study. Eligible families were then scheduled for a baseline assessment and received a packet in the mail containing measures for the study's outcome variables, along with instructions to complete the packet before their baseline assessment.

At the baseline assessment, parents turned in the completed packet of questionnaires. They then signed an informed consent and were interviewed by research staff to gather demographic data. After the interview, parents were randomly assigned to an immediate treatment or waitlist-control group. Although parents were informed that their participation in the mindfulness intervention could potentially reduce their stress, and that they were assigned to participate in this intervention either immediately or at a later time, parents were blind to the waitlist-control design of the study.

The MBSR intervention follows the manual outlined by Dr. Jon Kabat-Zinn (1990) at the University of Massachusetts Medical Center. The intervention included a didactic component in which participants learned about the concept of mindfulness and stress physiology, a practice component in which group members practiced mindfulness techniques, and a group discussion component. The MBSR program included eight weekly two-hour sessions, a daylong six-hour meditation retreat after the sixth session, and daily home practice based on audio CDs with instructions. The MBSR group leader was informed that he needed to deliver MBSR as manualized and was blind to the waitlist-control design of the study. See Chan and Neece (2018); Neece (2014) for more details regarding the procedures for the MBSR intervention used in the study.

As part of the waitlist-control design, parents from both the immediate treatment and waitlist group returned for a second assessment, during which only the immediate treatment group had received MBSR, and parents completed the same questionnaire measures collected at the baseline assessment. After the second assessment, parents in the waitlist group received MBSR and returned to the MAPS laboratory for a post-treatment assessment. Six months following the end of the intervention for each respective group, parents from each group received a follow-up assessment. After the completion of the project (i.e., all assessments were conducted), parents received a short summary and comparison of their child's behavioral functioning over the course of the intervention in order to reinforce parents' efforts to improve their parenting skills as well as raise awareness of remaining concerns.

Treatment Fidelity. Two trained research assistants assessed treatment fidelity each session using a treatment fidelity checklist developed for this project, which quantifies the number of items completed as anticipated per the manualized MBSR protocol as well as contact time reported in minutes (see Roberts & Neece, 2015, for details). Interrater reliability was high with 95.04% agreement between the two raters. In the treatment group, 73.27% ($SD = 16.60$) of the treatment content items were covered, compared to 78.03% in the control group ($SD = 9.93$), t (34) $= 1.046$, $p > 0.05$. Average contact time for the treatment group was 143.40 ($SD = 74.68$) and 141.75 ($SD = 76.17$) minutes for the control group, which was not significantly different, $t(34) = 0.065$, $p > 0.05$.

2.3 Measures

Demographics. Demographic variables were collected during an interview with the parents during the baseline assessment.

Big Five Personality Inventory. Personality traits were measured using the Big Five Inventory, which is a well validated 44-item self-report measure (BFI; John & Srivastava, 1999). The BFI includes the following subscales measuring five personality traits: extroversion, neuroticism, agreeableness, openness, and conscientiousness. Extraversion reflects the frequency and quality of interpersonal contact, capacity for joy, activity level, and stimulation-seeking behavior. Conscientious persons are best described as dutiful, scrupulous, perseverant, punctual, and organized. Agreeable individuals are compassionate, good-natured, complying, and trusting. Emotional stability is the opposite of neuroticism. As such, emotionally stable individuals are calm, unemotional, and self-satisfied, whereas neurotic persons are often nervous, touchy, anxious, depressed, and insecure. Finally, openness comprises characteristics such as curiousness, versatility, creativity, and originality. Each item is measured on a five-point likert-like scale ranging from strongly disagree (1) to strongly agree (2). All of the five subscales had acceptable reliability. In our sample, the Cronbach's alphas for all the subscales ranged from 0.70 to 0.86.

Subjective Units of Distress Scale. The subjective units of distress scale (SUDs; Roberts & Neece, 2015). We used question seven from the SUDS which asked participants "How much did you use your mindfulness this week?" This item was adapted from a subjective measure of maternal use of mindfulness in parents, the Subjective Units of Mindfulness (Singh et al., 2007), and was scored on a likert scale ranging from No use at all (0) to Very frequent, almost constant use (10). Participants filled out the SUDs measure at nine different time points including each weekly MBSR session, and at the weekend retreat which was following the sixth MBSR session.

Five Facets of Mindfulness. The Five Facets of Mindfulness Questionnaire (FFMQ) is a 39-item self-report questionnaire used to measure parents' development of specific mindfulness attributes, which suggests the use of mindfulness intervention skills in daily life (Baer et al., 2006). Parents rate items on a five-point Likert scale ranging from 1 (*never or very rarely true*) to 5 (*very often or always true*). The FFMQ contains five independent subscales: (1) Observe Scale, which measures an individual's sensory awareness or how the reporter sees, hears, and perceives the internal and external world (example item: "When I'm walking, I deliberately notice the sensations of my body moving"), (2) Describe Scale which measures how an individual labels experiences and expresses them to themselves and others (example item: "I'm good at finding words to describe my feelings"), (3) Act with Awareness Scale which measures how and if an individual chooses actions based on a attunement to a present moment situation (example item: "When I do things, my mind wanders off and I'm easily distracted [reverse coded]"), (4) Non-judgment Scale measuring an individual's own self-acceptance and unconditional empathy (example item: "I criticize myself for having irrational or inappropriate emotions [reverse coded]"), and (5) Non-react Scale which refers to an individual's ability to actively detach from negative thoughts and emotions while accepting them and choosing not to react (example item: "I perceive my feelings and emotions without having to react to them"). We administered the FFMQ measure at the baseline, session five, and post treatment. Cronbach's alpha for the subscales in our sample ranged from 0.73 to 0.91 across sessions.

2.4 Data analytic plan

Prior to testing our models, demographic variables were correlated with both the IV and DV for Aims 1 and 2. The demographic variables analyzed were those that are listed in the demographic table below (Table 1). No demographic variables were found to significantly correlate with both the IV and the DV. Therefore, no demographic covariates were included in the models.

2.4.1 Aim 1

Given that our analyses were exploratory in nature, we ran correlation analyses to examine which personality factors were related to use of mindfulness at baseline and at the last session of the intervention. If a personality factor was significantly correlated with either baseline or the last session use of mindfulness, then that personality factor was examined as a predictor of changes in use of mindfulness over the course of an eight-week MBSR intervention.

Two-level multilevel modeling for longitudinal data was used to test the hypothesis that the use of mindfulness would increase over the course of an 8-week MBSR intervention (sessions one through eight and retreat after week six) and that specific parent personality traits significantly correlated at baseline or post-treatment would predict changes in use of mindfulness over the course of the nine sessions. Analyses were performed using HLM-7 software and full maximum likelihood estimation. We also checked our data for outliers and assumptions of multi-level modeling including linearity, normality, and homoscedasticity of errors, which are described in further detail in the results section.

As recommended by Singer and Willett (2003), we evaluated a series of increasingly complex models leading up to the hypothesized final model. First, we examined the unconditional means model (Model A). This model allowed us to calculate how much variance occurred separately at Level 1 and Level 2 but did not include any predictor variables at either level of the model. Second, we added Time as a fixed predictor at Level 1 (Model B). We then evaluated the unconditional growth model (Model C), which allowed Time to vary randomly at Level 1. In Model D, we added personality factors as predictors of the intercept at Level 2, and in the final model we added personality as predictors of the slope at Level 2. Changes in deviance statistics were used to evaluate model fit, where a statistically significant decrease in deviance scores between tested models indicated superior fit (Singer & Willett, 2003).

2.4.2 Aim 2 and 3

Bivariate correlations were run in order to determine which personality factors were related to specific facets of mindfulness, given that our aims were exploratory in nature. If a personality trait was significantly related to either baseline or post-treatment score for any facet of mindfulness, then they were included in subsequent regression analyses. If any two personality traits were related to the same facet of mindfulness, both personality traits were included in the hierarchical linear regression. However, if the personality traits were correlated at higher than $r = 0.6$, the personality trait with the highest correlation to the mindfulness facet was solely used in the analysis, which was based on a recommendation by Gujarati and Porter (2009) to omit variables apriori in order to address multicollinearity concerns. Prior to running our regression analyses, we also tested for outliers and assumptions of regression. For each analysis, we obtained DFBetas, Leverage, and Studentized Deleted Residuals and evaluated them to test for leverage, discrepancy and influence of outliers. Cases were considered outliers if values for DFBetas, Leverage, and Studentized Deleted Residuals were outside of the following ranges: DFBetas ± 1, Leverage > 0.14, and Studentized Deleted Residuals ± 2.

For each personality trait that was significantly related to either baseline or post-treatment score for any facet of mindfulness, a hierarchical linear regression analysis was run with personality as the independent variable and post-treatment facet of mindfulness as the dependent variable, while controlling for baseline levels of the facet of mindfulness. Specifically, we added the baseline facet of mindfulness variable in block 1, personality facet in block 2, and post-treatment facet of mindfulness as the dependent variable. By controlling for baseline levels of the facet of mindfulness, we were able to examine if personality predicts changes in the facets of mindfulness between baseline and the last session of the intervention. Hierarchical linear regressions were used, rather than HLM as in Aim 1, given that five facet data were collected at fewer time points than SUDS use of mindfulness.

3. Results
3.1 Specific aim 1
3.1.1 Preliminary analyses
Bivariate correlation analyses were run in order to determine the relations between parent personality and parent use of mindfulness at baseline. Both parent Extroversion ($r=-0.31$) and parent Openness ($r=-0.34$) were significantly correlated with parent use of mindfulness at baseline ($ps<0.05$). Given that these were the only personality traits related to use of mindfulness, parent Extroversion and parent Openness were the only personality traits included in subsequent longitudinal analysis for Specific Aim 1. Bivariate correlations for personality traits and SUDS use of mindfulness were included in Table 3.

For each model, we examined the data for outliers and for violations of the assumptions of multilevel modeling including linearity, normality, and homoscedasticity of errors. We evaluated the data in the unconditional means model and the final model for outliers and assumptions of multilevel

Table 3 Bivariate correlations among of the Big Five personality traits and use of mindfulness during an MBSR intervention.

	1	2	3	4	5	6	7
1. BFI E	—						
2. BFI O	0.43[a]	—					
3. BFI C	0.32[a]	0.34[a]	—				
4. BFI A	0.24	0.34[a]	0.63[a]	—			
5. BFI N	0.02	−0.18	−0.40[a]	−0.52[a]	—		
6. SUDS Pre-Tx	−0.31	−0.34[a]	−0.18	−0.22	0.08	—	
7. SUDS Post-Tx	−0.11	0.16	0.14	0.05	−0.06	0.05	—

[a]$p<0.05$.
Note. BFI, Big Five personality inventory; BFI E, BFI extroversion; BFI O, BFI openness; BFI C, BFI conscientiousness; BFI A, BFI agreeableness; BFI N, BFI neuroticism; SUDS, subjective units of distress (use of mindfulneess); pre-Tx, pre-treatment; post-Tx, post-treatment.

modeling including homoscedasticity of errors, linearity, and normality. No outliers found or violations of assumptions of multilevel modeling were found.

3.1.2 Primary results

Two level multi-level modeling for longitudinal data was used to assess changes in use of mindfulness over the course of an MBSR intervention, and the effect of personality on changes in use of mindfulness. Results are presented in Table 3. The results of the unconditional means model were used to calculate the interclass correlation coefficient, which indicated that 24% of the variance in use of mindfulness was at Level 2 (individual level). Time was included as a fixed variable in the next model (Model B), and demonstrated superior fit to the unconditional means model. The unconditional growth model (Model C) was tested next, and demonstrated superior fit to Model B ($p < 0.05$). Adding Openness as a predictor of the intercept of use of mindfulness did not significantly improve model fit ($p > 0.5$), and was removed as a predictor of the intercept. Extraversion was then added as a predictor of the intercept, but also did not improve model fit, and was removed from the model ($p > 0.05$). However, allowing Openness to predict the slope at level 2 (Model D) fit the model best, as evidenced by the statistically significant decrease in the Deviance statistic ($p < 0.05$). Allowing Extroversion to predict the slope at level 2 did not improve model fit and was removed from the model ($p > 0.05$).

The average use of mindfulness at baseline for participants was 4.46 ($SD = 0.27$, $p < 0.001$). For the slope, parent use of mindfulness increased by 0.32 points per session for parents at the mean of Openness. For every one point increase in Openness, parent use of mindfulness increased by 0.11. Allowing parent use of mindfulness to vary across sessions accounted for 28% of the variance at Level 1, and allowing parent Openness to predict the rate of change in parent use of mindfulness at Level 2 accounted for 20% of the variance in the rate of change. Results for the multi-level model were included in Table 4.

3.2 Specific aim 2

3.2.1 Preliminary analyses

Bivariate correlations were used to examine the relations between parent personality traits (extroversion, agreeableness, openness, neuroticism, and conscientiousness) and the five facets of mindfulness (FFMQ; observe, describe, act with awareness, non-judgment, and non-reactivity) at baseline

Table 4 Results of fitting multilevel models for change in frequency of use of mindfulness over the course of an MBSR intervention.

		A	B	C	D (Openness)
		Est. (SE)	Est. (SE)	Est. (SE)	Est. (SE)
Initial status	Intercept	5.69[a] (0.20)	4.45[a] (0.27)	4.46[a] (0.27)	4.46[a] (0.27)
	Openness				
Rate of change	Intercept		0.32[a] (0.05)	0.32[a] (0.05)	0.32[a] (0.05)
	Openness				0.11[b] (0.04)
Variance components					
Level 1:	Within person	4.65	0.18	0.28	0.28
Level 2:	In initial status	1.43	−0.08	−0.60	−0.60
	In rate of change (slope)			0.05	0.20
Fit	Deviance	1645.20	1581.62	1573.70	1569.84

[a]$p < 0.001$.
[b]$p < 0.01$.

and post-treatment. Parent Openness was significantly related to FFMQ Observe at post-treatment ($r = 0.55$), $p < 0.05$. Parent Extroversion was significantly correlated with FFMQ Describe at baseline ($r = 0.31$) and post-treatment ($r = 0.42$), and Agreeableness was related to FFMQ Describe at post-treatment ($r = 0.33$), $ps < 0.05$. Parent Openness was significantly correlated with FFMQ Non-reactivity at post-treatment ($r = 0.42$), $ps < 0.05$. Parent Agreeableness ($r = 0.32$) and parent Conscientiousness ($r = 0.35$) were both related to FFMQ Acting with Awareness at post-treatment, $ps < 0.05$. Given that Agreeableness and Conscientiousness were intercorrelated at higher than 0.6 ($r = 0.63$), only Conscientiousness was used in the subsequent hierarchical linear regression due to concerns for multicollinearity. Conscientiousness was chosen due to being more highly correlated to FFMQ Acting with Awareness than Agreeableness. This rule was applied across all models for all aims, and no other predictors included in the same model were intercorrelated at > 0.60. Bivariate correlations between personality traits and the five facets of mindfulness at pre and post-treatment are included in Table 5.

Table 5 Correlations among the Big Five personality traits and five facets of mindfulness.

	1	2	3	4	5	6	7	8	9	10	11	12	13	14	15
1. BFI E	—														
2. BFI O	0.43^a	—													
3. BFI C	0.32^a	0.34^a	—												
4. BFI A	0.24	0.34^a	0.63^a	—											
5. BFI N	0.02	−0.18	$−0.40^a$	$−0.52^a$	—										
6. OB Pre	−0.11	0.16	0.00	−0.15	0.09	—									
7. OB Post	0.16	0.55^a	0.15	0.22	−0.04	0.40^a	—								
8. DS Pre	0.31^a	−0.01	0.00	−0.00	0.02	0.26^a	0.24	—							
9. DS Post	0.42^a	0.25	0.10	0.33^a	−0.08	0.03	0.42^a	0.64^a	—						
10. AA Pre	−0.12	−0.11	0.15	−0.04	−0.14	−0.06	−0.18	0.31^a	−0.07	—					
11. AA Post	0.01	0.11	0.35^a	0.32^a	−0.11	−0.05	0.21	0.16	0.28^a	0.52^a	—				
12. NJ Pre	−0.03	−0.08	0.02	0.04	−0.11	−0.14	−0.17	0.38^a	0.14	0.65^a	0.26	—			
13. NJ Post	0.13	0.14	0.11	0.20	−0.11	−0.03	0.18	0.31^a	0.46^a	0.29^a	0.48^a	0.61^a	—		
14. NR Pre	0.02	0.16	0.00	−0.11	−0.15	0.42^a	0.17	0.35^a	0.16	0.15	0.01	0.12	0.08	—	
15. NR Post	−0.02	0.42^a	0.13	0.14	−0.08	0.24	0.66^a	0.16	0.32^a	−0.19	0.16	−0.12	0.18	0.49^a	—

[a] $p < 0.05$.
Note. BFI, Big Five personality inventory; BFI E, BFI extroversion; BFI O, BFI openness; BFI C, BFI conscientiousness; BFI A, BFI agreeableness; BFI N, BFI neuroticism; pre/post, pre-treatment/post-treatment; OB, Observe; DS, describe; AA, acting with awareness; NJ, non-judgment; NR, non-reactivity.

Parent personality and MBSR   151

In order to evaluate for outliers, DfBetas, Leverage, and Studentized Deleted Residuals were saved and evaluated for each of the four regression analyses. For the analysis with parent Openness predicting changes in Observe, two outliers were found based on studentized residual scores >0.14 and by examining the residual plot using studentized deleted residuals. Two participants were deleted from this analysis. No other outliers or additional violations of the assumptions of regression were found in any of the other hierarchical linear regression analyses.

3.2.2 Primary analyses

In order to examine if personality traits predicted changes in five facets of mindfulness between baseline and post-treatment of the intervention, we ran four hierarchical linear regression analyses. Parent Openness significantly predicted FFMQ Observe, such that as parent Openness increased by one point, Observe increased by 3.50 ($p < 0.05$, $sr^2 = 0.25$). Conscientiousness significantly predicted FFMQ Acting with Awareness $p < 0.05$. Specifically, as parent Conscientiousness increased by one point, parent FFMQ Acting with Awareness increased by 2.21 points, 95% CI $= [0.01, 4.4]$, $sr^2 = 0.08$, $p < 0.05$. Parent Openness significantly predicted FFMQ Non-reactivity, such that as Openness increased by 1, FFMQ Non-reactivity increased by 2.40, ($p < 0.05$, $sr^2 = 0.18$). Neither parent Extroversion or Agreeableness significantly predicted FFMQ Describe, $p > 0.05$. Results of the hierarchical linear regression analyses are presented in Tables 6–9.

Table 6 Hierarchical linear regression predicting week 8 observe from openness.

	ΔR^2	β	b (SE)	95% CI	sr^2
Step 1	0.215[a]				
Baseline OB		0.464	0.442 (0.133)	[0.173, 0.712]	0.215
Step 2	0.246[a]				
Baseline OB		0.333	0.317 (0.116)	[0.083, 0.551]	0.103
Openness		0.513	3.50 (0.828)	[1.825, 5.175]	0.246

[a]$p < 0.01$.
Note. Openness, openness subscale on BFI; OB, Observe on the FFMQ.

Table 7 Hierarchical linear regression predicting week 8 acting with awareness from conscientiousness.

	ΔR^2	β	b (SE)	95% CI	sr^2
Step 1	0.172[a]				
Baseline AA		0.415	0.332 (0.133)	[0.105, 0.560]	0.172
Step 2	0.075[b]				
Baseline AA		0.363	0.291 (0.111)	[0.067, 0.514]	0.127
Conscientiousness		0.280	2.21 (1.088)	[0.008, 4.401]	0.075

[a]$p<0.01$.
[b]$p<0.05$.
Note. Conscientiousness, conscientiousness subscale on BFI; AA, acting with awareness on the FFMQ.

Table 8 Hierarchical linear regression predicting week 8 non-reactivity from openness.

	ΔR^2	β	b (SE)	95% CI	sr^2
Step 1	0.109[a]				
Baseline NR		0.330	0.426 (0.188)	[0.047, 0.806]	0.109
Step 2	0.150[a]				
Baseline NR		0.287	0.371 (0.175)	[0.018, 0.723]	0.081
Openness		0.389	2.537 (0.881)	[0.757, 4.316]	0.150

[a]$p<0.05$.
Note. Openness, Openness subscale on BFI; NR, Non-reactivity subscale on the FFMQ.

Table 9 Hierarchical linear regression predicting week 8 describe from extroversion and agreeableness.

	ΔR^2	β	b (SE)	95% CI	sr^2
Step 1	0.221[a]				
Baseline DS		0.470	0.523 (0.152)	[0.217, 0.829]	0.221
Step 2	0.127[b]				
Baseline DS		0.383	0.427 (0.151)	[0.121, 0.732]	0.130
Extroversion		0.215	1.290 (0.868)	[−0.464, 3.045]	0.036
Agreeableness		0.231	2.150 (1.268)	[−0.413, 4.712]	0.047

[a]$p<0.01$.
[b]$p<0.05$.
Note. Extroversion, Extroversion subscale on BFI; Agreeableness, Agreeableness subscale on BFI; DS, Describe subscale on the FFMQ.

4. Discussion

Research has shown that parents of children with DD who participate in MBSR interventions have significant reductions in stress post intervention (Neece, 2014). However, there is very little research on individual factors that impact how parents learn mindfulness skills over the course or the intervention and how often they utilize these skills. Given the high rates of stress evident in parents of children with DD (Baker et al., 2002), a better understanding of individual level factors that may impact who learns mindfulness will help to tailor future interventions. The current study was exploratory in nature given the dearth of literature on the relationship between personality and mindfulness in parents of children with DD, and highlighted personality as an important factor in how parents use mindfulness and acquire mindfulness facets over time. Specifically, for Aim 1 we found that both Extraversion and Openness were related to use of mindfulness at baseline, but that Openness was the only personality trait that predicted increases in use of mindfulness over the course of the intervention. For Aim 2, we found that Openness predicted increases in both Observe and Nonreactivity facets from baseline to post-treatment. Additionally, we found that Conscientiousness predicted increases in Acting with Awareness from baseline to post-treatment.

Our first aim addressed how personality impacts the trajectory of use of mindfulness over the course of an MBSR intervention. Parents' report of mindfulness use did significantly increase over the course of the intervention, which is consistent with previous research regarding MBSR interventions in various samples (de Vibe et al., 2015; Roberts & Neece, 2015). While parent Extroversion and Openness were both related to use of mindfulness at baseline, Openness was the only personality trait related to the trajectory of changes in parent's use of mindfulness. Individuals high in the openness trait are often more curious and creative, and may be more open to trying new skills (Barrick, Mount, & Judge, 2001). Some research has suggested that openness may be a particularly salient personality trait for MBSR (Latzman & Masuda, 2013), given that MBSR teaches skills and a way of thinking that is very unique and novel for most individuals. MBSR introduces a variety of skills over the course of the intervention, and it is possible that parents who are more open will continue to be willing to attempt new skills, which will add to their repertoire of mindfulness activities and increase use of mindfulness over the course of the intervention.

Openness is potentially an especially important trait for parents in the current study, given that many families likely participated due to interest in stress reduction and strategies to reduce child behavior, and may have been less informed regarding mindfulness. It is also possible that parents involved in the study are inherently more open to experiences given that the sample is treatment seeking. Regarding extroversion, it is possible that parents seeking a group intervention may also be inherently more extroverted, which may be why extroversion predicts use of mindfulness at baseline. However, given that mindfulness tends to be a more personal, introspective practice (Chambers, Gullone, & Allen, 2009), extroversion may have less to do with the trajectory of how parents learn mindfulness or how their use of mindfulness increases over time. Given that use of mindfulness increased over time, we would also predict that parent's specific facets of mindfulness would increase over the course of the intervention.

For Aim 2, we examined the relations between personality traits (Extroversion, Openness, Neuroticism, Conscientiousness, and Agreeableness) and changes in the five facets of mindfulness (Observe, Describe, Non-judgment, Non-reactivity, and Acting with Awareness) over the course of an MBSR intervention. Research has shown that specific facets of mindfulness increase over the course of an MBSR intervention for parents of children with DD (Roberts & Neece, 2015), but to our knowledge, there is no research addressing individual factors that impact increases in these facets. Specifically, we found that Conscientiousness and Openness were important predictors of changes in several of the five facets of mindfulness.

While findings regarding conscientiousness are mixed in the mindfulness literature (de Vibe et al., 2015; Jagielski et al., 2020), we found that increases in parent Conscientiousness significantly predicted increases in Acting with Awareness from pre to post MBSR intervention. Children with DD often display increased behavioral concerns (Baker et al., 2003; Neece et al., 2012) and are often much less independent throughout their lives in comparison to their TD peers (Kao, Kramer, Liljenquist, Tian, & Coster, 2012). As a result, parents of children with DD have to be diligent and often hypervigilant in the everyday care of their child, including advocating for services and participating in behavioral therapies for their child. Additionally, in order to respond appropriately to child needs and behavioral concerns, parents need to be aware of their child's needs and act accordingly. Individuals with high levels of conscientiousness are typically highly responsible, dependable, and rule-following (Barrick et al., 2001), which may make managing the needs of a child with DD more accessible. Given this, conscientiousness is likely a salient personality trait for parents of children with DD, and acting with awareness may be an especially important facet for parents of children with DD. When managing challenging behaviors, additional factors such as observing and non-reactivity may also be especially salient facets of mindfulness for parents of children with DD, given that more harsh or negative parenting behaviors occur when parents are more reactive (Niehaus, Chaplin, Turpyn, & Gonçalves, 2019).

Consistent with prior mindfulness research, we found that parent Openness was related to increases in mindful facets (Spinhoven et al., 2017; van den Hurk et al., 2011). Specifically, increased parent Openness predicted increases in both the Non-reactivity and Observe facets. Given that our study found that Openness predicted increases in use of mindfulness over the course of the study, it makes sense that Openness would also be related to increases in specific facets of mindfulness. Often higher levels of stress are associated with individuals reacting emotionally (stress reaction) to difficult situations, rather than being aware and choosing how to respond (stress response; Kabat-Zinn, 1990). For parents, this could mean reacting emotionally to negative child behavior without observing and paying attention to the function of a child's behaviors. In evidenced-based behavioral treatments, parents are taught that to eradicate negative child behavior, you first have to understand what is reinforcing the behavior (Webster-Stratton, 2001). Observing is likely a very important facet for parents of children with DD, as parents high in observing may be more able to be more actively aware of what their children are doing and respond in a way that is less reactive. Given that emotional reactivity in parenting is associated with more harsh or maladaptive parenting strategies (Niehaus et al., 2019), this facet is likely a very salient facet for parents of children with DD. As previously discussed, individuals high in openness tend to be more willing to engage in new activities (Barrick et al., 2001). Having higher levels of openness may help parents to be more willing to engage in new, mindful ways of thinking, thus improving facets such as observing and non-reactivity that may be salient for parenting a child with DD.

While literature consistently links neuroticism to stress outcomes from MBSR (Jagielski et al., 2020; Spinhoven et al., 2017; van den Hurk et al., 2011), less research has examined if neuroticism is related to changes in parents' use of mindfulness. For parents of children with DD, their high level of stress is chronic, beginning in the early years of the child's life and often increasing over the course of their child's life (Miodrag & Hodapp,

2010). Parents may learn to cope with their stress, but the stressor itself is stable. Neuroticism as a personality trait is often highly correlated with stress (Lahey, 2009). Thus, it is possible that given the chronic and stable nature of this parenting stress in the context of parenting a child with DD, parent neuroticism is less salient in how it affects how parents learn mindfulness or acquire any of the five facets of mindfulness.

4.1 Limitations

These results must be considered within the context of several study limitations. First and foremost, the current study utilized only self-report measures, which may be subject to bias. Future studies may benefit from utilizing more standardized measures of assessing personality such as the Minnesota Multiphasic Personality Inventory Second Edition (MMPI-2; Graham, 1993), which is not as subject to personal biases. Regarding measures of mindfulness, future studies may benefit from utilizing daily diaries which allow parents to track their daily mindfulness use, as well as observational measures, and corroborating reports from friends or family members.

Regarding statistical limitations, one possible limitation in the current study is our relatively small sample size in relation to the number of analyses run. Given that we ran four hierarchical linear regressions, as well as a multilevel model, there is a possibility of increased Type 2 error. Additionally, given the relatively high correlation between the Conscientiousness and Agreeableness trait ($r=0.63$), we chose to only include Conscientiousness as a predictor of Acting with Awareness in order to address potential multicollinearity. While removing Agreeableness does address multicollinearity concerns apriori, it is possible that there is some model specification bias as a result (Gujarati & Porter, 2009).

Another possible limitation to the current study is that we recruited primary caregivers of children with DD and our sample primarily consisted of female parents (96%). While it is common to have primarily mothers participate in parenting interventions, it is possible that we may have potentially missed certain gender effects on our findings. Some studies have found that different personality traits such as neuroticism and conscientiousness were more common in females than males and that there were differential effects of some personality on stress outcomes following MBSR for females versus males (de Vibe et al., 2015). Given these findings, it is possible that there are also different effects of gender when considering how a parent learns mindfulness. Future research may benefit from recruiting parents of various genders to better understand if there are gender differences in how certain personality traits relate to the use of mindfulness.

Lastly, while we did measure use of mindfulness weekly, at nine time points over the course of the MBSR intervention, which is a potential strength of the study, we only looked at five facets of data at baseline and post-MBSR treatment. Measuring changes in five facets at an increased number of time points across the intervention would allow us to track non-linear changes in the five facets, as well as within-person changes over time, which is a limitation of the current study. It is also possible that personality traits may impact continued use and retention of mindfulness skills and facets of mindfulness following the intervention, and future studies may benefit by utilizing follow-up data. However, despite these limitations we still believe that our findings are important for future studies targeting this vulnerable population.

4.2 Clinical implications and future directions

Overall, our results highlight openness and conscientiousness as particularly salient personality traits for parents of children with DD learning mindfulness in the context of an MBSR intervention. Specifically, our findings show that increases in parents' Openness predicts increased use of mindfulness, and more Openness and Conscientiousness lead to increases in individual facets of mindfulness including Observing, Non-reactivity, and Acting with Awareness. Knowing that Openness may contribute to how much parents increase in their use of mindfulness, as well as increases in Observing and Non-reactivity may help to inform clinical interventions. Clinically, if we know that an individual is lower in openness, they may be less willing to try new and novel mindfulness skills. Implementing interventions such as Motivational Interviewing prior to MBSR, which has been shown to improve commitment and motivation to change behaviors (Miller & Rollnick, 2013), may also improve parent's openness and willingness to engage in novel experiences. This increase in openness may also improve parent outcomes in intervention. Further, for clinicians, a greater understanding of client personality traits that may contribute to improvements in treatment may help to inform interventions, and prepare clinicians to adapt treatments in order to better serve clients.

Given the high rates of stress in parents of children with DD (Abbeduto et al., 1999; Baker et al., 2002), a greater understanding of individual factors that may contribute to reductions in stress outcomes in this vulnerable population is crucial. The current study highlighted Openness and Conscientiousness as important personality traits for the learning of mindfulness for parents of children with DD, which may help to inform future intervention research. By identifying personality factors that may impact participation in future interventions, researchers and clinicians can anticipate who may benefit from MBSR and provide appropriate support to those who may be less likely to engage.

Conflict of interest

The authors declare that they have no conflict of interest.

References

Abbeduto, L., Weissman, M. D., & Short-Meyerson, K. (1999). Parental scaffolding of the discourse of children and adolescents with intellectual disability: The case of, referential expressions. *Journal of Intellectual Disability Research, 43*(December), 540–557.

Baer, R. A., Smith, G. T., & Allen, K. B. (2004). Assessment of mindfulness by self-report: The Kentucky inventory of mindfulness skills. *Assessment, 11*(3), 191–206.

Baer, R. A., Smith, G. T., Hopkins, J., Krietemeyer, J., & Toney, L. (2006). Using self-report assessment methods to explore facets of mindfulness. *Assessment, 13*, 27–45.

Baker, B. L., Blacher, J., Crnic, K., & Edelbrock, C. (2002). Behavior problems and parenting stress in families of three-year-old children with and without DD. *American Journal on Mental Retardation, 107*, 433–444.

Baker, B. L., McIntyre, L. L., Blacher, J., Crnic, K., Edelbrock, C., & Low, C. (2003). Preschool children with and without developmental delay: Behaviour problems and parenting stress over time. *Journal of Intellectual Disability Research, 47*(4), 217–230.

Baker, B. L., Neece, C. L., Fenning, R., Crnic, K. A., & Blacher, J. (2010). Mental disorders in five-year-old children with or without intellectual disability: Focus on ADHD. *Journal of Child Clinical and Adolescent Psychology, 49*, 492–505.

Barkan, T., Hoerger, M., Gallegos, A. M., Turiano, N. A., Duberstein, P. R., & Moynihan, J. A. (2016). Personality predicts utilization of mindfulness-based stress reduction during and post-intervention in a community sample of older adults. *The Journal of Alternative and Complementary Medicine, 22*(5), 390–395.

Barrick, M. R., Mount, M. K., & Judge, T. A. (2001). Personality and performance at the beginning of the new millennium: What do we know and where do we go next? *International Journal of Selection and Assessment, 9*(1–2), 9–30.

Bazzano, A., Wolfe, C., Zylowska, L., Wang, S., Schuster, E., Barrett, C., et al. (2015). Mindfulness based stress reduction (MBSR) for parents and caregivers of individuals with developmental disabilities: A community-based approach. *Journal of Child and Family Studies, 24*(2), 298–308.

Beer, M., Ward, L., & Moar, K. (2013). The relationship between mindful parenting and distress in parents of children with an autism spectrum disorder. *Mindfulness, 4*(2), 102–112.

Brown, D. B., Bravo, A. J., Roos, C. R., & Pearson, M. R. (2015). Five facets of mindfulness and psychological health: Evaluating a psychological model of the mechanisms of mindfulness. *Mindfulness, 6*(5), 1021–1032.

Brown, K. W., & Ryan, R. M. (2003). The benefits of being present: Mindfulness and its role in psychological well-being. *Journal of Personality and Social Psychology, 84*, 822–848.

Bullis, J. R., Bøe, H. J., Asnaani, A., & Hofmann, S. G. (2014). The benefits of being mindful: Trait mindfulness predicts less stress reactivity to suppression. *Journal of Behavior Therapy and Experimental Psychiatry*, *45*(1), 57–66.

Carmody, J., & Baer, R. A. (2008). Relationships between mindfulness practice and levels of mindfulness, medical and psychological symptoms and well-being in a mindfulness-based stress reduction program. *Journal of Behavioral Medicine*, *31*(1), 23–33.

Cash, M., & Whittingham, K. (2010). What facets of mindfulness contribute to psychological well-being and depressive, anxious, and stress-related symptomatology? *Mindfulness*, *1*(3), 177–182.

Chambers, R., Gullone, E., & Allen, N. B. (2009). Mindful emotion regulation: An integrative review. *Clinical Psychology Review*, *29*(6), 560–572.

Chan, N., & Neece, C. L. (2018). Parenting stress and emotion dysregulation among children with developmental delays: The role of parenting behaviors. *Journal of Child and Family Studies*, *27*(12), 4071–4082.

Corthorn, C. (2018). Benefits of mindfulness for parenting in mothers of preschoolers in Chile. *Frontiers in Psychology*, *9*, 1443.

Crnic, K. A., Gaze, C., & Hoffman, C. (2005). Cumulative parenting stress across the preschool period: Relations to maternal parenting and child behaviours at age 5. *Infant and Child Development*, *11*(2), 201–209.

de Vibe, M., Solhaug, I., Tyssen, R., Friborg, O., Rosenvinge, J. H., Sørlie, T., et al. (2015). Does personality moderate the effects of mindfulness training for medical and psychology students? *Mindfulness*, *6*(2), 281–289.

Feldman, M., McDonald, L., Serbin, L., Stack, D., Secco, M. L., & Yu, C. T. (2007). Predictors of depressive symptoms in primary caregivers of young children with or at risk for developmental delay. *Journal of Intellectual Disability Research*, *51*(8), 606–619.

Feltman, R., Robinson, M. D., & Ode, S. (2009). Mindfulness as a moderator of neuroticism–outcome relations: A self-regulation perspective. *Journal of Research in Personality*, *43*(6), 953–961.

Gerstein, E. D., Crnic, K. A., Blacher, J., & Baker, B. L. (2009). Resilience and the course of daily parenting stress in families of young children with intellectual disabilities. *Journal of Intellectual Disability Research*, *53*(12), 981–997.

Giluk, T. L. (2009). Mindfulness, big five personality, and affect: A meta-analysis. *Personality and Individual Differences*, *47*(8), 805–811.

Graham, J. R. (1993). *MMPI-2: Assessing personality and psychopathology*. New York: Oxford University Press.

Grossman, P., Niemann, L., Schmidt, S., & Walach, H. (2004). Mindfulness-based stress reduction and health benefits: A meta-analysis. *Journal of Psychosomatic Research*, *57*(1), 35–43.

Gujarati, D. N., & Porter, D. C. (2009). *Basic econometrics* (5th ed.). McGraw-Hill Irwin.

Han, Z. R., Ahemaitijiang, N., Yan, J., Hu, X., Parent, J., Dale, C., et al. (2019). Parent mindfulness, parenting, and child psychopathology in China. *Mindfulness*, *3*, 1–10. https://doi.org/10.1007/s12671-019-01111-z.

Hastings, R. P., Daley, D., Burns, C., & Beck, A. (2006). Maternal distress and expressed emotion: Cross-sectional and longitudinal relationships with behavior problems of children with intellectual disabilities. *American Journal of Mental Retardation*, *111*(1), 48–61.

Jagielski, C. H., Tucker, D. C., Dalton, S. O., Mrug, S., Würtzen, H., & Johansen, C. (2020). Personality as a predictor of well-being in a randomized trial of a mindfulness-based stress reduction of Danish women with breast cancer. *Journal of Psychosocial Oncology*, *38*(1), 4–19.

John, O. P., & Srivastava, S. (1999). The big five trait taxonomy: History, measurement, and theoretical perspectives. In L. A. Pervin, & O. P. John (Eds.), *Handbook of personality theory and research* (pp. 102–138). New York: Guilford Press.

Johnson, N., Frenn, M., Feetham, S., & Simpson, P. (2011). Autism spectrum disorder: Parenting stress, family functioning and health-related quality of life. *Families, Systems & Health, 29*(3), 232–252.

Kabat-Zinn, J. (1990). *Full catastrophe living: The program of the stress reduction clinic at the University of Massachusetts Medical Center.* New York: Delta.

Kao, Y. C., Kramer, J. M., Liljenquist, K., Tian, F., & Coster, W. J. (2012). Comparing the functional performance of children and youths with autism, developmental disabilities, and no disability using the revised pediatric evaluation of disability inventory item banks. *American Journal of Occupational Therapy, 66*(5), 607–616.

Lahey, B. B. (2009). Public health significance of neuroticism. *The American Psychologist, 64*(4), 241–256.

Latzman, R. D., & Masuda, A. (2013). Examining mindfulness and psychological inflexibility within the framework of Big Five personality. *Personality and Individual Differences, 55*(2), 129–134.

McCrae, R. R., & Costa, P. T., Jr. (2013). Introduction to the empirical and theoretical status of the five-factor model of personality traits. In T. A. Widiger, & P. T. Costa Jr., (Eds.), *Personality disorders and the five-factor model of personality* (pp. 15–27). American Psychological Association.

Miller, W. R., & Rollnick, S. (2013). *Motivational interviewing: Helping people change.* The Guilford Press.

Miodrag, N., & Hodapp, R. M. (2010). Chronic stress and health among parents of children with intellectual and developmental disabilities. *Current Opinion in Psychiatry, 23*(5), 407–411.

Neece, C. L. (2014). Mindfulness-based stress reduction for parents of young children with developmental delays: Implications for parental mental health and child behavior problems. *Journal of Applied Research in Intellectual Disabilities, 27*, 174–186.

Neece, C. L., Green, S. A., & Baker, B. L. (2012). Parenting stress and child behavior problems: A transactional relationship across time. *American Journal on Intellectual and Developmental Disabilities, 117*(1), 48–66.

Niehaus, C. E., Chaplin, T. M., Turpyn, C. C., & Gonçalves, S. F. (2019). Maternal emotional and physiological reactivity: Implications for parenting and the parenting-adolescent relationship. *Journal of Child and Family Studies, 28*, 872–883.

Nyklíček, I., & Irrmischer, M. (2017). For whom does mindfulness-based stress reduction work? Moderating effects of personality. *Mindfulness, 8*(4), 1106–1116.

Orsmond, G. I., Seltzer, M. M., Krauss, M. W., & Hong, J. (2003). Behavior problems in adults with mental retardation and maternal well-being: Examination of the direction of effects. *American Journal on Mental Retardation, 108*, 257–271.

Roberts, L. R., & Neece, C. L. (2015). Feasibility of mindfulness-based stress reduction intervention for parents of children with developmental delays. *Issues in Mental Health Nursing, 36*(8), 592–602.

Robinson, E. A., Eyberg, S. M., & Ross, A. W. (1980). The standardization of an inventory of child conduct problem behaviors. *Journal of Clinical Child & Adolescent Psychology, 9*(1), 22–28.

Sanner, C. M., & Neece, C. L. (2017). Parental distress and child behavior problems: Parenting behaviors as mediators. *Journal of Child and Family Studies, 27*(2), 591–601. https://doi.org/10.1007/s10826-017-0884-4.

Shapiro, S. L., Carlson, L. E., Astin, J. A., & Freedman, B. (2006). Mechanisms of mindfulness. *Journal of Clinical Psychology, 62*(3), 373–386.

Singer, J. D., & Willett, J. B. (2003). *Applied longitudinal data analysis: Modeling change and event occurrence.* Oxford University Press.

Singh, N. N., Lancioni, G. E., Winton, A. S., Singh, J., Curtis, W. J., Wahler, R. G., et al. (2007). Mindful parenting decreases aggression and increases social behavior in children with developmental disabilities. *Behavior Modification, 31*(6), 749–771.

Spinhoven, P., Huijbers, M. J., Zheng, Y., Ormel, J., & Speckens, A. E. M. (2017). Mindfulness facets and Big Five personality facets in persons with recurrent depression in remission. *Personality and Individual Differences, 110*, 109–114.

van den Hurk, P. A. M., Wingens, T., Giommi, F., Barendregt, H. P., Speckens, A. E. M., & van Schie, H. T. (2011). On the relationship between the practice of mindfulness meditation and personality—An exploratory analysis of the mediating role of mindfulness skills. *Mindfulness, 2*(3), 194–200.

Webster-Stratton, C. (2001). *The incredible years: Parents, teachers, and children training series, leader's guide.* Seattle, WA: Author.

CHAPTER SIX

A public health approach to family supports: Empowering families of children with autism through the ECHO model

Eric J. Moody[a,*], Haley A. Sturges[b], Sarah Zlatkovic[a], Ethan Dahl[a], Sandra Root-Elledge[a], and Canyon Hardesty[a]

[a]Wyoming Institute for Disabilities, University of Wyoming, Laramie, WY, United States
[b]Department of Psychology, University of Wyoming, Laramie, WY, United States
*Corresponding author: e-mail address: eric.moody@uwyo.edu

Contents

1. The public health approach to supporting families of children with ASD   169
2. Raising a child with ASD and family well-being   171
3. Public health programs for families of children with ASD   175
4. The problem of scaling up family support programs and the unique approach of ECHO for families   178
5. Conclusion   185

Acknowledgments   186

References   187

Abstract

Children with autism spectrum disorder (ASD) often receive many direct services designed to improve their clinical outcomes. Indeed, direct service provision is critical to helping those with ASD reach their fullest potential. However, this approach often ignores the contextual factors that are likely to impact the effectiveness of those interventions. Given that a majority of the US health care system is not designed to support families, we argue (1) for taking a public health approach to supporting families and (2) that this will ultimately improve child outcomes. We use the Bioecological Theory of Human Development (Bronfenbrenner & Morris, 1998) as a model of how families, who are often responsible for coordinating care, providing in-home and long-term supports, and coordinating the services a child receives, should receive additional support. We use family well-being to frame the public health problem and review several family support programs. In particular, we use an innovative program, ECHO for Families, as an example of how families can be empowered to support their children, and how this improves family well-being. Additionally, we describe the importance of scaling up family support programs and how the ECHO for Families has been able to meet the unique

International Review of Research in Developmental Disabilities, Volume 59
ISSN 2211-6095
https://doi.org/10.1016/bs.irrdd.2020.07.006

© 2020 Elsevier Inc.
All rights reserved.

163

needs of a vast frontier state with limited resources. Finally, we argue that conceptualizing family supports as a matter of public health may lead to novel funding mechanisms that could improve well-being of the whole family, as well as improve outcomes for children with ASD.

The prevalence of autism spectrum disorder (ASD) has increased dramatically over the last several decades (Baio, 2012; Baio et al., 2018; Christensen et al., 2016; Maenner et al., 2020; Rice et al., 2010), resulting in significant public health burden. In fact, the projected annual cost of care for those with ASD is expected to reach $461 billion in the United States alone (Hurley-Hanson, Giannantonio, & Griffiths, 2020). As a result, it is only natural that there has been tremendous interest in creating effective clinical interventions to improve the developmental trajectories of those affected by ASD (e.g., Coren, Ramsbotham, & Gschwandtner, 2018; Reichow, Barton, Boyd, & Hume, 2012; Reichow & Wolery, 2009). While the evidence base for many interventions continues to grow, virtually all clinical approaches to ASD have an individual child-focused approach. That is, most services are offered directly to children who have ASD. Indeed, this direct-service approach is common across a wide range of clinical disciplines including behavioral supports, occupational and physical therapy, speech-language pathology and medicine. Even multi-tiered systems of support offered through educational systems ultimately result in direct service provision (Jimerson, Burns, & VanDerHeyden, 2015).

The direct-service approach makes perfect sense given that the goal of clinical interventions is to improve specific behaviors, functioning, or other clinical presentations of the child. Even the structure of the US healthcare system is set up to focus primarily on individual children and their clinical presentation. For example, clinicians are trained to assess and treat specific clinical problems directly, our reimbursement systems (e.g., Medicaid, private insurance) pay for treatments that will improve the child's functioning when administered directly, and parents are generally eager for their children to receive as many services as possible. While direct services are critical to improving child outcomes, this focus means that other contextual factors that may impact the child and family[a] functioning are largely not a target of intervention. Contextual factors could include a wide range of social

---

[a] Note that we use the term "family" in a broad sense. This can include biological, adoptive step or foster parents, extended family, legal guardians and other important individuals that are responsible for the day to day care of a child.

systems, including school systems, healthcare systems, including both payer and practice, family employment and job security, and overall family dynamics.

While not often the target of intervention, contextual factors can have an indirect impact on children with ASD. For example, if a parent of a child with ASD is extremely concerned about the family's financial well-being due to the burden of paying for the child's treatment, this may cause the parent to take on an exceedingly large workload or a second job with the hope of increasing the family's income. Ironically, if the added workload causes the parent to focus less attention on core job-duties this could ultimately hurt the parent's overall job performance. If this leads to disciplinary action or termination, this could then negatively impact the child, even though the child has no direct exposure to those more distal systems (i.e., the parent's work environment). Further, working more might also limit the amount of time the parent has with the child at home, further reducing the amount of support the parent can provide the child to improve behaviors or functioning. Thus, it is crucial to consider how broader social systems might impact a child's development and ultimately their clinical outcomes.

Bronfenbrenner's Bioecological Theory of Human Development (Bronfenbrenner, 1977, 1979; Bronfenbrenner & Morris, 1998) provides a useful framework for conceptualizing how contextual factors impact the outcomes of children with ASD. Although, the theory underwent substantial revision up to Bronfenbrenner's death (Tudge, Mokrova, Hatfield, & Karnik, 2009), all versions of this theory point out that children exist within increasingly complex systems that influence the development of the child (Bronfenbrenner & Morris, 1998). Like layers of an onion, larger, more complex, and broader contextual systems build on the smaller and more intimate systems (see Fig. 1). Importantly, there are constant interactions between and within these contextual systems (Bronfenbrenner & Morris, 1998). The smallest unit of influence of these systems is called the microsystem, followed by the meso, exo and macrosystems. Given that the microsystem is the most proximal system to the child, it is the primary focus of this paper; although, broader systems can have important effects as well.

A large number of social structures are included at the microsystem level, including schools, caregivers, friends, and others that interact with each other and the child. Given the proximity of the microsystem to the child, the social structures within this system are particularly important to child development. That is, the more proximal a system is to a child, the more

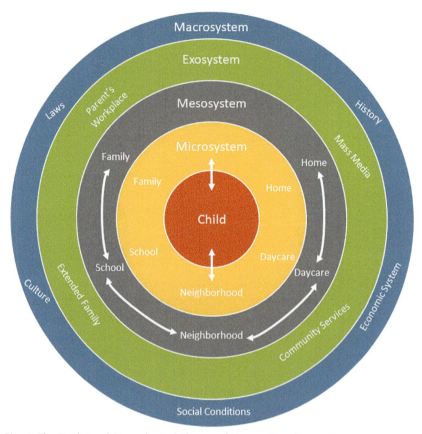

Fig. 1 The Traditional Bioecological Theory of Human Development.

that the processes that derive from those social structures are likely to impact the child's development (Tudge et al., 2009). In most versions of this theory, the family system is on par with other systems in the microsystem. For instance, families are put on equal footing with schools, and other microsystems as depicted in Fig. 1. However, we argue that given the importance of proximal processes (Tudge et al., 2009), the family system should be considered as a critical component of the microsystem, especially for younger children. In particular, the family is the system in which the child spends the most time, and the family often mediates the child's interactions with other microsystems. Therefore, it is the most proximal social structure of all microsystems. For example, parents coordinate the child's schooling, healthcare, and community interactions. They put the child to bed, help brush teeth, cook meals, play with and comfort the child. These are roles that other structures in the microsystem cannot replace. Therefore, the family system plays a disproportionately large role in the development of children relative to other social structures in the microsystem.

Given this, we suggest that families play a unique role within the microsystem. That is, instead of being equivalent to all other social structures in the microsystems, we argue that family systems should be placed in the most proximal position to the child (see Fig. 2). That is, family systems are often the most proximal of all microsystems to the child and therefore play a mediating role between the child and other microsystem structures. Indeed, families are given a privileged place in many legal systems (e.g., the American legal system usually argues that the best interests of children is to remain with their parents, Elrod & Dale, 2008; "Meyer v Nebraska,"

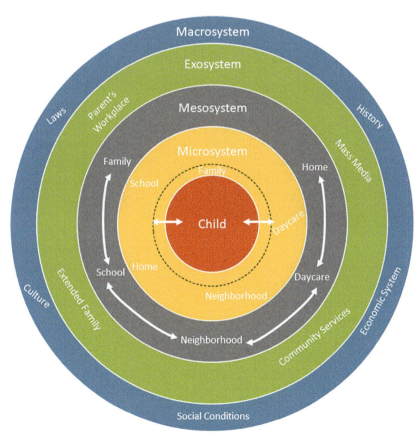

Fig. 2 The Bioecological Theory of Human Development with families situated most proximally to the child.

1923) highlighting the exceptional importance that families play in the lives of children. For example, parents must work with all the other microsystems, whether healthcare providers, educators, or community groups, to mediate the broader impact of the microsystem on their children. Hence, parents are almost always expected to play an exceptionally proximal role in their children's lives.

Despite the critical importance of families in children's development, our healthcare system generally focuses directly on the child rather than any system surrounding the child. Certainly, some disciplines (e.g., social work; education systems) place a greater importance on families and other microsystems, and parent-training can be a valued enhancement to existing behavioral interventions (Minjarez, Karp, Stahmer, & Brookman-Frazee, 2020; Turner-Brown, Hume, Boyd, & Kainz, 2019). For instance, the Early Start Denver Model (Rogers & Dawson, 2010) trains parents to provide supports for the child that are similar to what the clinician does, but it does not try to directly improve family functioning, family stress levels, work-life balance, or any other microsystems that provide a critical context for the child's overall development. Despite this, families of children with ASD often report that they receive little support that is designed to improve their functioning (Vohra, Madhavan, Sambamoorthi, & St Peter, 2014) and this may lead to lower levels of family functioning overall (e.g., Higgins, Bailey, & Pearce, 2005). Further, because the child's development is embedded within increasingly complex contextual environments that all interact, completely ignoring the child's family system comes with some peril. For example, consider the ambiguity parents of children with ASD must navigate. While the evidence base of effective interventions is growing, there is still relatively weak evidence to support any singular treatment (Reichow et al., 2012, updated in 2016), and each child's individual response to treatment is difficult to predict (Warren et al., 2011). Certainly, clinicians will provide recommendations that are consistent with their discipline (e.g., Stansberry-Brusnahan & Collet-Klingenberg, 2010); however, this is not a standard of care, nor is this recommendation appropriate for all children (Mottron, 2017). Moreover, there is little consensus on what treatments are most effective (Warren et al., 2011; Weitlauf et al., 2014). This means that families of children with ASD must search for the treatment(s) that will work best for their child. As a result, the average number of interventions tried per family is seven to nine (Goin-Kochel, Myers, & Mackintosh, 2007), suggesting that parents are often not satisfied with their child's progress. Moreover, there are often residual symptoms that affect their functioning even after intervention (Warren et al., 2011). With very little information on which approach is most likely to lead to a specific outcome, parents may never know when their child's development has reached its full potential. Further, this leads to parents trying numerous interventions that may be costly and time consuming. Therefore, with little direct support to the family it is not surprising that parents often report extremely high levels of stress that can ultimately impact their own health and well-being, as well as the well-being of their children with ASD.

Certainly, direct clinical support for the child continues to be critical to ensure that every child develops to his or her full potential, which will subsequently reduce the overall public health burden of ASD (e.g., lifetime cost of care, reduced health and well-being). However, ignoring the child's microsystems has the potential to negatively impact family functioning, and thereby hinder the goals of direct clinical interventions as well. Unfortunately, there is little ability for direct clinical services to devote significant resources to anything other than the child. For this reason, we advocate for a comprehensive public health approach to family supports. That is, rather than thinking of family supports as a clinical service, either as an add-on to the child's treatment or in its own right, we should consider supporting families with children with ASD as a matter of public health. This approach advocates for a systems level and iterative approach to program implementation that impacts microsystems that support the child, especially the family. As with all public health approaches, the goal is not to supplant more clinically driven services, but rather to create environments that are conducive to optimal health outcomes. In this case, public health programs promote family well-being through community-based programs which target risk and protective factors to create environments that allow the family to better support their children with ASD. This approach, combined with high-quality clinical care, has the potential to create more empowered and resilient families that are better equipped to support their child's developmental trajectory.

1. The public health approach to supporting families of children with ASD

The discipline of public health is generally concerned with promoting the health and well-being of communities, rather than direct intervention at an individual level (Frieden, 2010). This goal is achieved by reducing population exposures to factors that are known to make diseases or conditions more likely (risk factors) and increasing the prevalence of factors that are known to protect populations from specific conditions (protective factors; Coie et al., 1993). As these interventions are targeted at communities, public health interventions primarily operate in the micro, meso, and exo system levels to reduce exposure to risk factors and enhance exposure to protective factors. Importantly, because the public health approach focuses on larger systems, it is perfectly acceptable to engage with numerous societal organizations such as education, community living systems, and other non-governmental organizations to improve exposure to risk factors. For example, a program that tries to improve the health of children who have inadequate food security could work through school systems to reduce the cost of school lunches (microsystem). A program targeting the mesosystem might include neighborhood food pantries that provide access to food in areas that have few grocery stores. Here we focus primarily on the microsystem given it is most proximal to the child and the family is part of that system.

Most public health programs are developed through some sort of deliberate process that includes a rationale for how the program's activities will reduce the public health burden experienced by a community that is associated with a given condition. While there is variability in the processes used to develop and implement public health programs, generally four iterative steps are used to understand and respond to a given issue (Mercy, Rosenberg, Powell, Broome, & Roper, 1993): (1) the scope of the public health problem must be defined, including understanding key characteristics and consequences, (2) the risk and protective factors associated with the problem must be understood, (3) programs that impact the problem or its risk and protective factors must be developed and evaluated, and (4) these programs must be implemented broadly in a cost-effective way. This is a cyclical process; therefore, ongoing evaluation and monitoring of the programs' effects must be used to further refine understanding of the underlying problem, its causes, and steps that are effective to prevent it.

This general framework has been used successfully to improve public health problems, such as interpersonal violence (Rosenberg & Fenley, 1991), substance use disorder (Substance Abuse and Mental Health Services Administration, 2016), and asthma (Davis & Herman, 2011) to name a few. We will, therefore, use this framework to describe how the public health approach can be used to improve outcomes of families that have a child with ASD. This includes defining the public health problem of reduced family well-being for families of children with ASD, noting some of the risk and protective factors, and outlining public health programs that can be used to improve this problem. In particular, as an example of how family programs can fit into this framework and positively impact communities, we will describe the ECHO for Families program offered through the Wyoming Institute for Disabilities at the University of Wyoming. This program was developed using this public health framework and is designed to primarily impact families within the microsystem level so they can be more empowered and effective at supporting their children with ASD. Given the flexibility of ECHO for Families and the ease with which it can be scaled up to meet demand from diverse communities and other disabilities, it has the potential to improve the well-being of families who have loved ones with a wide range of disabilities.

2. Raising a child with ASD and family well-being

To adopt a public health approach to family supports for ASD, the public health problem must first be identified. The literature on families of children with ASD provides numerous descriptions of how having a child with ASD can increase parental or family stress (Twoy, Connolly, & Novak, 2007), reduce quality of life (Brown, MacAdam-Crisp, Wang, & Iarocci, 2006; Ezzat, Bayoumi, & Samarkandi, 2017) and impact parent mental health (Benson, 2010, 2012; Jellett, Wood, Giallo, & Seymour, 2015). Given that there are a wide range of factors that relate to these outcomes, we use the concept of *well-being* to describe this public health problem. That is, having a child with ASD may negatively impact a family's well-being. Well-being is a broad concept which encompasses an array of social, physical, emotional, and economic components and is of primary concern for families who have children with ASD. For example, a recent scoping review (Tint & Weiss, 2016) revealed that poor family well-being is associated with several problematic outcomes, including decreases in mental and physical health, feelings of social isolation, and financial hardship or burden. Moreover, many risk factors disproportionately impact the well-being of families of children with ASD (Herring et al., 2006; Oelofsen & Richardson, 2006; Tehee, Honan, & Hevey, 2009; Woodman, 2014). Importantly, many factors associated with reduced well-being are contextual factors that are situated in the microsystem. Therefore, it is imperative to consider broader public health approaches that are more able to mitigate these contextual challenges when developing programs focused on helping families as well as programs that focus on delivering services to the family unit as a whole rather than the child alone.

The risk and protective factors associated with family well-being are quite diverse. One particularly problematic impact on family well-being results from financial hardship (Herring et al., 2006; Oelofsen & Richardson, 2006; Tehee et al., 2009; Woodman, 2014). Financial hardship is a known predictor of parental stress for families of children with disabilities (Minnes, Perry, & Weiss, 2015) and unfortunately, families of these children are more likely to face financial hardships due to the unique caregiving needs of their children. For instance, there are significant differences in income levels between families with children who are delayed and families with non-delayed children (Baker, Blacher, Crnic, & Edelbrock, 2002). Reduced family income could be due to one parent having to stay at home to care for their child with ASD (Blanche, Diaz, Barretto, & Cermak, 2015; Brobst, Clopton, & Hendrick, 2009; Horlin, Falkmer, Parsons, Albrecht, & Falkmer, 2014) or because of the added financial burden associated with paying for interventions and services for their child. Indeed, the lifetime cost of caring for individuals with ASD is enormous, ranging from 1.4 to 3.6 million dollars per individual (Buescher, Cidav, Knapp, & Mandell, 2014; Cakir, Frye, & Walker, 2020). Although this figure includes public funding, there is a significant cost to families as well (Buescher et al., 2014; Horlin et al., 2014; Knapp, Romeo, & Beecham, 2009). While income and care costs vary widely, this means that families of children with ASD will be at risk for decreased well-being as a result of financial issues. Further, while many public health programs do address indirect aspects of financial difficulty such as vocational rehabilitation and job training for the child with ASD, the issues directly pertaining to financial hardship that would improve family well-being (e.g., direct support related to reduced family income) may not be effectively addressed, resulting in a lack of effective change for the family unit.

Social stigma is also a major risk factor for the well-being of families with children with ASD. While parents often report that receiving an ASD diagnosis for their child is a positive incident because it allows them to resolve parenting concerns, the ASD diagnosis can also lead to feelings of separation from the rest of their community. Reports of losing friendships following their child's diagnosis or being disconnected from others who do not have a child with ASD is unfortunately common (e.g., Farrugia, 2009; Kinnear, Link, Ballan, & Fischbach, 2016). This may be due, in part, to a lack of acceptance or understanding of ASD in the surrounding community which frequently seems to result in social stigma (Farrugia, 2009). Ultimately, this contributes to feelings of social isolation and exclusion for families of children with ASD (Kinnear et al., 2016) and reduced social engagement in typical social opportunities because of their caregiving responsibilities or misunderstandings regarding the appropriateness of their child's behavior (Marsack & Perry, 2018; Myers, Mackintosh, & Goin-Kochel, 2009). This stigma and social isolation similarly extends to typically developing siblings of children with ASD (Myers et al., 2009), who can also experience reduced well-being (Chan & Goh, 2014; Dauz Williams et al., 2010).

Beyond social isolation and stigma, a family's inability to access services that are most appropriate for their child can be extremely challenging. First, service systems are so complex that many families struggle to access ASD-specific services without the assistance of care coordinators (Vohra et al., 2014). Indeed, families must interact with a wide range of service systems, including healthcare providers (e.g., medicine, allied health, dental and mental health), payors (e.g., insurance and Medicaid), educational systems (Part B and C, special education, IEPs and 504 plans), vocational support programs, and legal systems (e.g., guardianship, advocacy). Challenges to accessing supports is further compounded with limited income and insurance coverage (Pearson & Meadan, 2018). Additionally, the lack of clear information about the most effective services for their child can harm overall family well-being as individualizing care to meet their child's specific needs is incredibly difficult for most families of children with ASD (Anderson, Lupfer, & Shattuck, 2018). To further complicate this issue, there may be geographic barriers to accessing care. For instance, families in rural states often have to travel much further to receive frontline services such as applied behavior analysis and speech-language pathology relative to their non-rural counterparts (Mello, Goldman, Urbano, & Hodapp, 2016; Pearson & Meadan, 2018). Additionally, given that response to treatment is difficult to predict in children with ASD (Warren et al., 2011) and that most families try upward of seven different types of interventions to improve outcomes (Goin-Kochel et al., 2007), scarcity of information about which services would be most effective (Warren et al., 2011; Weitlauf et al., 2014) could exacerbate any negative impacts of accessing services on family well-being.

It is also important to note that along with all of these contextual impacts on family well-being, child behavioral problems continue to be an important risk factor for decreased family well-being. For example, child executive functioning difficulties and social impairments are contributors to parental stress (Tsermentseli & Kouklari, 2019), and a larger number of behavioral problems and more pervasive behavioral problems are strongly associated with higher levels of parental stress (Burke & Hodapp, 2014; Firth & Dryer, 2013; Herring et al., 2006; Plant & Sanders, 2007; Robinson & Neece, 2015; Woodman, 2014). Moreover, the type of disability present in a child can be indicative of how much stress is faced by parents. Specifically, there seems to be higher levels of parental stress for families of children with ASD relative to other intellectual and developmental disabilities (IDD; Burke & Hodapp, 2014; Hayes & Watson, 2013; Kirby, White, & Baranek, 2015). The unique caregiving aspects associated with the behavioral problems in children with ASD can also impact well-being in that higher difficulty of caregiving is associated with higher levels of parental stress (Plant & Sanders, 2007). Therefore, clinical intervention continues to be a critical part of improving the well-being of families. Although, this process is most effective when families are involved (Salazar, 2020) and parents may have goals for their children that may not be effectively addressed by certain clinical interventions (Singh, Moody, Rigles, & Smith, 2018). Thus, it is important for clinicians and parents to have a robust and meaningful partnership as the child's needs are addressed.

Fortunately, there are also a number of protective factors that safeguard families of children with ASD against decreases in well-being. Self-compassion (Robinson, Hastings, Weiss, Pagavathsing, & Lunsky, 2018), hardiness (Weiss, 2002), sense of competency (Weiss, Tint, Paquette-Smith, & Lunsky, 2016) and maternal positivity (Jess, Totsika, & Hastings, 2018) are all associated with well-being in that greater levels of these factors are correlated with lower levels of parental stress. While some personal characteristics, such as these, can prove difficult to change on their own, parental empowerment that is developed through parental support is also a strong predictor of family well-being (Guralnick, Hammond, Neville, & Connor, 2008; Minnes et al., 2015; Plant & Sanders, 2007; Woodman, 2014). Moreover, this protective factor is more easily modified than are personality characteristics. That is, parental support can be introduced at any time in order to increase a family's sense of empowerment, thus protecting against stress and improving well-being. Most frequently, this form of support is provided through an expansion of community resources, a network of knowledge, and access to other parents who have had a similar experience, which reduces feelings of social and/or geographical isolation (Guralnick et al., 2008; Plant & Sanders, 2007; Woodman, 2014). Parental support has been shown to predict successful levels of adaptation (Weiss, 2002), increase parental resilience (Peer & Hillman, 2014), and can even predict parental stress in a child's elementary school years (Guralnick et al., 2008).

While there are numerous risk and protective factors that impact family well-being, it is important to remember that there are complex relationships between the involved social structures that may not easily be altered. For example, many clinical interventions—while providing expert care to the child with ASD and focusing on risk factors such as behavioral problems—often do not sufficiently address familial concerns that contribute to well-being as only a small number of these contributors can be addressed by clinical interventions or trainings. For example, Applied Behavior Analysis (ABA), child toilet trainings, and behavioral interventions can address some child behavioral problems while psychosocial therapy can improve parents' mental health. However, support that is only offered within clinical systems is likely to conform to the limits and structures of the healthcare system and will, therefore, focus predominantly on a limited subset of the factors that impact parent stress and well-being.

Further, there are likely to be residual symptoms that cannot be eliminated by direct clinical services (e.g., stimming) and thus should be addressed within the family setting, or microsystem to alleviate parental stress and improve family well-being. Considering the malleability of parental support and its contributions to well-being as established by previous literature, this is an important opportunity for family support programs to help families of children with ASD to improve outcomes. Given that the current approach to clinically supporting children does not usually have concomitant effects on the parents or family, we argue that there should be a shift in how family supports are structured.

3. Public health programs for families of children with ASD

With the scope of the public health problem identified, the next step is to examine strategies and develop public health programs that address that need. Given the diversity of factors contributing to family well-being, it is critical that programs are able to respond to the range of needs a family may face. Direct clinical intervention will continue to address child behavioral characteristics through our existing healthcare systems. However, many of the risk and protective factors are part of microlevel systems that cannot be easily impacted through a clinical approach. As such, many family support programs have been developed to provide parents with tools to help their child and family succeed. For example, inclusion programs (Baker-Ericzén, Brookman-Frazee, & Stahmer, 2005), parent education, intervention, training, and support groups (Al-Khalaf, Dempsey, & Dally, 2014; Iida et al., 2018; Kuravackel et al., 2018; McConkey & Samadi, 2013; Niinomi et al., 2016; Turner-Brown et al., 2019), respite care (Chou, Tzou, Pu, Kröger, & Lee, 2008), home-based support services (Heller, Miller, & Hsieh, 1999), and center-based trainings (Roberts et al., 2011) are forms of programs that have been developed for families of children with ASD or other related IDD.

Programs of this nature appear to be highly acceptable and have encouraging outcomes data on well-being. These existing programs seem to improve family functioning (Moody et al., 2019), reduce parental stress (Al-Khalaf et al., 2014; Baker-Ericzén et al., 2005; Heller et al., 1999; Niinomi et al., 2016; Turner-Brown et al., 2019), increase parental satisfaction with community functioning and service needs (Heller et al., 1999), improve parents' mental well-being (Iida et al., 2018; McConkey & Samadi, 2013; Roberts et al., 2011; Turner-Brown et al., 2019), enhance parental feelings of social support (Kuravackel et al., 2018), and increase self-reported quality of life (Niinomi et al., 2016; Roberts et al., 2011). There is even evidence that impacting family functioning can lead to decreases in children's problematic behaviors (e.g., Iida et al., 2018; Kuravackel et al., 2018), further suggesting that improving microsystem factors can improve child functioning. Indeed, this emphasizes the interaction between contextual factors and the child's development and provides additional confirmation that supporting families is critical to the outcomes of the whole family unit.

While there are numerous family support programs available, those that are most likely to have lasting and meaningful impact on families, and their children, are those that enhance family-empowerment (Ashcraft et al., 2019; Factor et al., 2019). Family-empowerment refers to the degree to which parents feel in control of the decisions and choices related to the health of their child (Ashcraft et al., 2019). More importantly, family-empowerment is associated with several outcomes that enhance parents' ability to support their children, including increasing involvement in daily care, symptom management, enhanced advocacy and decision making (Ashcraft et al., 2019). Not only does family-empowerment have significant impacts on children, but programs that enhance empowerment are generally highly regarded by parents, and therefore more likely to encourage sustained participation. Additionally, programs that are able to incorporate numerous aspects of the child's microsystem—for example, their medical provider, their educators, and their parents—may be more effective in creating a strong sense of family empowerment. One novel and innovative parent-support program that is designed to enhance parent-empowerment, called ECHO for Families, leverages a larger capacity building model called Project ECHO™.

The ECHO Model was originally created to address the lack of access to specialized care for patients with hepatitis C across the state of New Mexico (Arora et al., 2007, 2011, 2014; Arora, Thornton, Jenkusky, Parish, & Scalctti, 2007). Employing a hub-and-spoke design, hepatitis C specialists at the hub would provide training to other healthcare providers at spoke sites. Employing video-conferencing technology, participants and experts would meet from all around the state to learn from and teach others through didactic presentations, case-based learning, and mentoring through the formation of a community of practice. Specialists at the hub-site would present a didactic training on a topic of interest while participants interact through questions and discussions. Participants at spoke sites would have the opportunity to present a case regarding a current problem of practice or challenge. The specialists at the hub as well as other participants at spoke sites would then provide recommendations and suggestions for addressing the concerns of the practitioner.

In this way, participants receive personalized support to help them provide the specialized care their patients need without requiring patients to travel long distances or wait for months to see specialists. During ECHO sessions, hub and spoke participants engage in two-way sharing of knowledge and experience as well as mentoring and a social support network developed through this community of practice (Arora et al., 2011, 2014; Arora, Geppert, et al., 2007; Arora, Thornton, et al., 2007). The ECHO Model has since been adopted by many organizations and institutions and has been used to address other health disparities such as mental health (Fisher et al., 2017; Mehrotra et al., 2018; Sockalingam et al., 2017), education (Root-Elledge et al., 2018), and a wide array of medical concerns (e.g., pain managment, Ball, Wilson, Ober, & Mchaourab, 2018; geriatrics, Bennett et al., 2018; cancer, Lopez et al., 2017). Most recently, the Wyoming Institute for Disabilities has adapted the ECHO model to create ECHO for Families. This network provides families of children with ASD with additional support to improve empowerment via the same four elements as all ECHO networks: (1) short information sessions delivered by experts on topics of need in the community, (2) presentations from the community about issues they are currently facing, (3) delivery through teleconferencing technology so that participants can join regardless of their location, and (4) ongoing evaluation to ensure that the content of the network continues to meet the needs of participants.

ECHO for Families is an exciting innovation in family supports for several reasons. First, it is a parent-empowerment based model. The whole program is designed to provide parents with resources that they can use to make decisions on their own terms. This is accomplished by providing high-quality information as well as providing them with connections to other parents who share their experience. This allows for the creation of meaningful community among participants and allows each participant to advocate for their child as they see fit. Further, because they are provided a venue to talk about the challenges they are currently experiencing, parents are able to develop actionable strategies to address those challenges. Further, because the content of each ECHO for Families session is set by the participants, the program is able to adapt to the changing needs of the community. This is all accomplished without direct clinical intervention, and instead focuses on risk and protective factors associated with microsystem structures. Therefore, this model employs a public health framework to support families of children with ASD. ECHO for Families will be described in more detail below.

4. The problem of scaling up family support programs and the unique approach of ECHO for families

The final step in the public health approach is to scale up the program so that it can reduce the public health burden more broadly and therefore impact the population as a whole. Critically, scaling up allows for the benefits of this approach to be impact public health. Yet, this step in the public health process is arguably the most challenging for family support programs. Many of the barriers to the scaling-up process require systems-level changes, or even shifts in societal thinking about the role of family supports. However, while challenging, these are not insurmountable challenges and we argue that creating a more favorable landscape for the implementation of family support programs is the most important factor in improving family well-being for those who have children with ASD. For instance, the public health approach to public health may lead to accessing novel funding streams, such as through state, local or federal public health agencies, implementation grants or similar mechanisms.

That said, it is important to understand the barriers to scaling up family support programs. For instance, by nature of the diversity of risk and protective factors that impact family well-being, most programs are not able to impact all risk and protective factors. As a result, there are a wide range of family programs that are designed to focus on a subset of factors associated with family well-being. This approach can be extremely beneficial to parents experiencing a particular risk factor at a specific time. For instance, a family that needs respite care immediately may derive enormous benefit from a program that can provide this service. However, family needs may change, and other risk and protective factors may not be addressed by a given program. As a result, the family may still experience decreases in overall well-being despite positive impacts on a subset of risk or protective factors. This also means that the family may need to have access to a diverse family programs so they can access different services as their needs change. However, this puts the family back in the position of needing to coordinate a variety of services, similar to what they face with their child's clinical care.

Second, the funding mechanisms used to sustain family support programs are often challenging. For example, these programs are frequently funded through charitable contributions or grants and may not have a reliable revenue stream. As a result, many family support organizations may struggle financially, which may make it difficult for these organizations to remain solvent, let alone scale up their programs. This ultimately results in many family support programs struggling to help all families in need of their services (Heller et al., 1999; Hudson, Cameron, & Matthews, 2008). Of course, financing of healthcare services is a complex and critical issue right now. However, in the absence of reliable revenue streams such as reimbursement through insurance or Medicaid, many families may not have the financial resources to pay for the real cost of some family services (e.g., Hudson et al., 2008).

Additionally, the format of many existing family support programs can present issues for scaling up programs to meet the needs of rural or low-resource families. For instance, many programs are based on in-person trainings, and interventions may rely on a family's ability to attend all sessions. However, resource limitations such as problems with finding a caretaker, an inability to travel long distances, and rural isolation (Kuravackel et al., 2018; Turner-Brown et al., 2019) can impair the potential effectiveness of these programs and make it impossible to scale these models up to the whole community. Further, as with clinical treatments, the idiosyncratic nature of ASD can also present a barrier to success, as there is often a lack of fit between standardized programs and the specific needs of some children and families (Roberts et al., 2011). Thus, many families need to explore numerous programs to determine an appropriate fit for their child, but this may be difficult to accomplish if access to programs or resources is limited.

Finally, even when implemented within clinical programs, problems arise in relation to sustained funding, conflict between clinical structures, and the appropriate place of family advocacy or support within those structures.

Although scaling up programs may be difficult, it is possible. However, to be successful, programs must develop innovative delivery models that allow for greater impact, and they must be built on strong partnerships with the community and funders to ensure that the impact can be sustained. One example of this is the University of Wyoming (UW) ECHO for Families of children with ASD. This network was developed in 2018, in collaboration with families from around the state of Wyoming to ensure that it would meet their current needs. Accordingly, the network's identity was crafted with direction from families as they identified what they wanted to achieve through participation in an ECHO network. Additional input was gathered from state agencies, community organizations and autism experts to ensure that the content would be relevant for state systems and was consistent with current best practices. ECHO for Families is guided by a family-determination perspective that is built on the belief that families are in the best position to identify what they need and can determine what strategies or resources to use to improve their well-being. The formation of the network, the session training, topic planning, and the case presentation feedback and suggestions are all guided by this belief.

ECHO for Families sessions utilize the same format as the original medical model for ECHO: a didactic presentation followed by a case presentation, delivered over video conferencing (e.g., Zoom ™) with ongoing program evaluation. The only changes made in this adaptation of the ECHO model (1) were modifying the language used to remove clinical terminology in order to become more family-friendly and (2) adding procedures to ensure the confidentiality and safety of participants. For example, "didactic presentations" became "training topics" and "case presentations" became "family narratives." Additionally, participants are repeatedly informed that this is not a clinical service, and measures were taken to allow family members to present cases. However, all other features of the ECHO sessions remain the same: the cultivation of a community, two-way exchange of knowledge and ideas, and personalized support through mentoring and a social support network.

The goal for each ECHO session is to address a concern identified by families and provide actionable, high-quality health information so that families can utilize their learning immediately. Training topics have included behavioral strategies, transition planning, s self-advocacy, workplace readiness skills, social skills, and roles and responsibilities at IEP meetings, among others. Family narratives have varied widely and have touched on a number of situations and challenges. Morning routines, behavior struggles, parent-teacher coordination, family-agency coordination, advocating for needs, and many others have been topics of family narratives. Importantly, family narratives are always about a concern that a parent is currently facing, regardless of the day's training topic, and the whole network is given an opportunity to provide suggestions based on their own unique experiences. While content experts are available to provide guidance on best practices, this model is based on collaborations among parents, rather than professional recommendations.

As such, the success of ECHO for Families depends on strong family-professional partnerships that use the belief in family-determination as a guidepost. While this ECHO network is focused on supporting families of children with ASD, it is often the case that individuals from different professions who work with these families are also in attendance. For example, behavioral specialists, case managers, social workers, special education teachers, and many others have attended ECHO for Families sessions, either as training presenters, content experts, or simply as participants interested in working with families in this community of practice. Importantly, the quality of family-school partnerships is incredibly impactful on parental well-being (Burke & Hodapp, 2014) given that the school transition period (i.e., transitioning an adult child out of school) is highly correlated with greater levels of stress (McKenzie, Ouellette-Kuntz, Blinkhorn, & Démoré, 2017). Thus, by including a wide variety of specialists in ECHO sessions, obstacles relating to a child's school environment or transition period can be sufficiently addressed with direct support from relevant professionals.

While the ethos of ECHO for Families is important, the ECHO model has been key to scaling up the program to reach the whole state, and region. In particular, the ECHO model is based on teleconferencing technology. This allows for substantial cost and time savings to parents. For instance, Wyoming, the primary implementation site for ECHO for Families, is a large, sparsely populated state and, with the exception of Cheyenne and Casper, most communities are considered rural or frontier (Wyoming Department of Health, 2020). With the use of videoconferencing technology as the primary mode of conducting ECHO sessions, the ECHO Model is uniquely situated to reach far more communities around the state of Wyoming than would be possible with programs that meet in-person. Families do not need to travel in order to attend sessions and can join from wherever they may be, which minimizes the indirect costs to families to participate (e.g., childcare, commute time, travel expenditures). This is particularly important during the winter months in which there are frequent storms and road closures. The negative effects of social and geographical isolation are also mitigated through the cultivation of this community of practice.

Further, ECHO for families is an extremely cost-effective strategy which makes it attractive to funders who are primarily interested in maximizing the impact of each dollar used by the program. For instance, after initial costs for staffing and equipment, there are few additional costs required to expand ECHO programs. In terms of the equipment needed, hubs are encouraged to outfit a videoconferencing space where the hub team can facilitate ECHO sessions with video and audio, though this is not required. Hub team members can meet from their personal devices, many of which may already be equipped with video cameras and microphones. After initial setup, there are few costs for expanding an ECHO network and facilitating additional ECHO sessions or even creating additional ECHO networks focused on addressing other health disparities. Though, as ECHO programs expand and begin facilitating several networks, additional staff may be needed. As for equipping participants, depending on the videoconferencing platform chosen by the program coordinators, all that is usually required is an internet connection. According to the Pew Research Center, 90% of adults in 2019 have access to an internet-capable device, and this number is expected to continue to grow (Pew Research Center, 2019). Programs may choose to allocate funds for video cameras and microphones to be sent to participants in need. Other programs may elect to make other arrangements that are either free or low-cost such as arranging for local libraries or community college campuses to provide computer access during the scheduled ECHO sessions.

While the ability to reach a large number of families in a cost-efficient manner makes this model attractive, it must still be appealing and useful to the families that use the program. Program evaluation data suggests that parents and family members find ECHO for Families valuable and worthwhile. For example, participants from the 2018–2019 ECHO for Families network reported increases in knowledge and skills to use new strategies (see Table 1) as well as increased motivation for and implementation of new autism strategies (see Table 2). More importantly, families reported feelings of self-efficacy and a connection to other families (see Table 3). Qualitative interviews with participants of the ECHO for Families network

Table 1 Participant self-rating of knowledge and skills from the 2018–2019 ECHO for families network.

Knowledge/skill	Mean post-level	Mean retrospective pre-level	Mean difference	SD	t	n	P value
Structuring directions	3.96	3.08	0.89	1.03	4.37	26	<0.001
Setting up effective and appropriate consequences	3.85	3.19	0.65	1.09	3.05	26	0.005
Giving positive feedback to children	4.38	3.92	0.46	0.86	2.74	26	0.01
Teaching rules, routines, and expectations	4.04	3.62	0.42	1.03	2.10	26	0.05
Strengthen relationships/ connecting to child to prevent behavior	3.88	3.50	0.39	1.17	1.68	26	0.11
Transition planning	3.35	3.00	0.35	1.02	1.74	26	0.10
Self-advocacy and student-led IEP meetings	3.35	3.04	0.31	0.79	1.99	26	0.06
Workplace readiness skills	3.15	2.77	0.39	0.70	2.81	26	0.01

Table 2 Participant increases in knowledge, skills, motivation, and use of new strategies from the 2018–2019 ECHO for families network.

As a result of your participation, to what extent...	% Who said...					
	"Did not participate enough"	"Hardly at all"	"A little bit"	"Some"	"Quite a bit"	"A lot"
Has your knowledge about autism increased?	7.7%	11.5%	23.1%	30.8%	15.4%	11.5%
Have your skills related to autism increased?	15.4%	11.5%	15.4%	38.5%	7.7%	11.5%
Has your motivation related to autism increased?	11.5%	7.7%	11.5%	42.3%	11.5%	15.4%
Have you implemented any autism strategies at home?	11.5%	11.5%	15.4%	38.5%	11.5%	11.5%

Table 3 Participant ratings of self-efficacy and connectedness from the 2018–2019 ECHO for families network.

Statement	% Strongly disagree	% Disagree	% Agree	% Strongly agree	% Not applicable
"I am planning to try something I've learned today."	0%	3%	33%	58%	6%
"I believe I can successfully apply what I've learned today."	0%	1%	36%	58%	5%
"Attending today's session has helped me feel connected to other families."	0%	4%	40%	47%	9%
"I feel like I have expanded my network by participating in today's session."	0%	6%	40%	46%	8%

further support the program's impact on family well-being. Notably, anecdotal reports from parent participating in ECHO suggests that it reduces stress, improves community connections, increases social support, and result in higher self-efficacy for families. Even for parents with lower levels of self-reported familial stress and higher degrees of knowledge relating to ASD prior to participation in ECHO, the increases in confidence gained through participation, mainly because of the opportunity to expand their personal and professional networks, enabled families to feel more confident in their decision-making. As stated by one participant, ECHO "provides an 'extra layer' of knowledge to help inform decision-making." Additionally, in considering the differences between clinical interventions and ECHO for Families, while participants did acknowledge the importance of clinical interventions, they also noted that parent education is often lacking, whereas ECHO focuses on parent education. Further, ECHO allows for real-life skill building, and can even "trigger ideas or intentions related to clinical treatment or outcomes," as detailed by one participant. In other words, clinical interventions are like the "medicine" while ECHO is the "therapy," and the combination of the two results in better outcomes relative to clinical outcomes alone.

Overall, from evaluation and interview results, it appears that ECHO for Families is able to provide social support to families, which may lead to increased confidence in decision-making, knowledge of trainings and interventions, and reduced levels of stress. Thus, ECHO for Families addresses challenges with family well-being and provides appropriate supports to reduce the impact of risk factors and stressors related to having a child with ASD. Simply put, as a public health approach to family supports that is based on family empowerment, ECHO for Families offers a non-clinical alternative to parents that delivers actionable information which is relevant to the family's current needs. Further, this allows for families to make choices based on their own desires while assuming family outcomes are the result of complex interaction of knowledge, emotional and social support, access to resources, and sense of competence.

Also, it is important to note, the ECHO Model is easily adaptable and can be used to address a number of other family concerns. For example, the ECHO for Families network has addressed in-home behavioral supports, IEPs versus 504 plans, transitions to the workforce, sibling and spousal issues, navigating healthcare systems, and even emotional difficulties. WIND has scaled up the ECHO for Families program to help support families of children with other special healthcare needs. For example, families of children with ADHD, depression, and intellectual and development disabilities can also attend the ECHO for Families sessions for support. Given the prevalence of IDD in children, approximately 1 in 6 (e.g., Boyle et al., 2011), and the issues with residing in geographically or socially isolated areas, ECHO for Families provides an exciting opportunity for parents of children with other conditions who have similarly experienced impediments to family well-being.

5. Conclusion

Children with ASD will continue to need direct clinical intervention to improve developmental outcomes, specifically behavioral problems, especially when considering how the US healthcare system refers and reimburses clinicians based on direct-support services. However, there is little evidence for best practice in clinical interventions, with many families of children with ASD left to experiment with different interventions until they find the right fit for their child. Clearly, more research is needed to develop individualized, evidence-based clinical interventions for children with ASD. Yet, this cannot come at the expense of family well-being.

Due to the lack of a clear standard of care based on strong research, parents may struggle to determine when their child has reached full growth potential. However, the Bioecological Theory of Human Development (Bronfenbrenner, 1977, 1979; Bronfenbrenner & Morris, 1998) and public health frameworks (Mercy et al., 1993) provide support for enhancing contextual factors in a child's microsystem in order to improve overall family well-being. In fact, enhancing family well-being, especially through empowering the family to be an effective caregiver in a way that makes sense for their unique family circumstances will ultimately benefit the child. Parental support programs that are built on an empowerment approach will reduce the public health burden as well as the lifetime cost of care for those with ASD. But more importantly, it will improve the lives of families of children with ASD, including the outcomes of the children themselves.

Therefore, we argue for the adoption of a public health approach to family supports. By doing so, this will create healthcare, educational and community systems that will be more effective at delivering care to the child with ASD, supporting development, and ensuring that the family will be able to effectively mediate the child's ongoing development and care. Further, this approach allows existing interventions to be more impactful (e.g., Iida et al., 2018; Kuravackel et al., 2018; Salazar, 2020), especially as they are scaled up. ECHO for Families is one example of how public health programs can effectively and efficiently support families. ECHO for Families also has the added benefit of being flexible enough to work within rural or urban settings, and the ability to focus on a variety of changing family needs while still empowering parents to develop skills to support their children. However, regardless of the program, by reconceptualizing family supports as a matter of public health, we will create environments that promote the health and well-being of the families, while empowering the family to create change within their microsystem that leads to better outcomes for their children. This is the goal for all children with ASD; however, no single intervention can accomplish this on its own. Families will continue to be central to reaching this objective. By empowering families to be effective partners with the clinical community we can better achieve our common goals and create the social structures that will lead to the best outcomes for all those touched by ASD.

Acknowledgments

This work was supported by Wyoming Family to Family Health Information Center. (Health Resources and Services Administration, 2 H84MC24069-05-00) and University Centers for Excellence in Developmental Disabilities Education, Research, and Service Core, Health Resources and Services Administration (90DDUC0011-01-00).

References

Al-Khalaf, A., Dempsey, I., & Dally, K. (2014). The effect of an education program for mothers of children with autism spectrum disorder in Jordan. *International Journal for the Advancement of Counselling, 36*(2), 175–187.

Anderson, C., Lupfer, A., & Shattuck, P. T. (2018). Barriers to receipt of services for young adults with autism. *Pediatrics, 141*(Suppl. 4), S300–S305.

Arora, S., Geppert, C. M., Kalishman, S., Dion, D., Pullara, F., Bjeletich, B., et al. (2007). Academic health center management of chronic diseases through knowledge networks: Project ECHO. *Acadademic Medicine, 82*(2), 154–160. https://doi.org/10.1097/ACM. 0b013e31802d8f68.

Arora, S., Thornton, K., Jenkusky, S. M., Parish, B., & Scaletti, J. V. (2007). Project ECHO: Linking university specialists with rural and prison-based clinicians to improve care for people with chronic hepatitis C in New Mexico. *Public Health Reports, 122*(Suppl. 2), 74–77. https://doi.org/10.1177/00333549071220S214.

Arora, S., Thornton, K., Komaromy, M., Kalishman, S., Katzman, J., & Duhigg, D. (2014). Demonopolizing medical knowledge. *Academic Medicine, 89*(1), 30–32.

Arora, S., Thornton, K., Murata, G., Deming, P., Kalishman, S., Dion, D., et al. (2011). Outcomes of treatment for hepatitis C virus infection by primary care providers. *New England Journal of Medicine, 364*(23), 2199–2207. https://doi.org/10.1056/NEJMoa 1009370.

Ashcraft, L. E., Asato, M., Houtrow, A. J., Kavalieratos, D., Miller, E., & Ray, K. N. (2019). Parent empowerment in pediatric healthcare settings: A systematic review of observational studies. *The Patient—Patient-Centered Outcomes Research, 12*(2), 199–212. https://doi.org/10.1007/s40271-018-0336-2.

Baio, J. (2012). Prevalence of autism spectrum disorders: Autism and Developmental Disabilities Monitoring Network, 14 sites, United States, 2008. *Morbidity and Mortality Weekly Report Surveillance Summaries, 61*(3), 1–19.

Baio, J., Wiggins, L., Christensen, D. L., Maenner, M. J., Daniels, J., Warren, Z., et al. (2018). Prevalence of autism spectrum disorder among children aged 8 years—Autism and Developmental Disabilities Monitoring Network, 11 Sites, United States, 2014. *Morbidity and Mortality Weekly Report Surveillance Summaries, 67*(6), 1.

Baker, B. L., Blacher, J., Crnic, K. A., & Edelbrock, C. (2002). Behavior problems and parenting stress in families of three-year-old children with and without developmental delays. *American Journal on Mental Retardation, 107*(6), 433–444.

Baker-Ericzén, M. J., Brookman-Frazee, L., & Stahmer, A. (2005). Stress levels and adaptability in parents of toddlers with and without autism spectrum disorders. *Research and Practice for Persons with Severe Disabilities, 30*(4), 194–204.

Ball, S., Wilson, B., Ober, S., & Mchaourab, A. (2018). SCAN-ECHO for pain management: Implementing a regional telementoring training for primary care providers. *Pain Medicine, 19*(2), 262–268.

Bennett, K. A., Ong, T., Verrall, A. M., Vitiello, M. V., Marcum, Z. A., & Phelan, E. A. (2018). Project ECHO-geriatrics: Training future primary care providers to meet the needs of older adults. *Journal of Graduate Medical Education, 10*(3), 311–315.

Benson, P. R. (2010). Coping, distress, and well-being in mothers of children with autism. *Research in Autism Spectrum Disorders, 4*(2), 217–228.

Benson, P. R. (2012). Network characteristics, perceived social support, and psychological adjustment in mothers of children with autism spectrum disorder. *Journal of Autism and Developmental Disorders, 42*(12), 2597–2610.

Blanche, E. I., Diaz, J., Barretto, T., & Cermak, S. A. (2015). Caregiving experiences of Latino families with children with Autism Spectrum Disorder. *American Journal of Occupational Therapy, 69*(5). https://doi.org/10.5014/ajot.2015.017848.

Boyle, C. A., Boulet, S., Schieve, L. A., Cohen, R. A., Blumberg, S. J., Yeargin-Allsopp, M., et al. (2011). Trends in the prevalence of developmental disabilities in US children, 1997–2008. *Pediatrics, 127*(6), 1034–1042. https://doi.org/10.1542/peds.2010-2989.

Brobst, J. B., Clopton, J. R., & Hendrick, S. S. (2009). Parenting children with autism spectrum disorders: The couple's relationship. *Focus on Autism and other Developmental Disabilities, 24*(1), 38–49.

Bronfenbrenner, U. (1977). Toward an experimental ecology of human development. *American Psychologist, 32*(7), 513.

Bronfenbrenner, U. (1979). *The ecology of human development.* Harvard University Press.

Bronfenbrenner, U., & Morris, P. A. (1998). The ecology of developmental processes. In W. Damon & R. M. Lerner (Eds.), *Handbook of child psychology: Theoretical models of human development* (pp. 993–1028). John Wiley & Sons Inc.

Brown, R. I., MacAdam-Crisp, J., Wang, M., & Iarocci, G. (2006). Family quality of life when there is a child with a developmental disability. *Journal of Policy and Practice in Intellectual Disabilities, 3*(4), 238–245.

Buescher, A. V., Cidav, Z., Knapp, M., & Mandell, D. S. (2014). Costs of autism spectrum disorders in the United Kingdom and the United States. *JAMA Pediatrics, 168*(8), 721–728.

Burke, M. M., & Hodapp, R. M. (2014). Relating stress of mothers of children with developmental disabilities to family–school partnerships. *Mental Retardation, 52*(1), 13–23.

Cakir, J., Frye, R. E., & Walker, S. J. (2020). The lifetime social cost of autism: 1990–2029. *Research in Autism Spectrum Disorders, 72.* https://doi.org/10.1016/j.rasd.2019.101502.

Chan, G. W., & Goh, E. C. (2014). 'My parents told us that they will always treat my brother differently because he is autistic': Are siblings of autistic children the forgotten ones? *Journal of Social Work Practice, 28*(2), 155–171.

Chou, Y. C., Tzou, P. Y., Pu, C. Y., Kröger, T., & Lee, W. P. (2008). Respite care as a community care service: Factors associated with the effects on family carers of adults with intellectual disability in Taiwan. *Journal of Intellectual and Developmental Disability, 33*(1), 12–21.

Christensen, D. L., Bilder, D. A., Zahorodny, W., Pettygrove, S., Durkin, M. S., Fitzgerald, R. T., et al. (2016). Prevalence and characteristics of Autism Spectrum Disorder among 4-year-old children in the Autism and Developmental Disabilities Monitoring Network. *Journal of Developmental and Behavioral Pediatrics, 37*(1), 1–8. https://doi.org/10.1097/DBP.0000000000000235.

Coie, J. D., Watt, N. F., West, S. G., Hawkins, J. D., Asarnow, J. R., Markman, H. J., et al. (1993). The science of prevention: A conceptual framework and some directions for a national research program. *American Psychologist, 48*(10), 1013.

Coren, E., Ramsbotham, K., & Gschwandtner, M. (2018). Parent training interventions for parents with intellectual disability. *Cochrane Database of Systematic Reviews, 7.*

Dauz Williams, P., Piamjariyakul, U., Carolyn Graff, J., Stanton, A., Guthrie, A. C., Hafeman, C., et al. (2010). Developmental disabilities: Effects on well siblings. *Issues in Comprehensive Pediatric Nursing, 33*(1), 39–55.

Davis, A., & Herman, E. (2011). Considerations and challenges for planning a public health approach to asthma. *Journal of Urban Health: Bulletin of the New York Academy of Medicine, 88*(Suppl. 1), 16–29. https://doi.org/10.1007/s11524-010-9515-8.

Elrod, L. D., & Dale, M. D. (2008). Paradigm shifts and pendulum swings in child custody: The interests of children in the balance. *Family Law Quarterly, 42*, 381.

Ezzat, O., Bayoumi, M., & Samarkandi, O. (2017). Quality of life and subjective burden on family caregiver of children with autism. *American Journal of Nursing Science, 6*, 33–39.

Factor, R. S., Ollendick, T. H., Cooper, L. D., Dunsmore, J. C., Rea, H. M., & Scarpa, A. (2019). All in the family: A systematic review of the effect of caregiver-administered autism spectrum disorder interventions on family functioning and relationships. *Clinical Child and Family Psychology Review, 22*(4), 433–457. https://doi.org/10.1007/s10567-019-00297-x.

Farrugia, D. (2009). Exploring stigma: Medical knowledge and the stigmatisation of parents of children diagnosed with autism spectrum disorder. *Sociology of Health and Illness, 31*(7), 1011–1027. https://doi.org/10.1111/j.1467-9566.2009.01174.x.

Firth, I., & Dryer, R. (2013). The predictors of distress in parents of children with autism spectrum disorder. *Journal of Intellectual and Developmental Disability, 38*(2), 163–171.

Fisher, E., Hasselberg, M., Conwell, Y., Weiss, L., Padrón, N. A., Tiernan, E., et al. (2017). Telementoring primary care clinicians to improve geriatric mental health care. *Population Health Management, 20*(5), 342–347.

Frieden, T. R. (2010). A framework for public health action: The health impact pyramid. *American Journal of Public Health, 100*(4), 590–595. https://doi.org/10.2105/AJPH.2009.185652.

Goin-Kochel, R. P., Myers, B. J., & Mackintosh, V. H. (2007). Parental reports on the use of treatments and therapies for children with autism spectrum disorders. *Research in Autism Spectrum Disorders, 1*(3), 195–209. https://doi.org/10.1016/j.rasd.2006.08.006.

Guralnick, M. J., Hammond, M. A., Neville, B., & Connor, R. T. (2008). The relationship between sources and functions of social support and dimensions of child-and parent-related stress. *Journal of Intellectual Disability Research, 52*(12), 1138–1154.

Hayes, S. A., & Watson, S. L. (2013). The impact of parenting stress: A meta-analysis of studies comparing the experience of parenting stress in parents of children with and without autism spectrum disorder. *Journal of Autism and Developmental Disorders, 43*(3), 629–642.

Heller, T., Miller, A. B., & Hsieh, K. (1999). Impact of a consumer-directed family support program on adults with developmental disabilities and their family caregivers. *Family Relations*, 419–427.

Herring, S., Gray, K., Taffe, J., Tonge, B., Sweeney, D., & Einfeld, S. (2006). Behaviour and emotional problems in toddlers with pervasive developmental disorders and developmental delay: Associations with parental mental health and family functioning. *Journal of Intellectual Disability Research, 50*(12), 874–882.

Higgins, D. J., Bailey, S. R., & Pearce, J. C. (2005). Factors associated with functioning style and coping strategies of families with a child with an autism spectrum disorder. *Autism, 9*(2), 125–137.

Horlin, C., Falkmer, M., Parsons, R., Albrecht, M. A., & Falkmer, T. (2014). The cost of autism spectrum disorders. *PLoS One, 9*(9).

Hudson, A., Cameron, C., & Matthews, J. (2008). The wide-scale implementation of a support program for parents of children with an intellectual disability and difficult behaviour. *Journal of Intellectual and Developmental Disability, 33*(2), 117–126.

Hurley-Hanson, A. E., Giannantonio, C. M., & Griffiths, A. J. (2020). The Costs of Autism. In *Autism in the workplace: Creating positive employment and career outcomes for generation A* (pp. 47–66). Springer International Publishing. https://doi.org/10.1007/978-3-030-29049-8_3.

Iida, N., Wada, Y., Yamashita, T., Aoyama, M., Hirai, K., & Narumoto, J. (2018). Effectiveness of parent training in improving stress-coping capability, anxiety, and depression in mothers raising children with autism spectrum disorder. *Neuropsychiatric Disease and Treatment, 14*, 3355.

Jellett, R., Wood, C. E., Giallo, R., & Seymour, M. (2015). Family functioning and behaviour problems in children with autism spectrum disorders: The mediating role of parent mental health. *Clinical Psychologist, 19*(1), 39–48.

Jess, M., Totsika, V., & Hastings, R. P. (2018). Maternal stress and the functions of positivity in mothers of children with intellectual disability. *Journal of Child and Family Studies, 27*(11), 3753–3763.

Jimerson, S. R., Burns, M. K., & VanDerHeyden, A. M. (2015). *Handbook of response to intervention: The science and practice of multi-tiered systems of support.* Springer.

Kinnear, S. H., Link, B. G., Ballan, M. S., & Fischbach, R. L. (2016). Understanding the experience of stigma for parents of children with autism spectrum disorder and the role stigma plays in families' lives. *Journal of Autism and Developmental Disorders, 46*(3), 942–953.

Kirby, A. V., White, T. J., & Baranek, G. T. (2015). Caregiver strain and sensory features in children with autism spectrum disorder and other developmental disabilities. *American Journal on Intellectual and Developmental Disabilities, 120*(1), 32–45.

Knapp, M., Romeo, R., & Beecham, J. (2009). Economic cost of autism in the UK. *Autism, 13*(3), 317–336.

Kuravackel, G. M., Ruble, L. A., Reese, R. J., Ables, A. P., Rodgers, A. D., & Toland, M. D. (2018). COMPASS for Hope: Evaluating the effectiveness of a parent training and support program for children with ASD. *Journal of Autism and Developmental Disabilities, 48*, 404–416. https://doi.org/10.1007/s10803-017-3333-8.

Lopez, M. S., Baker, E. S., Milbourne, A. M., Gowen, R. M., Rodriguez, A. M., Lorenzoni, C., et al. (2017). Project ECHO: A telementoring program for cervical cancer prevention and treatment in low-resource settings. *Journal of Global Oncology, 3*(5), 658–665.

Maenner, M. J., Shaw, K. A., Baio, J., Washington, A., Patrick, M., DiRienzo, M., et al. (2020). Prevalence of autism spectrum disorder among children aged 8 years—Autism and Developmental Disabilities Monitoring Network, 11 sites, United States, 2016. *Morbidity and Mortalith Weekly Report, 69*(SS-4), 1–12. https://doi.org/10.15585/mmwr.ss6904a1.

Marsack, C. N., & Perry, T. E. (2018). Aging in place in every community: Social exclusion experiences of parents of adult children with autism spectrum disorder. *Research on Aging, 40*(6), 535–557.

McConkey, R., & Samadi, S. A. (2013). The impact of mutual support on Iranian parents of children with an autism spectrum disorder: A longitudinal study. *Disability and Rehabilitation, 35*(9), 775–784.

McKenzie, K., Ouellette-Kuntz, H., Blinkhorn, A., & Démoré, A. (2017). Out of school and into distress: Families of young adults with intellectual and developmental disabilities in transition. *Journal of Applied Research in Intellectual Disabilities, 30*(4), 774–781.

Mehrotra, K., Chand, P., Bandawar, M., Sagi, M. R., Kaur, S., Aurobind, G., et al. (2018). Effectiveness of NIMHANS ECHO blended tele-mentoring model on integrated mental health and addiction for counsellors in rural and underserved districts of Chhattisgarh, India. *Asian Journal of Psychiatry, 36*, 123–127.

Mello, M. P., Goldman, S. E., Urbano, R. C., & Hodapp, R. M. (2016). Services for children with autism spectrum disorder: Comparing rural and non-rural communities. *Education and Training in Autism and Developmental Disabilities*, 355–365.

Mercy, J. A., Rosenberg, M. L., Powell, K. E., Broome, C. V., & Roper, W. L. (1993). Public health policy for preventing violence. *Health Affairs, 12*(4), 7–29. https://doi.org/10.1377/hlthaff.12.4.7.

Meyer v Nebraska, 262 US US 390 (1923).

Minjarez, M. B., Karp, E. A., Stahmer, A. C., & Brookman-Frazee, L. (2020). Empowering parents through parent training and coaching. In *Naturalistic developmental behavioral interventions for autism spectrum disorder* (pp. 77–98). Paul H. Brookes Publishing Co.

Minnes, P., Perry, A., & Weiss, J. A. (2015). Predictors of distress and well-being in parents of young children with developmental delays and disabilities: The importance of parent perceptions. *Journal of Intellectual Disability Research, 59*(6), 551–560. https://doi.org/10.1111/jir.12160.

Moody, E. J., Kaiser, K., Sharp, D., Kubicek, L. F., Rigles, B., Davis, J., et al. (2019). Improving family functioning following diagnosis of ASD: A randomized trial of a parent mentorship program. *Journal of Child and Family Studies, 28*(2), 424–435.

Mottron, L. (2017). Should we change targets and methods of early intervention in autism, in favor of a strengths-based education? *European Child and Adolescent Psychiatry, 26*(7), 815–825. https://doi.org/10.1007/s00787-017-0955-5.

Myers, B. J., Mackintosh, V. H., & Goin-Kochel, R. P. (2009). "My greatest joy and my greatest heart ache": Parents' own words on how having a child in the autism spectrum has affected their lives and their families' lives. *Research in Autism Spectrum Disorders, 3*(3), 670–684.

Niinomi, K., Asano, M., Kadoma, A., Yoshida, K., Ohashi, Y., Furuzawa, A., et al. (2016). Developing the "Skippu-Mama" program for mothers of children with autism spectrum disorder. *Nursing & Health Sciences, 18*(3), 283–291.

Oelofsen, N., & Richardson, P. (2006). Sense of coherence and parenting stress in mothers and fathers of preschool children with developmental disability. *Journal of Intellectual and Developmental Disability, 31*(1), 1–12.

Pearson, J. N., & Meadan, H. (2018). African American parents' perceptions of diagnosis and services for children with autism. *Education and Training in Autism and Developmental Disabilities, 53*(1), 17–32.

Peer, J. W., & Hillman, S. B. (2014). Stress and resilience for parents of children with intellectual and developmental disabilities: A review of key factors and recommendations for practitioners. *Journal of Policy and Practice in Intellectual Disabilities, 11*(2), 92–98.

Pew Research Center. (2019). *Internet/Broadband Fact Sheet.* https://www.pewresearch.org/internet/fact-sheet/internet-broadband/#find-out-more.

Plant, K. M., & Sanders, M. R. (2007). Predictors of care-giver stress in families of preschool-aged children with developmental disabilities. *Journal of Intellectual Disability Research, 51*(2), 109–124.

Reichow, B., Barton, E. E., Boyd, B. A., & Hume, K. (2012). Early intensive behavioral intervention (EIBI) for young children with autism spectrum disorders (ASD). *Cochrane Database of Systematic Reviews, 10.* CD009260. https://doi.org/10.1002/1465 1858.CD009260.pub2.

Reichow, B., & Wolery, M. (2009). Comprehensive synthesis of early intensive behavioral interventions for young children with autism based on the UCLA young autism project model. *Journal of Autism and Developmental Disorders, 39*(1), 23–41. https://doi.org/10.1007/s10803-008-0596-0.

Rice, C., Nicholas, J., Baio, J., Pettygrove, S., Lee, L. C., Van Naarden Braun, K., et al. (2010). Changes in autism spectrum disorder prevalence in 4 areas of the United States. *Disability and Health Journal, 3*(3), 186–201. https://doi.org/10.1016/j.dhjo.2009.10.008.

Roberts, J., Williams, K., Carter, M., Evans, D., Parmenter, T., Silove, N., et al. (2011). A randomised controlled trial of two early intervention programs for young children with autism: Centre-based with parent program and home-based. *Research in Autism Spectrum Disorders, 5*(4), 1553–1566.

Robinson, S., Hastings, R. P., Weiss, J. A., Pagavathsing, J., & Lunsky, Y. (2018). Self-compassion and psychological distress in parents of young people and adults with intellectual and developmental disabilities. *Journal of Applied Research in Intellectual Disabilities, 31*(3), 454–458.

Robinson, M., & Neece, C. L. (2015). Marital satisfaction, parental stress, and child behavior problems among parents of young children with developmental delays. *Journal of Mental Health Research in Intellectual Disabilities, 8*(1), 23–46.

Rogers, S. J., & Dawson, G. (2010). *Early start Denver Model for young children with autism: Promoting language, learning, and engagement.* Guilford Press.

Root-Elledge, S., Hardesty, C., Hidecker, M. J. C., Bowser, G., Ferguson, E., Wagner, S., et al. (2018). The ECHO Model for enhancing assistive technology implementation in schools. *Assitive Technology Outcomes and Benefits, 12*, 37–55.

Rosenberg, M. L., & Fenley, M. A. (1991). *Violence in America: A public health approach.* Oxford University Press on Demand.

Salazar, R. M. (2020). Full circle autism care includes family relationships and dynamics. In *Autism 360°* (pp. 219–234). Elsevier.

Singh, R., Moody, E. J., Rigles, B., & Smith, E. B. (2018). What it takes to raise a child with autism in a rural state: An appreciative inquiry. *Advances in Neurodevelopmental Disorders* online first.

Sockalingam, S., Arena, A., Serhal, E., Mohri, L., Alloo, J., & Crawford, A. (2017). Building provincial mental health capacity in primary care: An evaluation of a Project ECHO mental health program. *Academic Psychiatry.* https://doi.org/10.1007/s40596-017-0735-z.

Stansberry-Brusnahan, L. L., & Collet-Klingenberg, L. L. (2010). Evidence-based practices for young children with autism spectrum disorders: Guidelines and recommendations from the National Resource Council and National Professional Development Center on Autism Spectrum Disorders. *International Journal of Early Childhood Special Education, 2*(1), 45–56.

Substance Abuse and Mental Health Services Administration. (2016). *Facing addiction in America: The surgeon general's report on alcohol, drugs, and health.* Retrieved from https://addiction.surgeongeneral.gov/sites/default/files/surgeon-generals-report.pdf.

Tehee, E., Honan, R., & Hevey, D. (2009). Factors contributing to stress in parents of individuals with autistic spectrum disorders. *Journal of Applied Research in Intellectual Disabilities, 22*(1), 34–42.

Tint, A., & Weiss, J. A. (2016). Family wellbeing of individuals with autism spectrum disorder: A scoping review. *Autism, 20*(3), 262–275.

Tsermentseli, S., & Kouklari, E.-C. (2019). Impact of child factors on parenting stress of mothers of children with autism spectrum disorder and intellectual disability: A UK school-based study. *Early Child Development and Care*, 1–12.

Tudge, J. R. H., Mokrova, I., Hatfield, B. E., & Karnik, R. B. (2009). Uses and misuses of Bronfenbrenner's bioecological theory of human development. *Journal of Family Theory & Review, 1*(4), 198–210.

Turner-Brown, L., Hume, K., Boyd, B. A., & Kainz, K. (2019). Preliminary efficacy of family implemented TEACCH for toddlers: Effects on parents and their toddlers with autism spectrum disorder. *Journal of Autism and Developmental Disorders, 49*(7), 2685–2698.

Twoy, R., Connolly, P. M., & Novak, J. M. (2007). Coping strategies used by parents of children with autism. *Journal of the American Academy of Nurse Practitioners, 19*, 251–260.

Vohra, R., Madhavan, S., Sambamoorthi, U., & St Peter, C. (2014). Access to services, quality of care, and family impact for children with autism, other developmental disabilities, and other mental health conditions. *Autism, 18*(7), 815–826.

Warren, Z., McPheeters, M. L., Sathe, N., Foss-Feig, J. H., Glasser, A., & Veenstra-Vanderweele, J. (2011). A systematic review of early intensive intervention for autism spectrum disorders. *Pediatrics, 127*(5), e1303–e1311. https://doi.org/10.1542/peds.2011-0426.

Weiss, M. J. (2002). Hardiness and social support as predictors of stress in mothers of typical children, children with autism, and children with mental retardation. *Autism, 6*(1), 115–130.

Weiss, J. A., Tint, A., Paquette-Smith, M., & Lunsky, Y. (2016). Perceived self-efficacy in parents of adolescents and adults with autism spectrum disorder. *Autism, 20*(4), 425–434.

Weitlauf, A., McPheeters, M., Peters, B., Sathe, N., Travis, R., Aiello, R., et al. (2014). Therapies for children with autism spectrum disorder: Behavioral interventions update. In *Comparative effectiveness review.* www.effectivehealthcare.ahrq.gov/reports/final.cfm.

Woodman, A. C. (2014). Trajectories of stress among parents of children with disabilities: A dyadic analysis. *Family Relations, 63*(1), 39–54.

Wyoming Department of Health. (2020). *What is rural.* Retrieved from https://health.wyo.gov/publichealth/rural/officeofruralhealth/what-is-rural/.

Printed in the United States
By Bookmasters